WORLD CHAMPION OPENINGS

WORLD CHAMPION OPENINGS

Eric Schiller

CARDOZA PUBLISHING

ACKNOWLEDGEMENTS

I'd like to thank the following people who directly or indirectly helped bring this project to fruition: World Champion Garry Kasparov and Grandmaster Raymond Keene, who gave me my start as an author back in 1980. Frequent collaborators Grandmaster Joel Benjamin, Grandmaster Leonid Shamkovich and International Master John Watson, who have refined my skills at analysis. Thanks too to National Master Hal Bogner for friendly and helpful advice and Sandi Marx for helping me to keep organized. Finally, and by no means least, publisher Avery Cardoza, who provided all the resources I needed to get the job done. And a nod to Half Moon Bay Coffee Company and Café Classique, where I received sustenance and fuel, not to mention a great deal of needed caffeine, Bruce, Phil, Mickey, Bob and guests who restored my spirits at Shoreline during the brutal final phase of working on the book.

PRINTING HISTORY

First Printing	March 1997
Second Printing	June 1998
Third Printing	April 2000

Libray of Congress Catalog Card No: 96-85740
ISBN: 0-940685-69-8
Front Cover Photograph by Paul Eisenberg

CARDOZA PUBLISHING
PO Box 1500 Cooper Station, New York, NY 10276
Phone (718)743-5229 • Fax(718)743-8284 •
Email:cardozapub@aol.com
Web Site - www.cardozapub.com

Write for your free catalogue of gaming and chess books, equipment, software and computer games.

ABOUT THE AUTHOR

Eric Schiller, widely considered one of the world's foremost chess analysts, writers and teachers, is internationally recognized for his definitive works on openings. He is the author of 80 chess books including Cardoza Publishing's definitive series on openings, *World Champion Openings, Standard Chess Openings*, and *Unorthodox Chess Openings*—an exhaustive opening library of more than 1700 pages, and the companion book to this work, *World Champion Combinations*, written with Grandmaster Raymond Keene. He's also the author of *Encyclopedia of Chess Wisdom, Gambit Opening Repertoire for White, Gambit Opening Repertoire for Black, Complete Defense to King Pawn Openings, Complete Defense to Queen Pawn Openings*, and multiple other chess titles for Cardoza Publishing. (For listings of all chess titles published by Cardoza Publishing, go online to www.cardozapub.com.)

Eric Schiller is a National and Life Master, an International Arbiter of F.I.D.E., and the official trainer for many of America's top young players. He has recently been appointed as official coach of America's best players under 18 to represent the United States at the Chess World Championships. He has also presided over world championship matches dating back to 1983, runs prestigious international tournaments, and been interviewed dozens of times in major media throughout the world. His games have been featured in leading chess journals and newspapers including the venerable New York Times. Eric Schiller's web site is www.chessworks.com.

*To Hadas, Adam, Jessica, Abby, Emily, and Melissa,
who I hope will grow up to be fine chess players.*

Eric Schiller with World Champion Garry Kasparov

TABLE OF CONTENTS

CHARTS OF THE CHAMPIONS

1. INTRODUCTION

This book examines the repertoires of the greatest chessplayers and shows you how they have treated virtually all of the important chess openings. We reveal the opening strategies that Paul Morphy and the 13 official World Champions have used to earn the number one spot in the chess rankings. The basic concepts of each of these openings are described and illustrated with complete games played by the World Champions themselves, so that you can easily absorb their secrets and use them successfully in your own games.

There are hundreds of common chess openings strategies, with names ranging from Sicilian Dragon, Hedgehog, and Rat through the more esoteric Flohr-Mikenas Attack. Most top chessplayers only play a dozen or so at a time, and make major changes only a few times in their professional career. Their choices are generally conservative, leaving experimental approaches for an occasional outing when the mood fits. The range of openings chosen by each player may be small, but there is a great deal of variety when comparing the repertoires of various superstars.

Chess opening strategy still remains more of an art than a science, and fashion often dictates popularity, rather than any objective standard. Openings fade in and out. In the 1990s, for example, we have seen a revival of variations which were only common in the last century! We find current champions Garry Kasparov and Anatoly Karpov adopting plans which have only rarely been seen since the heyday of Paul Morphy in the 1850s and 60s.

In the various chapters of this book you will see the opening play of Paul Morphy, Wilhelm Steinitz, Emanuel Lasker, Jose Capablanca, Alexander Alekhine, Max Euwe, Mikhail Botvinnik, Vasily Smyslov, Mikhail Tal, Tigran Petrosian, Boris Spassky, Bobby Fischer, Anatoly Karpov and Garry Kasparov. These players have been the undisputed champions of the world from the period covering 1857 to the present day. We will examine all the major openings and see whether or not they liked to play them, and how they reacted when confronted with them from the other side of the board.

In each section, you will learn a bit of the history and basic ideas of the opening, and how big a role it played in the individual careers of the champions. You'll be provided one or two complete games with commentary, so that you can see how a small advantage can turn into a masterful brilliancy with good technique, or how opportunities can be squandered by bad technique.

After reading this book, you can go on to incorporate openings that you find interesting into your own repertoire. There are thousands of books available on specific opening strategies. You can also deepen your understanding of the ideas behind the openings by examining collections of games by the champions who used them.

Once you learn to achieve good positions from the start, many of your opponents will start to crumble and you'll have all you need to bring home the point and be a winner!

2. HISTORY OF THE CHAMPIONS

THE BACKGROUND

There have been many claims to the title of World Champion, and with the exception of the period from 1948 to 1992, the process of selecting the champion has been controversial. In the early days of chess, there were few international competitions to determine the best player in the world. Official matches did not begin until 1886, and since 1993 there have been two rival organizations designating their own champions.

Most world championship matches were closely contested, usually being decided by two points or less. In world championship play, matches decided by four points or more in a 24 game match were considered one-sided and decisive. The scoring system in championship matches, as in regular tournaments, is to award one point for wins, one half point for draws.

THE PLAYERS

Paul Morphy was without question the best player of his day, and is generally considered to have held the unofficial championship title until his death in 1884. To determine his successor, a match was held between two worthy candidates, Wilhelm Steinitz and Emil Zukertort. That match was played in America. Steinitz won by a score of 12.5-7.5 in a match held in New York, St. Louis, and New Orleans.

With an undisputed champion at last, challengers arose to attempt to wrest the title from Steinitz. The first challenger was Mikhail Chigorin, the Russian star, who lost a match in Havana in 1889 by a score of 10.5-6.5. Then Steinitz dispatched Isidore Gunsburg in New York (10.5-8.5) in 1891, and then won a rematch against Chigorin (12.5-10.5) in Havana. But in 1894 he ran into Lasker.

Emanuel Lasker's more refined and balanced style proved decisively superior to Steinitz's more primitive play, and in 1894 Lasker won the title by a score of 12-7 in a match held in New York, Philadelphia and Montreal. A rematch in 1897 in Moscow was a complete mismatch, with Lasker winning by 12.5-4.5. Lasker went on to trounce American Frank Marshall 11.5-3.5 in a contest battled in New York, Philadelphia, Memphis, Chicago and Baltimore. In 1908 the great Dr. Siegbert Tarrasch tried his hand, only to go down to defeat 10.5-5.5 in Duesseldorf and Munich. Karl Schlechter was next in line, and he fared better, splitting the 1910 Vienna and Berlin match 5-5. That left the title with Lasker, however, and later in the same year he took care of David Janowski by a score of 9.5-1.5, in Berlin.

Lasker held the title for almost three decades, part of which was consumed by World War I, but eventually he had to yield to the rising Cuban star Jose Capablanca, who won in Havana in 1921 by 9-5. Capablanca lost his initial defense to Alexander Alekhine in Buenos Aires in 1927. It was a long match, won by Alekhine with 18.5 to Capablanca's 15.5.

Alekhine picked inferior opposition for his defenses, and easily took care of Efim Bogoljubow in a match in Germany and Holland, 1929, with a score of 15.5-9.5. A rematch in Germany in 1934 was also a blowout, 15.5-10.5. The next year, however, Alekhine traveled to Holland to battle against Dutchman Max Euwe, and left the title behind by a score of 15.5-14.5. A rematch two years later ended in favor of Alekhine, 15.5-9.5.

Then World War II intervened. When it was over, Alekhine died before another match could be held. The World Chess Federation (FIDE) took control of the championship and held a great tournament to determine the title. This was the first and last time a tournament format was used instead of match play. It was held in The Hague and Moscow.

Mikhail Botvinnik won the 5-player event with 14 out of 20 points, followed by Vasily Smyslov (11), Paul Keres and American Samuel Reshevsky (10.5). Max Euwe only managed four points. The title headed to the Soviet Union, where it would remain for many years.

FIDE put in a system of qualifying tournaments to choose the next challenger, and it seemed to work. Botvinnik managed only a 12-12 tie in his defense against the creative genius David Bronstein, a result which was strongly influenced by "off-the-board" maneuvers according to Bronstein. The 24-game match format would remain in effect for a long time. The three-year cycle, unique in competition, was established.

WORLD CHAMPION OPENINGS

The 1948 runner-up didn't quit, however, and in 1954 Smyslov again challenged for the title in Moscow, with a less controversial 12-12 tie keeping the championship in Botvinnik's hands. Three years later they met again, and this time Smyslov prevailed 12.5-9.5. Botvinnik was granted a rematch a year later, and again won the title, this time by 12.5-10.5. The title remained Soviet, and Moscow became the default venue for championship matches.

The winner of the next qualifying cycle was Mikhail Tal, from Riga, who returned from Moscow with the championship title after defeating Botvinnik in 1960 by the convincing margin of 12.5-8.5. Again Botvinnik was entitled to a rematch, and he won a year later by 13-8.

Next in line, in 1963, was Tigran Petrosian, and Botvinnik's unlucky streak of defenses continued as Petrosian won 12.5-9.5. This time the title was gone for good. Petrosian managed to retain the title in the 1966 match against Boris Spassky by 12.5-11.5, but in 1969 Spassky won 12.5-2.5. Still in Soviet hands, the title seemed inaccessible to the rest of the world.

Then came Fischer. Bobby Fischer obliterated all opposition in a searing path to the title match. He then turned the contest into a psychological and political thriller, even giving up one game by forfeit. Nevertheless, in a match the whole world watched, Fischer scored 12.5 points to only 8.5 by Spassky and became World Champion. In a dispute with FIDE he refused to defend the title and remained out of the professional chess scene for twenty years.

As the anointed challenger, Anatoly Karpov inherited the title by default in 1975. He proved his worth in a set of matches against Soviet defector Viktor Korchnoi, who had settled in Switzerland. Six victories were needed to earn the championship. In Baguio City, Philippines, Karpov won 16.5-15.5. He almost failed, as Korchnoi went from 5-2 down to 5-5 (draws did not count) before Karpov achieved his final victory. Three years later, in Merano, Karpov won more convincingly by a score of 11-7.

By 1984, Karpov was looking over his shoulder at Garry Kasparov, whose rise through the ranks was meteoric. This time the match dragged on forever, despite a 4-0 lead enjoyed by Karpov after just 9 games. Then Kasparov became a rock, drawing every game, and Karpov's lead was extended to 5-0 only in the 27th game. The drawing streak resumed, and Karpov started to fade. After 48 games, Florencio Campomanes, the FIDE President, made the most controversial decision in the history of the games. He simply stopped the match, with the score 5-3 after Kasparov had won two games in a row. Outrage was expressed by both players, the media and the public, but Campomanes would not budge. He ordered a rematch seven months later, in September of 1985.

Kasparov was ready, and won by a score of 13-11 in the old 24-game format. In 1986, the match was split between London and Leningrad, and Kasparov won 12-11. The 1987 defense against Karpov was even closer. Kasparov had to win the final game to keep his title, and he did so to earn the 12-12 tie and retain the championship despite all the pressure. In 1990, the match finally returned to America, with the first half of the Kasparov-Karpov battle held in New York and the remainder in Lyon, France. This time Kasparov squeeked by with a 12.5-11.5 score. That match was the last undisputed World Championship.

A feud between the professional players of the world and FIDE President Campomanes had been simmering for some time, since at least 1986. Kasparov had founded the Grandmasters Association to wrest control of the championship from FIDE, but was not able to achieve the goal due to internal divisions in the organization. He regrouped in 1993 by forming the Professional Chess Association. With money provided by the American company Intel, the PCA organized a championship and England's Nigel Short, who had defeated Karpov in the FIDE cycle, was the challenger. Short played some interesting chess but was unable to present a serious challenge to Kasparov, who won 12.5-7.5 in the famous Savoy Theater in London's Strand district.

FIDE refused to acknowledge any of this, and held its own match, with Karpov facing an overmatched Jan Timman in a contest held in various cities in Holland and Jakarta. Karpov won by 12.5-8.5.

The two champions survived challenges in 1995, when Kasparov defeated Indian superstar Viswanathan Anand in New York 10.5-7.5. The following year Karpov prevailed against a new American challenger, Gata Kamsky, 10.5-7.5. That match was held in the home town of the new FIDE President, Kirsten Iljumzhingov, who lives in Elista, the capital of the former Soviet Republic of Kyrghizia. Iljumzhingov was not only the host, he was also the President of the country!

As this book is written, neither FIDE nor the PCA have secured funding and developed plans for future World Championships. The legitimacy of the World Championship title is as insecure as it was in Alekhine's day.

Having covered the history of the championship, let me present thumbnail sketches of the champions we have met. There are many books devoted to each of them, so rather than present biographical details, I'll just comment on their styles and the significance of their opening play.

3. THE WORLD CHAMPIONS

PAUL MORPHY

Paul Morphy, the American legend, was born on June 22, 1837 in New Orleans. 'The Pride and the Sorrow of Chess' was his nickname, and it fits. His active career was short, but impressive. He defeated Lowenthal, Harrwitz, and Anderssen in matches but couldn't get a match with Staunton. Staunton was seen as having ducked a match, and his reputation has always suffered as a result. There was no official World Championship at the time, and only a Staunton vs. Morphy match would have resolved the issue.

Morphy brought the spicy flavor of his New Orleans Creole heritage to the chessboard, sacrificing pieces whenever a reasonable opportunity arose. It didn't hurt that his opponents were so lacking in defensive skills that it did not make much difference whether the sacrifices are correct or not. Morphy developed pieces quickly, then provoked a weakness and tried to exploit it as quickly as possible.

While his play is an excellent model for beginners, and can be instructive in the art of attack, his opening play is not suited to modern tournament since the opposition tends to be much better prepared than in the 19th century.

Morphy did not make many contributions to opening theory. He basically just set up the pieces to attack the enemy king. Though he is credited with some opening variations, he did little to earn them. Morphy's opening play is virtually indistinguishable from many other players of his day.

WILHELM STEINITZ

Wilhelm Steinitz (1836-1900) was born in Prague, lived in Vienna, and then headed to the New World, emigrating to the United States. His travels exposed him to most of the leading chess ideas of the day, and he became a player who was at least as effective in defense as in the art of attack. This made him very difficult to defeat, especially for opponents who were used to opponents simply folding in a bad position.

Steinitz's superiority on defense allowed him to play some openings which are considered suspect by modern standards, but his play as White is often worthy of emulation. He followed classical principles, but did enjoy a few more eccentric openings, and was almost reckless in his disregard for king safety.

Steinitz was a great innovator in the opening, and many of his inventions remain in the Grandmaster repertoire. The Steinitz Variation of the French Defense (1.e4 e6; 2.d4 d5; 3.Nc3 Nf6; 4.e5) is once again the most popular way of dealing with Black's formation.

On the Black side, Steinitz promoted the variations of the Spanish Game which involve an early ...d6 by Black. Steinitz's appreciation of structural weaknesses and defensive resources enabled him to greatly enrich the opening library, and his *Modern Chess Instructor* is considered a classic.

Steinitz was arguably the first great thinker in the game, and his writings greatly influenced the development of chess. After an early "mandatory" phase as a swashbuckling attacker, Steinitz became more and more of a strategical player, and eventually one with exaggerated respect for the dynamic potential of cramped, defensive positions. He is considered the first official world champion, thanks to his defeat of Zukertort in 1886. His play left an indelible mark on the game.

EMANUEL LASKER

Dr. Emanuel Lasker, (1868-1941) was born on Christmas eve in Berlinchen, Germany. He was World Champion for 27 years, a record not likely to be broken. He gained the title by beating Steinitz 12-7 in 1894. He beat Marshall, Tarrasch, and Janowski in matches and drew Schlechter. In 1921, he finally lost the title to Capablanca 5-9 in a match in Havana. Interestingly, Fischer didn't consider Lasker worthy of his top ten list, calling him a 'coffee-house' player.

The German style developed by Lasker, a distinguished mathematician, was a more scientific approach to the game and his mastery of the endgame led him to appreciate the importance of pawn structures in the opening. He was a very classical player, avoiding weaknesses as much as possible. This is contrasted with more modern players who are willing to accept weaknesses in return for counterplay.

Although this description seems to indicate a dry style, Lasker was one of the first great opening theoreticians. There are very few openings which have not been enriched by his games and extensive writings. His best known variation is the Lasker Variation of the Queen's Gambit Declined, which features an early invasion of the e4-square by a Black knight. Lasker also developed a safe method of accepting the Queen's Gambit too.

He adopted gambits from time to time, even as Black, taking great risks in such openings as the Albin Countergambit. Well ahead of his time, he appreciated Black's resources in the Lasker-Pelikan Variation of the Sicilian Defense, a strategy now employed by top World Championship contenders such as Vladimir Kramnik.

Any player would be well-advised to study the handling of the opening by Lasker. His plans are structurally sound and lead to solid positions. Following Lasker's example in the opening is as sound now as it was a century ago.

JOSE RAUL CAPABLANCA

Who could replace Lasker but an even stronger endgame player? Havana-born Jose Raul Capablanca (1888-1942) fit the bill. 'The Chess Machine' was his nickname, and he was probably the closest in style to that epithet. He gained the title against Lasker in a match without a loss in 1921. He also went nine years without a loss in tournament play! He finally lost his title in 1927 to Alekhine and was never to be given another chance at the title.

His opening repertoire was not unlike Lasker's, especially as Black. The classical approach prevailed, and only slight changes in fashion led to a shift to some of the newer, hypermodern openings.

As with Lasker, it is hard to go wrong with any of the openings Capablanca played regularly. Keep in mind that his endgame prowess allowed him to play for minimal advantages, counting on his formidable technique to deliver the point in the end.

ALEXANDER ALEKHINE

Alexander Alexandrovich Alekhine (1892-1946) was born on Halloween in Moscow and lived in several European countries. He had a very aggressive style which led to many games where even Grandmasters were surprised with his tactical vision.

He defeated Capablanca to win the title in 1927 but his relations with Capablanca were so bad that they were not even on speaking terms and he never gave Capablanca a chance to regain the title. He held on to the title by defeating weaker opposition until Max Euwe took it from him in 1935, but then he regained the title from the Dutchman in 1937 and held it, without a title defense, until his death in 1946.

With Alekhine, the path was clear for the Hypermoderns, whose ideas we'll meet when we start discussing the openings, and other experimenters. While Alekhine did not adopt the kingside fianchetto plans espoused by the Hypermodern school, he did allow the creation of a strong enemy pawn center only to use it as a target for his middlegame operations. So he was certainly influenced by their radical ideas.

Living in an experimental age in general, Alekhine played a wide variety of openings, several of which were quite disrespectable at the time. He is best remembered as the inventor of the Alekhine Defense, although he didn't use it often, but was equally at home in many lines of the Queen's Gambit, both accepted and declined.

He often tried new gambit ideas, but had the good sense to abandon those experiments which proved to be unreliable. He liked to explore the byways of opening theory, and often found that a particular experiment should not be repeated. For this reason you should be careful not to take all of his opening moves as models to be followed.

Alekhine's creativity was seen throughout the opening inventory, with contributions to the Spanish Game, Vienna Game, French Defense, Dutch Defense, Queen's Gambit, Queen's Indian Defense, Semi-Slav and many other time-tested openings.

MAX EUWE

Machgielis (Max) Euwe (1901-1981) was World Champion from 1935-37, and was also the president of FIDE, the chess world's political body. He won his title from Alekhine, and then lost it to Alekhine. Both matches were imaginative fights.

Euwe is best known for his writings on chess, the body of which covered the entire range of opening, middlegame and endgame strategies. He made many major contributions to our understanding of the opening. Although hypermodern ideas were often seen in his games as White, Euwe returned to the Classical style of play as Black. His contributions to the opening were more of specific moves than general strategy, and he raised some openings, such as the Slav, to a more respectable level of play.

Euwe was an opening *theoretician*. (A theoretician studies the game scientifically, examining many specific items and evaluating them.) He was a widely published author, and was responsible for many broad research projects on the opening. He really knew what he was doing, and his opening play is of generally high quality.

MIKHAIL BOTVINNIK

Mikhail Moisiyevich Botvinnik (1911-1994), born in Kuokkala, USSR, was the premier figure of chess from 1948 until 1963. His style was based on logic, and he was an engineer by training. He gained the title with a victory in what may have been the strongest tournament in history, split between The Hague and Moscow in 1948. He had a habit of losing the title only to reclaim it. He dropped the match to Smyslov in 1957, but won the rematch in 1958. Botvinnik then lost a match to Tal in 1960, only to win in 1961. Petrosian finally put him away for good in 1963.

Botvinnik was a dedicated student of the opening. He has variations named after him in most of the major openings, but his name is most closely associated with the French Defense, Dutch Defense, Semi-Slav and English Opening. In each he developed new ideas which remain in common use today.

The Classical style dominated Botvinnik's play, and he was dedicated in his pursuit to control the center of the board. He rarely experimented, and clung to a narrow opening repertoire for most of his career. He used the English Opening (1.c4) more effectively than any previous World Champion.

Even now, many players adopt Botvinnik's repertoire almost exclusively. It contains a pleasant variety of very sound openings. The only drawback for some players is that it is not always as confrontational as more modern approaches.

VASILY SMYSLOV

Vasily Vasiliyevich Smyslov was born March 24, 1921 in Moscow. Smyslov played three matches against Botvinnik for the title over the years 1954-58. While his overall score was 18 wins, 17 losses, and 34 draws, he won only the 1957 match, losing the other two. His amazing longevity was demonstrated when he made it to the Candidates' final against Kasparov in 1984.

Smyslov liked many of the same openings as Euwe, and fully understood the nuances of hypermodern play. At the same time, he is one of the greatest exponents of the Classical openings, in particular, the Spanish Game. His slow, patient maneuvering style has always been punctuated by outbursts of sacrificial brilliance. Still an active player, Smyslov now prefers to introduce new ideas in the middlegame rather than the openings.

Equally at home in flexible flank openings, classical defenses, and the labyrinth of the Sicilian Defenses, Smyslov was responsible not so much for new moves, but rather for new strategic approaches to the opening. Many of his innovations radically changed the nature of the middlegame structures, as in the case of his early kingside fianchetto in the Slav and Queen's Gambit Accepted. These openings had not previously seen that plan in action.

He is specifically credited with new approaches to the English Opening, Gruenfeld, Nimzoindian, Slav, Sicilian Defense and Spanish Game, for both Black and White.

The subtle nature of the positions preferred by Smyslov makes his opening repertoire far from ideal for the beginner or intermediate player, but as one approaches mastery, it is a wonderful model.

MIKHAIL TAL

The most beloved of champions, Mikhail Tal (1936-1992), was born in Riga, Latvia and quickly rose to international prominence. World champion for only one year, he beat Botvinnik in 1960 and lost in 1961 in matches for the title. His style was imaginative and attacking; understandably, he was a favorite of the fans. He battled ill health throughout his life and this had an effect on his results, but he was universally admired by the entire chess community.

Tal could play just about any opening well. All he needed was a chance to attack and the position would soon explode in fireworks. He traveled many paths in the openings, often taking risks that would never be chanced by a modern champion.

Treat Tal's repertoire with the same suspicion which applies to Alekhine's. Many of the openings he played have been refuted or relegated to the fringes of serious play.

TIGRAN PETROSIAN

Tigran Vartanovich Petrosian (1929-1984) was born in Tbilisi, Georgia. He won the title from Botvinnik in 1963 with a 12.5/9.5 score and successfully defended it against Spassky in 1966. He lost his title to Spassky in 1969. He was noted for a defensive and maneuvering style that was hard for amateurs to understand and was perhaps the least favorite champion in history, at least from a fan's point of view.

Petrosian had a distinctive style. It is easy to recognize Petrosian at the wheel early in the game. He often erected pawn barriers and hid behind them, waiting for the opponent to play with just a shade too much ambition. Petrosian's ideas in the opening were quite original, but often led to positions only one with an obsessive love for constricted positions could tolerate. His cramped positions would have driven Morphy, Alekhine or Tal crazy, but this was home turf for the Georgian wizard.

Nevertheless, in the mainstream openings with 1.d4 he added a lot of firepower to the White side of the King's Indian, Queen's Indian, and Queen's Gambit.

As Black, he was fond of the French Defense but was willing to accept almost complete immobility of his forces in positions where his defensive counterattacking genius could exploit overambitious play on the part of his opponent.

Beginners should avoid playing the constricted positions Petrosian favored, but once the importance of the center and piece mobility are learned, these openings can prove very effective in practical play.

BORIS SPASSKY

Boris Vasiliyevich Spassky (1937-), from Leningrad, USSR, needed two matches against Petrosian to gain the title. In 1966, he lost 11.5/ 12.5, but, in 1969, he won 12.5/10.5. He lost his title to Fischer in 1972 and a rematch against Fischer 20 years later in 1992. Spassky now resides in France.

Spassky is known as a universal player, comfortable in many different types of positions. He has often sought out the byways of opening theories, and has preferred openings which are more idea-based than move-based. Intense opening preparation is not in Spassky's character, though he could rise to the occasion in match play, especially when competing for the World Championship.

Spassky's openings are by and large unambitious. He enjoys variations which involve comfortable development, such as his line in the Queen's Indian Defense (1.d4 Nf6; 2.c4 e6; 3.Nf3 b6; 4.e3, followed by Bd3 and kingside castling) and the Leningrad Variation of the Nimzoindian (1.d4 Nf6; 2.c4 e6; 3.Nc3 Bb4; 4.Bg5). It is no accident that these openings depart from the major continuations at the fourth move. Such an early deviation leaves less theory to be absorbed.

As Black, Spassky was responsible for the resurrection of the Tarrasch Defense, another opening with easy development and clear strategic goals.

His repertoire is ideal for the beginner or intermediate player who is more interested in learning how to play the opening than in memorizing variations.

BOBBY FISCHER

Robert James "Bobby" Fischer, was born March 9, 1943 in Chicago. His accomplishments included: World Champion (defeating Boris Spassky in 1972); a perfect score in the US championship; and 20 straight wins against top opposition. He has been a controversial figure throughout his career with his forfeiture of the title in 1975 as one example, his 1992 match against Spassky in Yugoslavia in violation of UN sanctions and US govenment threats (Fischer boasts about not paying taxes) as another.

Fischer was a major theoretician. His refinements, sprung at the board against unsuspecting opponents, remain scattered throughout the treatises on the most important openings. He liked to engage the battle early, whipping up complicated, inscrutable positions which he had already studied at home.

As White, Fischer mostly followed the accepted main lines, primarily in openings starting with 1.e4. He was a master of the Spanish Game, both in the traditional forms and with an early exchange of bishop for knight at c6. In the Sicilians, he deployed a bishop at c4 against the Dragon, Scheveningen and Najdorf formations, and was devastatingly effective.

When seated on the Black side, he used the Najdorf Sicilian and in particular the Poisoned Pawn Variation with no fear of enemy opening preparation. The Indian Games served him just as well when the opponent ventured 1.d4. He flirted with "reversed" openings such as the King's Indian Attack, where his understanding of the power of a fianchettoed bishop combined with a kingside attack felled many impressive opponents.

Fischer almost never played a bad opening. His repertoire is suitable for all level of players. It is not as topical now as it was 20 years ago, but that is not to say that it is not just as good.

ANATOLY KARPOV

Anatoly Yevgenyevich Karpov, was born May 23, 1951 in Zlatoust in the former Soviet Union. Karpov ranks amongst the greatest in the pantheon. Unfortunately, he has won the FIDE title twice by default, in

1975, when Fischer refused to defend, and 1993, when Kasparov bolted FIDE for his own organization. This is misleading in that his tournament results have been every bit fitting for a world champion. His victory in Linares 1994 was overwhelming and the field included almost all possible contenders for the title. His series of matches against Kasparov has set the record for most games by two opponents.

Karpov plays conservative openings, with long pedigrees and a history of success. He seeks a small but persistent advantage in the opening, confident that he will be able to maintain and exploit it. For this reason, Karpov's repertoire can be recommended only to advanced players whose technique will not let them down. Lesser players will watch in despair as their advantage slowly disappears, unsupported by Karpov's inexorable logic and understanding.

The opening preferences of Anatoly Karpov would not be unfairly described as boring. The most positional line of the Spanish and quietest lines of the Caro-Kann and Queen's Indian Defenses are just his cup of tea. He is a bit more aggressive as White, relying primarily on 1.e4 and choosing solid positional openings such as the Italian Game, and the Modern Variation against the Alekhine Defense, systems with the modest Be2 against the Sicilians, etc.

Although his trainer, Igor Zaitsev, is properly credited with developing what is now the main line of the Spanish Game (1.e4 e5; 2.Nf3 Nc6; 3.Bb5 a6; 4.Ba4 Nf6; 5.0-0 Be7; 6.Re1 b5; 7.Bb3 d6; 8.c3 0-0 9.h3 Re8; 10.d4 Bb7), it is Karpov who brought it to its lofty stature by his consistent mastery of the system in tournament and match competition.

GARRY KASPAROV

Garry Kimovich Kasparov was born on April 13, 1963, and 13 is his lucky number. Kasparov is of Armenian and Jewish heritage, and was born in the Azerbaijan capital of Baku.

Perhaps the greatest player in history, he is currently the PCA title holder. He has played many matches with Karpov, all successful save the first one, a marathon match in 1984 and 1985 that spanned 6 months and 48 games. Kasparov's first victory came later that year against Karpov, and he hasn't lost a title match since. He recently defeated Anand for the title in New York, having previously defended his title against Short in London 1993. A "reunification" match with Karpov is under discussion for 1997 or 1998.

Kasparov has had a profound effect on opening theory. He will often amaze spectators and his opponents by choosing ancient openings, or playing a sharp topical opening for the very first time. The youngest champion has a broader repertoire than any Champion since Alekhine, and already has contributed heavily to the theory of his favorite openings, including the Scheveningen and Najdorf Sicilians, Gruenfeld and King's Indian as Black, and just about every opening as White.

His most lasting contributions to date are in the Kasparov Variation of the Queen's Indian Defense and Saemisch Variation of the King's Indian Defense. Kasparov brought the Tarrasch Defense up to a new level of interest and sophistication in the 1980s.

Recently he has trotted out old and discarded openings such as the Evans Gambit, and once again the world is paying attention!

If you play almost any normal opening, you will find excellent models in Kasparov's games. It should be remembered, however, that his choices are made with his particular skill set in mind. If you cannot store masses of specific opening lines in your head, you may want to avoid openings Kasparov plays.

4. SUMMARY OF OPENING TYPES

Chess writers usually group openings according to a hierarchy based on the typical positions of each opening. This classification isn't perfect, but it helps to organize the discussion in a rational way. We speak of Open Games, Semi-Open Games, Closed Games, Indian Games, Flank Games, and Unorthodox Games.

Later in the book we will discuss the typical characteristics of each grouping, but here is a summary by way of introduction:

OPEN GAMES

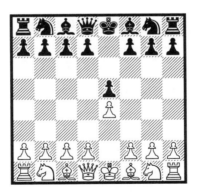

White starts with 1.e4 and Black responds with 1...e5. White continues with rapid development, sometimes in the form of gambits where White gives up a pawn to increase the pace of attack. These are the most traditional openings and dominated chess until the period just after World War 1. Black risks very little in the Open Games, but is unlikely to win quickly.

SEMI-OPEN GAMES

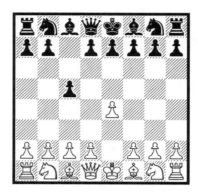

These openings also start with 1.e4 by White, but Black chooses moves other than 1...e5. Technically, all replies other than 1...e5 belong to this category, but very strange and usually bad moves are relegated to the "Unorthodox" group. From Black's perspective, Semi-Open games are in no way inferior to Open Games. While they are a little sharper and involve a bit more risk, they also offer greater rewards.

CLOSED GAMES

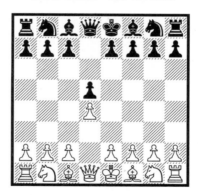

When White plays 1.d4 and Black answers with 1...d5, we have a Closed Game. The pace of these games is slower and less flashy than in the Open Games. It is hard for Black to achieve full equality, but the defenses are very solid.

INDIAN GAMES

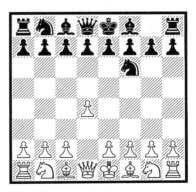

A more popular reply to 1.d4 is 1...Nf6, which has dominated the scene for the last 50 years or so. White then can prevent Black from taking early measures in the center of the board, but Black has sufficient resources to undermine White's control of the center.

Most of the Indian Games are hypermodern in style. This means that one of these players does not start by occupying a central square with pawns, but instead places the knights and bishops on squares which control parts of the center.

FLANK GAMES

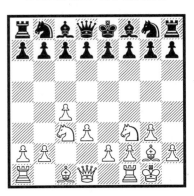

A typical flank formation for White

Flank games are a hypermodern development. The fianchetto is the most popular device, stationing a bishop in the corner of the board along one of the long diagonals.

UNORTHODOX GAMES

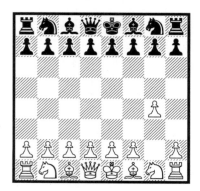

Depending on who you ask, Unorthodox Games are either the ones that just don't fit in the categories above, really bad moves that no one should play, or uncharted areas for exploration by creative minds. World Champions rarely employ these openings, and are usually effective when playing against them.

5. TRANSPOSITIONS

We have to consider the positions typical of an opening, not just the first moves played in a game when we're examining an opening or a variation. Often a game begins in one opening but shifts into another by reaching a position that is more typical of the latter. This is called a **transposition**. It's the *destination position* that's important, not necessarily the route taken to get there.

For example, suppose White plays 1.Nf3 and Black responds 1...c5.

We would consider both of these moves typical of a flank game. But if White now plays 2.e4, then we have the Sicilian Defense, usually reached by 1.e4 c5; 2.Nf3.

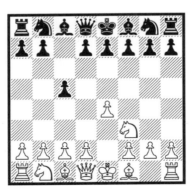

Of course it does not matter at this point which move order was used, but it is sometimes the case that these transpositions are seen even late in the opening, perhaps at move 10 or 12. In addition, it is possible to reach the same position by a different number of moves!

For example 1.e4 d5; 2.exd5 Qxd5; 3.Nc3 Qd6; 4.d4 c6 is a variation of the Scandinavian Defense which I have frequently played, though it isn't quite "respectable." It can also arise from the Alekhine Defense after 1.e4 Nf6; 2.e5 Ng8; 3.d4 d6; 4.exd6 Qxd6; 5.Nc3 c6. Same position, two move orders. Here is another I have used: 1.e4 c6; 2.d4 d5; 3.exd5 Qxd5; 4.Nc3 Qd6. Many paths, all leading to my pet defense — covered in my forthcoming book, *Unorthodox Chess Openings*.

Because there are so many possible transpositions, it is not easy to determine which opening characterizes a particular game. When we talk about the King's Indian Defense, for example, we are not concerned with whether the game begins 1.d4 Nf6; 2.c4 g6; 3.Nc3 Bg7. If Black plays an early ...d5, we will be in Gruenfeld territory, while an early ...c5 may shift us to a Modern Benoni.

It is only after Black has completed development, including ...d6 and ...0-0 (in most cases) that we can be fairly certain of remaining in the realm of the King's Indian.

Here is a practical example from Kasparov, who uses a very roundabout method to reach the Tarrasch Defense:

(1) CHABANON - KASPAROV
French Team Championship, 1993

1.c4. This game undergoes some remarkable transformations in the opening. We start out as an English Opening.

1...Nf6; 2.Nc3 e5. The reversed Sicilian appeals to Kasparov. **3.g3 c6; 4.d4 exd4; 5.Qxd4 d5.**

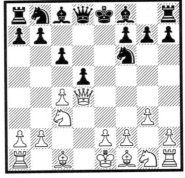

Now the pawn structure is that of a reversed Alapin Sicilian, where the fianchetto plan is not among the best. **6.Bg2 Be6; 7.cxd5 cxd5.**

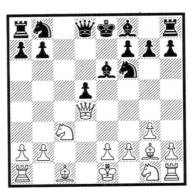

Now we have a Tarrasch, which usually begins 1.d4 d5; 2.c4 e6; 3.Nc3 c5. Notice that none of Black's pawns followed the same path in this game. Kasparov used to play the Tarrasch, so this was nothing new to him. **8.Nf3 Nc6; 9.Qa4.** On 9.Qd1 White is a full tempo down on the normal Tarrasch. **9...Bc5; 10.0–0 0–0; 11.Ne1 d4!**

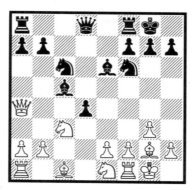

Black's play is normal Tarrasch strategy, and White's minor pieces, already badly placed, don't wind up on much better squares even after quite a bit of maneuvering. **12.Nd3 Bb6; 13.Nb5 Bd5; 14.Bh3 Re8; 15.Nf4.**

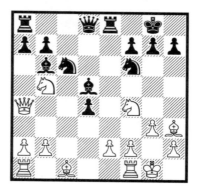

15...Be4! White's pieces are still ineffective. Watch how Kasparov quickly exploits the position. **16.Rd1 Qe7; 17.Na3 d3!; 18.exd3 Bf3.** Black is setting up threats on the back rank, but f2 is also weak. Kasparov smells blood and swims quickly toward the enemy king. **19.Rf1 Ng4!; 20.Bd2.** Perhaps White should have just traded the light-squared bishop for the knight at g4. **20...Nce5!; 21.Bg2.**

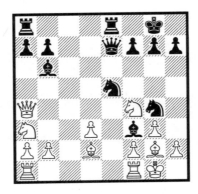

Now Kasparov just chops a lot of wood and opens up a path to the enemy king, taking advantage of the position of the knight at f4 to win time later with ...g5. **21...Nxf2!; 22.Rxf2 Bxg2; 23.Kxg2 Bxf2; 24.Kxf2 g5!** If the knight moves, then the pawn at d3 falls with check and nasty consequences. **25.Qe4 gxf4; 26.gxf4 Qh4+** and White resigned.

So keep in mind that the boundaries between different openings are quite fuzzy and that the general remarks we read will not apply to all positions arising from the opening under discussion.

6. FINDING THE BEST FIRST MOVE

WHAT'S THE BEST FIRST MOVE?

Almost five centuries of play with modern rules has so far failed to reach any sort of consensus on the best move to start the game. This is testimony to the lasting power of chess as a game. Although many arguments have been advanced for the several obvious candidates, and leading authorities have sometimes proclaimed the clear superiority of one opening over another, in fact the question remains open.

The first pair of obvious candidates are 1.e4 and 1.d4. Each occupies and controls important central territory and allows a bishop to get into the game. The pawn at d4 is protected by the queen, and this is sometimes used to argue for **1.d4**.

But this is not an important factor because the goal of either opening is to establish pawns at both squares. Here is the picture after **1.e4**.

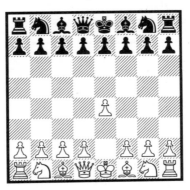

Since e4 is slightly more difficult to control, it could be argued that White should seize this square first. Black can try to prevent the White pawn from safely occupying e4 by playing ...d5 as soon as possible. Of White's first moves, only 1.e4 and 1.c4 discourage this reply, while 1.d4 allows it.

1.c4. gets an honorable mention because it does hinder 1...d5, since 2.cd5 Qxd5; 3.Nc3, gives White a clear initiative. On the other side of the board, 1.f4 is not as useful, because Black can reply 1...d5 and control the e4 square. Controlling e5 is not as important, and in fact when White does play 1.f4, 1...e5! is a very strong reply, known as the From Gambit. After 2.fxe5 d6; 3.exd6 Bxd6; White already has to worry about weaknesses on the kingside.

1.c4, on the other hand, does not endanger the king.

1.Nf3 is often seen, but again 1...d5 is a good reply and White has no real chance of establishing and maintaining the ideal pawn center. It is often used as a transpositional device to be followed by an early advance of White's pawn to d4.

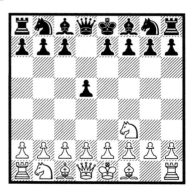

THE PREFERENCES OF THE CHAMPIONS

Let's look at the preferences of our World Champions. Most have had a strong preference for either 1.e4 or 1.d4, though a few have a more balanced view. Some like to use a flank strategy but vary the initial move between 1.d4, 1.c4, and 1.Nf3, often reaching similar positions as play develops.

Even in these cases, however, no champion has used moves other than 1.e4 and 1.d4 for more than about a quarter of their games.

Following is a chart prepared with the help of the DejaVu Chess Library database. It shows the ratio of 1.e4 to all other moves. There is no need to distinguish 1.d4 from the other alternatives, both because of the problems with transpositions and also because unorthodox strategies play no significant role in the repertoire of any of the players, never exceeding a couple of percentage points.

So we'll just use two groups, 1.e4, and all other moves.

WORLD CHAMPION OPENINGS

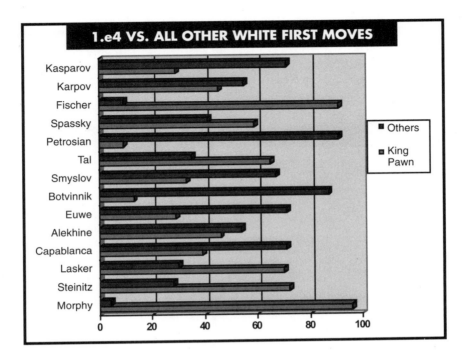

1.e4 VS. ALL OTHER WHITE FIRST MOVES

Kasparov, Karpov, Fischer, Spassky, Petrosian, Tal, Smyslov, Botvinnik, Euwe, Alekhine, Capablanca, Lasker, Steinitz, Morphy

Legend: ■ Others   ■ King Pawn

Horizontal axis: 0, 20, 40, 60, 80, 100

We can see 1.d4 has grown in popularity, but that 1.e4 remains a popular choice. Alekhine, Karpov, and Spassky have the most balanced repertoires, while Morphy, Botvinnik, Petrosian and Fischer are the most extreme. Yet even the extremists are divided on the subject!

Looking from the other side of the board, we can ask what opening moves are most frequently played against the World Champions. We'll use three categories: 1.e4, 1.d4, and the rest. This time we break out the alternatives to the main choices into a separate group, because many of these openings do not transpose into 1.d4 games. Sometimes players try to trick World Champions with unusual opening strategies, though these rarely succeed.

Perhaps we could resort to statistics to solve the question by asking which move provides the better results. That seems a reasonable approach, but you will find no deluge of numbers in this book. Statistics on chess openings, for several reasons, are simply meaningless. The result of a chess game is not directly tied to the result of the opening. Many twists, turns, blunders and brilliancies lie on the road between the opening and the endgame, and sometimes a game is lost by overstepping the time control in a winning position. Also keep in mind that the players may have been mismatched from the start.

Next, consider that an opening may win game after game until a refutation is found, and then disappear quickly. The *DejaVu Chess Library* database will simply show that one side won, say, 95% of the games with this opening. Yet once the refutation is established, no serious player will use the opening in competitive play.

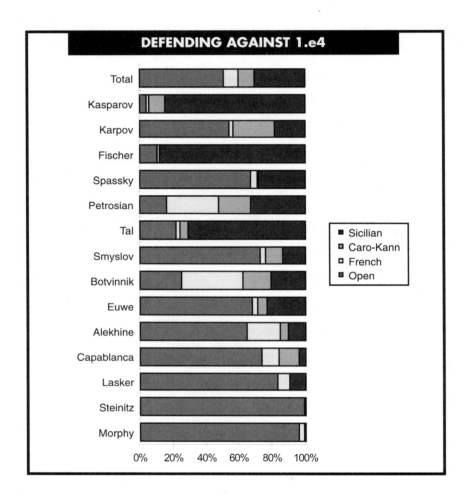

In this book, statistics and charts will only be used to illustrate points of preference for certain openings, not to make objective claims about the merits of each variation. Still, when we see that World Champions all avoid some lines to the point of excluding them entirely from their repertoires, it is safe to infer that there is at least a perceived problem with the opening.

WHAT ARE THE BEST DEFENSES?

Among World Champions there is no consensus on the best response to 1.e4 and 1.d4. Historically, the Open Games prevailed, but over time the Sicilian Defense has risen to prominence, and both the French and Caro-Kann defenses have their advocates among the champions. The chart on the previous page summarizes these preferences.

Working our way up from the (historical) bottom, we see that 1...e5 is the overwhelming favorite against 1.e4 from Paul Morphy through Max Euwe. With Euwe, this "classicism" is joined by the excitement of the Sicilian Defense. After the Second World War we see both the Open Games and the Sicilians controlling much of the action, though the French was a trusty weapon for Botvinnik and Petrosian, who also used the Caro-Kann. It is Anatoly Karpov, however, who has been the most enthusiastic supporter of 1...c6.

The top row shows the overall picture at a glance: Open Games and Sicilians dominate, and the French and Caro Kann are the only "acceptable" alternatives. True, the World Champions sometimes experiment with other plans. Alexander Alekhine brought 1...Nf6 to serious competition, but it appeared in a mere two percent of his outings as Black. Most of the champions played it at least once, but none, save Alekhine, thought it worthy of a dozen uses before being discarded.

Meeting 1.d4 leads to quite a different picture. Here the World Champions concentrate on three groups of openings. The first group is the Closed Games, typically starting 1.d4 d5, including the Queen's Gambits, Slav and Stonewall Dutch. The remaining two groups belong to the Indian family, characterized by the reply 1...Nf6.

Among the Indians there is a clear split between those which involve fianchettoing a bishop at g7, including the King's Indian, Benoni, Gruenfeld, and a second group where Black plays ...e6 and deploys the bishop at b4 or e7. We might call these groups the "King's Indians" and "Queen's Indians" but in fact those names are reserved for specific defenses.

If we view the board from Black's perspective as the "south" looking "north" at White, we can talk about the first group as West Indians (the bishop at g7 being Black's "West") and the second group as East Indians. This makes sense to me, since it is Black who determines whether a West Indian or East Indian is reached. Thus, it makes sense to view the board from Black's perpective. (These are convenient terms, but could cause confusion if you translate them into French, where they are reversed.) Here is a typical East Indian formation.

Notice that Black is battling for the e4-square with knight and bishop, while the other bishop pins the White knight, which would otherwise be able to influence the battle for e4.

In the West Indians, Black concedes the battle for e4, but concentrates on the d4-square and the entire h8-a1 diagonal. For example:

WORLD CHAMPION OPENINGS

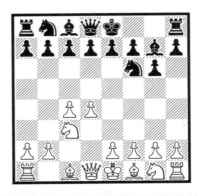

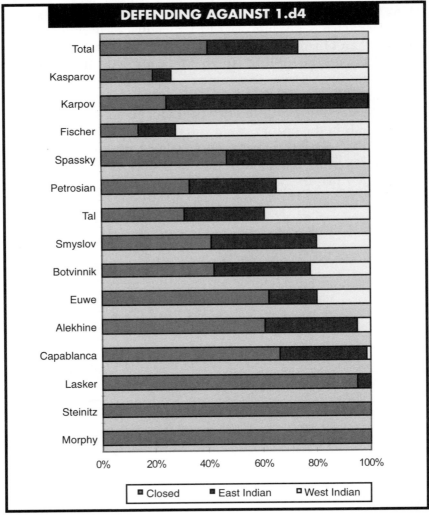

DEFENDING AGAINST 1.d4

- Total
- Kasparov
- Karpov
- Fischer
- Spassky
- Petrosian
- Tal
- Smyslov
- Botvinnik
- Euwe
- Alekhine
- Capablanca
- Lasker
- Steinitz
- Morphy

0%   20%   40%   60%   80%   100%

■ Closed   ■ East Indian   □ West Indian

In any case, we see from the chart on the previous page that in the overall experience of the World Champions, the three groups of openings hold a roughly level place, though the Closed games have been in decline ever since Morphy's day. Bobby Fischer and Garry Kasparov are the leading exponents of the King's Indian and Gruenfeld Defenses of the West Indians, while Anatoly Karpov, Boris Spassky and Vasily Smyslov prefer the Queen's Indian and Nimzoindians of the East. Mikhail Tal and Tigran Petrosian, rather surprisingly, had the most balanced repertoires.

DICTATING THE OPENING POSITION

We've seen that World Champions play both 1.e4 and 1.d4, as well as flank openings. At this level of classification, the choice switches over to Black. That is, if White plays 1.e4, then Black will choose whether the game is an Open Game or Semi-Open Game. If 1.d4, Black will choose a Closed Game, Indian Game, or other reply. If 1.c4 or 1.Nf3, Black can choose to play with symmetry, fight for the center, or adopt a fixed formation.

By understanding the different types of formations, and seeing how the best minds in the history of chess have played them, you'll be able to control the flow of the opening and achieve positions that you like to play. You'll enjoy the game a lot more, and of course, become a much stronger player.

Now let's move on to the openings themselves.

7. OPEN GAMES

INTRODUCTION

Ever since pawns earned the right to march forward two squares in one turn, the move 1.e4 has been a favorite at all levels of play. It is the first opening choice of most players, and for good reason. The White pawn at e4 occupies an important square and controls both d5 and f5. If Black places a piece at f6, White can attack it by further advancing the pawn to e5.

When Black responds with 1...e5, we have an **Open Game**. The point is not to maintain symmetry for its own sake, but rather to contest important squares in the center. By occupying e5, the pawn presents an obstacle to the further advance of the White pawn at e4. There are no real drawbacks to 1...e5, save that it can serve as a target for White's pieces.

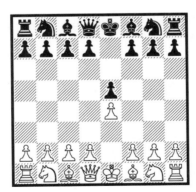

Indeed, the battle for control of e5 is the most significant aspect of the Open Games, and one which distinguishes them from all others. The most natural continuation, the **Spanish Game**, keeps the central battle raging for many moves. This has become the most established continuation, but White has also explored more direct methods of attack. Most of them have fallen from fashion, and only surface on rare occasions. There are a few, such as the **Italian Game**, that have attracted the serious attention of World Champions.

The pace of development in the Open Games is generally quite rapid, with all pieces comfortably developed and both kings castled safely well before the 15th move. If Black does not attend to the safety of the king early in the game, then the game can quickly end in disaster. White can afford the luxury of a few inaccurate moves, but Black must exercise more care. This is one of the aspects of Open Games that appeals to players as White, but can be annoying as Black.

Actually, the Open Games are fairly simple to play correctly if the pieces are developed actively by Black.

OVERVIEW

The Open Games have a long history and many branches have developed from the main lines. Nevertheless, the **Spanish Game** (1.e4 e5 2.Nf3 Nc6 3.Bb5), known in America as the **Ruy Lopez**, is the most respected of the Open Games. It contains a wealth of stylistic possibilities, and many players feel quite comfortable on either side of the board. It is rare to find a chessplayer who has never played it, and one can only pity those unfortunates, since the Spanish Game leads to some of the most profound positions in chess, which retain secrets even when analyzed well past move thirty.

The **Italian Game** (1.e4 e5 2.Nf3 Nc6 3.Bc4) is also ancient, with a great deal of theory accumulated well before the twentieth century. Nevertheless, new ideas are constantly being introduced, and both the present PCA World Champion, Garry Kasparov, and the FIDE World Champion, Anatoly Karpov, have played it in top-level competition. From the Italian Game, White can direct the play into the Scotch Gambit (1.e4 e5 2.Nf3 Nc6 3.Bc4 Nf6 4.d4, also reached via 3.d4 exd4 4.Bc4) or Evans Gambit (1.e4 e5 2.Nf3 Nc6 3.Bc4 Bc5 4.b4!?).

The **King's Gambit** (1.e4 e5 2.f4) retains its vitality even though it was supposedly analyzed to death over 75 years ago. The **Vienna Game** (1.e4 e5 2.Nc3), a rather stodgy approach, can take on gambit characteristics after 3.f4. Other gambits are no longer seen in high-level play, except as surprise weapons.

Black has some gambits available too, such as the **Latvian Gambit** (1.e4 e5 2.Nf3 f5), though they are generally considered inferior and are not played by World Champions in serious circumstances. For the most part it is too risky to invest a pawn when behind in development.

After 1.e4 e5 2.Nf3 Black has more reasonable alternatives, for example 2...Nf6, the **Russian Game**, in which piece symmetry can be maintained only briefly, but pawn structure can remain symmetrical throughout the game. Another interesting option is the **Philidor Defense** (1.e4 e5 2.Nf3 d6), which can lead to exciting positions with castling on opposite wings. The **Bishop's Opening** is a largely transpositional tool usually leading to the Italian Game.

SPANISH GAME

1.e4   e5
2.Nf3 Nc6
3.Bb5

The **Spanish Game**, also known as the **Ruy Lopez**, has figured prominently in the repertoire of several World Champions, especially Fischer, Lasker, Alekhine and Capablanca. Each of them played it in at least one out of every 6 games as White!

And when opponents ventured 1.e4 as White, the Spanish was often the result, except for Morphy and Steinitz, because the Spanish was out of favor then, considered too slow. Other 19th century masters preferred more direct attacking methods, such as the Italian Game or King's Gambit, for defensive technique was poor, and it was possible to win many games quickly in the opening. As chess evolved, defensive technique improved, and the Spanish took over the scene.

Notice in the graph on the following page how even when the Open Games did not figure prominently in the repertoire of a champion, the Spanish still usually featured in more games than all the remaining Open Games combined.

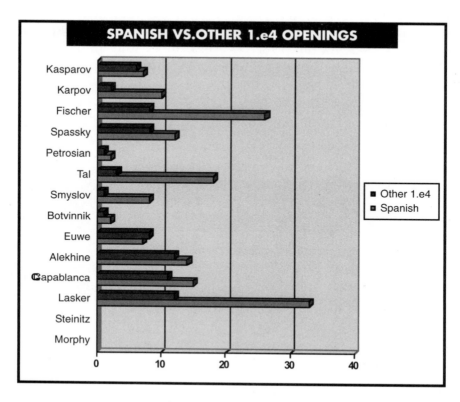

The Spanish Game is characterized by almost infinite variety, from quiet maneuvering games to savage kingside attacks. It is very easy to understand, and the typical ideas surface over and over again, giving the advantage to serious players. For me, the Spanish Game is like an old friend. I may travel the paths of many openings in the sheer joy of exploration, but there is always a satisfying feeling when I am back in Spanish territory again.

This is in many ways the most logical of chess openings. White plants a pawn at e4, hoping to send its companion to d4 as soon as possible. Black responds by occupying the important central square e5, while at the same time clamping down on d4. White then targets the enemy pawn at e5 while simultaneously developing a knight, and Black defends, but also gains development for the knight. Since the knight at c6 now defends the pawn at e5, White undermines the defense by threatening to capture the knight at c6 with the bishop that is now at b5.

Black usually reacts by provoking the exchange, playing 3...a6. Although this seems to fall in with White's plans, in fact after 4.Bxc6, the

Exchange Variation, Black plays 4...dxc6. Now 5.Nxe5 fails to 5...Qd4!. Of the World Champions, only Bobby Fischer has used the Exchange Variation as White with any regularity.

Normally, White retreats the bishop to a4, being unwilling to trade the powerful bishop for a mere knight. Then Black usually attacks the pawn at e4 with 4...Nf6, and White can afford to castle, since after 5.0-0 Nxe4 the pawn can be regained either quickly with 6.Re1, or with the superior 6.d4! b5; 7.Bb3, as we'll see in the section on the **Open Variation**. So instead of 5...Nxe4, the simple 5...Be7 is more common, leading to the **Closed Variation**.

Black does not have to play 3...a6. There are plenty of alternatives, even in the repertoires of the World Champions. We'll take a look at the active **Modern Steinitz Defense** and the wild **Schliemann Variation**, too.

CLOSED VARIATION

1.e4	e5
2.Nf3	Nc6
3.Bb5	a6
4.Ba4	Nf6
5.0-0	Be7

In the **Closed Variation**, both sides develop all of their forces before undertaking any active operations. The style of play is slow, maneuvering, and positional. If either side creates a serious weakness, however, the game can become vicious. Karpov is a leading exponent of the Black side. Kasparov once gave a convincing demonstration as Black, but is more often found playing White. It is fair to say that most great players have played both sides of the Closed Variation at some point in their career, if only when quite young.

Let's look at how Mikhail Tal handled the Black side:

10/21/7 ✓

1.e4 e5; 2.Nf3 Nc6; 3.Bb5 a6; 4.Ba4 Nf6; 5.0–0 Be7; 6.Re1 b5; 7.Bb3 0–0. Black should play 7...d6 if the Breyer Variation is the goal, because against this move Kasparov has demonstrated the power of 8.a4! **8.c3 d6; 9.h3** White plays this to keep the enemy bishop away from g4, when the pin on the knight is annoying. Now Black has many different strategies, including combining ...Bb7 and ...Re8, repositioning minor pieces with ...Nd7 and ...Bf6, or playing on the queenside with ...Na5. Tal chooses another, very respectable path. **9...Nb8.**

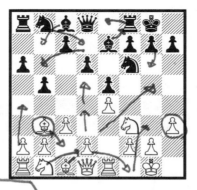

The Breyer Variation, which has held up well throughout the century. **10.d4 Nbd7; 11.Nbd2 Bb7; 12.Bc2 Re8; 13.Nf1 Bf8; 14.Ng3 g6; 15.b3.** An old fashioned line. Now 15.Bg5 and 15.a4 are preferred. **15...Bg7; 16.d5 Nb6; 17.Qe2?** A serious error which allows Tal to undermine White's center. The best plan is to play Be3 in order to put pressure on the dark squares and bring the other rook to a more active position. **17...c6; 18.c4 cxd5; 19.cxd5.**

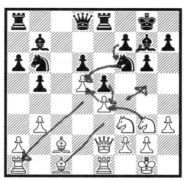

Time for Tal to create some fireworks. White's center looks very strong, but it crumbles quickly. **19...Nfxd5; 20.exd5 e4** The bishop on g7 now springs to life. **21.Nxe4 Bxa1; 22.Bg5 f6; 23.Be3.** Some people never learn. Over three decades later, White tried to improve with 23.Bh4 but suffered a similar fate after 23...Bxd5; 24.Rxa1 Bxe4; 25.Bxe4 d5 and Black, in another game played in Germany, had a big advantage. **23...Nxd5; 24.Rxa1 Nxe3; 25.Qxe3 Bxe4; 26.Bxe4 d5.**

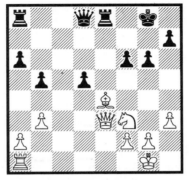

White resigned, since the bishop is lost. Note that Rd1 doesn't help because Black can capture the bishop with the rook anyway, with a decisive advantage.

One of the most exciting variations in the Closed Spanish is the Marshall Attack, seen here in a game between Frank Marshall and World Champion Capablanca.

(3) CAPABLANCA - MARSHALL
New York, 1918

1.e4 e5; 2.Nf3 Nc6; 3.Bb5 a6; 4.Ba4 Nf6; 5.0–0 Be7; 6.Re1 b5; 7.Bb3 0–0; 8.c3. Kasparov has demonstrated recently that 8.a4 may be more accurate, keeping the initiative by attacking at b5. **8...d5!?**

The now-famous Marshall Attack, is still popular in contemporary chess, with Viswanathan Anand the leading advocate. It was quite a shock when this game was played with the inventor handling the Black pieces. **9.exd5 Nxd5; 10.Nxe5 Nxe5; 11.Rxe5.**

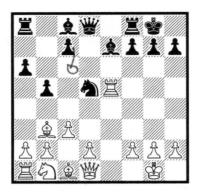

11...Nf6. As a result of this game, 11...Nf6 fell out of favor, and 11...c6 has become the standard continuation. The evaluation of the Marshall remains unclear, but as noted in the note to move 8, White may have a way of avoiding it and obtaining an advantage at the same time. **12.Re1 Bd6; 13.h3 Ng4; 14.Qf3!** 14.hxg4 Qh4; 15.g3 Bxg3; 16.fxg3 Qxg3+; 17.Kf1 Bxg4 and Black wins. **14...Qh4; 15.d4!** 15.Re8 is met by 15...Bb7! **15...Nxf2; 16.Re2** 16.Qxf2? would be a blunder because of 16...Bh2+; 17.Kf1 Bg3; 18.Qxf7+ Rxf7+ and, because it is check, White has no time for 19.Re8 mate.

16...Bg4. 16...Ng4; 17.Nd2. Taking the rook leads to disaster because Black infiltrates with the queen at g3. 17...Bd7; 18.Nf1 Nf6; 19.Be3 and White is clearly better. **17.hxg4 Bh2+; 18.Kf1 Bg3;** 18...Nh1; 19.Be3 Ng3+; 20.Ke1 Nxe2+; 21.Kxe2 Rae8; 22.Nd2 is a position Black wouldn't wish on his mother-in-law. The h-file will be an expressway to disaster, and the pressure on the e-file is irrelevant. **19.Rxf2 Qh1+.**

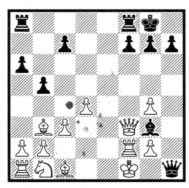

20.Ke2. Capablanca is conducting the defense with utmost precision and Black's attack is falling apart. **20...Bxf2;** 20...Qxc1; 21.Rf1 Qxb2+; 22.Nd2 Bd6; 23.Bxf7+ and White wins. **21.Bd2 Bh4; 22.Qh3.** If Black exchanges queens, then there is no more attack and resignation is inevitable. **22...Rae8+; 23.Kd3 Qf1+; 24.Kc2.**

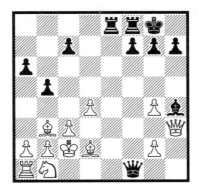

White is not worried. Black has too little in the way of attacking force, and all Capablanca has to do is activate the rook at a1. **24...Bf2; 25.Qf3 Qg1; 26.Bd5 c5; 27.dxc5 Bxc5; 28.b4 Bd6** White has two pieces for a rook, but the rook has been sitting on a1 the entire game.

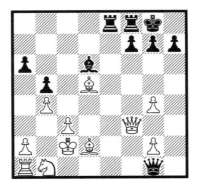

Now Capablanca brings it out. **29.a4! a5; 30.axb5 axb4; 31.Ra6! bxc3; 32.Nxc3 Bb4** Capablanca's king is completely safe, and his attack is stronger than it looks . **33.b6 Bxc3; 34.Bxc3 h6; 35.b7 Re3.** Here Capablanca finished off the game with a brilliant move, announcing mate in 6. **36.Bxf7+;** 36.Qxf7+!? Rxf7; 37.b8Q+ Kh7; 38.Rxh6+ Kxh6; 39.Qh8+ Kg5; 40.Qh5+ Kf4; 41.Qxf7+ would have been pretty, but much slower. **36...Rxf7;** 36...Kh8; 37.Rxh6 mate. **37.b8Q+.** A new queen brings the game to a swift conclusion. **37...Re8; 38.Qxe8+ Kh7; 39.Qfe4+ Rf5; 40.Qxf5+ g6; 41.Qexg6 mate.**

OPEN VARIATION

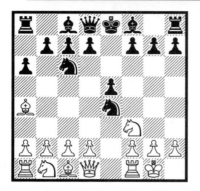

1.e4	e5
2.Nf3	Nc6
3.Bb5	a6
4.Ba4	Nf6
5.0-0	Nxe4

The **Open Variation** gives Black temporary custody of a pawn. Most World Champions strongly prefer to be White in this opening, and in championship competition both Anatoly Karpov and Garry Kasparov have given their opponents a sever spanking in these lines.

One of the most famous games in the Open Spanish was played quite recently.

(4) KASPAROV - ANAND
New York (PCA World Championship, 10th game), 1995

1.e4. This game was in many ways the most memorable of the 1995 PCA World Chamnpionship Match. Kasparov's home preparation was fantastic, and he didn't need to break a sweat to earn his point at the board. It illustrates how powerful new (or forgotten) ideas can bring about a devastating psychological blow in addition to any objective merits the idea may have. **1...e5; 2.Nf3 Nc6; 3.Bb5 a6; 4.Ba4 Nf6; 5.0–0 Nxe4; 6.d4 b5.** This counterattack is always seen, to release the pressure on the queenside. **7.Bb3** White threatens to move the bishop to d5. **7...d5; 8.dxe5 Be6.**

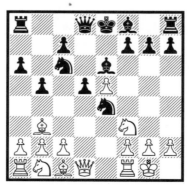

The last few moves are firmly established as best, but now White has several plans. **9.Nbd2.** This move has moved up to an equal position with 9.c3 as the main line of the Open Spanish. **9...Nc5; 10.c3 d4.** The most aggressive, but also the riskiest line. After 10...Bg4, intending to retreat the knight to e6, Black has a decent game. **11.Ng5.** This introduces a piece sacrifice which leads to unclear complications if accepted. Anand had prepared an alternative line. **11...dxc3; 12.Nxe6 fxe6; 13.bxc3 Qd3.** This much had been seen in game 6 of the match, but in this game Kasparov was ready with an old new move from the magical hand of Mikhail Tal.

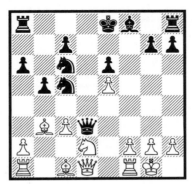

14.Bc2!! Tal's idea is to set up a magnificent rook sacrifice. Kasparov claimed that the idea had only come to his attention a few days before this game. **14...Qxc3.** Anand responded quickly and seemed to be well within his own preparation. **15.Nb3.** This seemed to catch Anand by surprise. Kasparov sacrifices the rook at a1 for a fierce attack. **15...Nxb3.**

Amazingly, even this much is not new. An obscure postal game between Berg and Nevestveit in 1990 reached the same position, and varied with 15...Rd8. After 16.Bd2 Qxc5; 17.Re1 Qd5, Kasparov would have played not 18.Nxc5, as in the cited game, but rather 18.Qg4! which would have brought victory quickly. **16.Bxb3.**

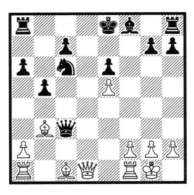

16...Nd4. Anand defers acceptance of the sacrifice until the next move. After 16...Qxa1; 17.Qh5+ it is hard to find a defense for Black. **17.Qg4 Qxa1; 18.Bxe6 Rd8.** At this point there doesn't seem to be any way to save the game for Black.

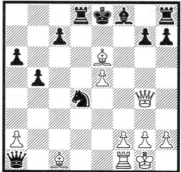

19.Bh6 Qc3. Not 19...Qxf1+?; 20.Kxf1 gxh6; 21.Qh5+. **20.Bxg7 Qd3; 21.Bxh8 Qg6;** 21...Ne2+ only postpones the inevitable. **22.Bf6 Be7; 23.Bxe7 Qxg4** Or 23...Kxe7; 24.Qh4+. **24.Bxg4 Kxe7; 25.Rc1.** By now Kasparov is out of his opening preparation and has a winning position, but it still requires accurate play, which the World Champion carries out with efficiency. **25...c6; 26.f4 a5; 27.Kf2 a4; 28.Ke3 b4.**

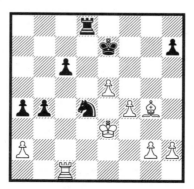

29.Bd1. The bishop gets out of the way so that the g-pawn can advance. **29...a3; 30.g4 Rd5; 31.Rc4 c5; 32.Ke4 Rd8; 33.Rxc5 Ne6; 34.Rd5 Rc8; 35.f5 Rc4+; 36.Ke3 Nc5; 37.g5 Rc1; 38.Rd6. White won.**

MODERN STEINITZ DEFENSE

Boris Spassky was a specialist in a variation on a theme by Steinitz. The **"Modern" Steinitz** is an improved version of 1.e5 e5; 2.Nf3 Nc6; 3.Bb5 d6?!, which has fallen into disrepute. By interpolating ...a6 and

Ba4, Black now has the option of driving back the enemy bishop with
...b5 when necessary.

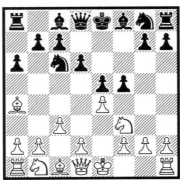

1.e4	e5
2.Nf3	Nc6
3.Bb5	a6
4.Ba4	d6

(5) RETI - CAPABLANCA
Berlin, 1928

1.e4. Reti took a break from his preferred flank openings for this game.
1...e5; 2.Nf3 Nc6; 3.Bb5 d6. An old and discredited defense, but the game
quickly transposes to a more popular line. **4.c3.** Laziness, perhaps. 4.d4 is the
correct way to get an advantage for White. **4...a6; 5.Ba4.** We are now in the
Modern Steinitz Variation, a respectable weapon which was adopted by several Champions, including Spassky. **5...f5.** This is the famous Siesta Variation.
It is not considered fully playable for Black, but is a fun surprise weapon and
demonstrates some of the exciting possibilities of the Spanish Game.

6.d4. Modern authorities prefer capturing at f5, which leads to rapid development for White. 6.exf5 Bxf5 7.0–0 Bd3 To try to prevent d4, after which
White would have a clear advantage. 8.Re1 Be7 9.Bc2! Bxc2 10.Qxc2 Nf6 11.d4!
and White has the initiative. **6...fxe4; 7.Ng5 exd4; 8.Nxe4.** White might do
better to castle and make a gambit of the opening. **8...Nf6.** Black uses the

exposed White knight to develop with tempo. **9.Bg5 Be7; 10.Qxd4.** White miscalculates that Black won't be able to take advantage of his exposed queen. **10...b5.** Winning material, but White must have felt that Black's many pawn moves would give White enough counterplay. **11.Nxf6+ gxf6; 12.Qd5 bxa4.**

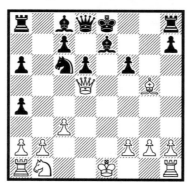

13.Bh6. 13.Qxc6+ achieves nothing against 13...Bd7 **13...Qd7.** This fine move defends the knight as well as the bishop on e7, prepares to attack White's kingside by a later ...Qg4 or Qh3 and gets ready to castle queenside. **14.0-0 Bb7.** Aiming his extra piece straight at White's king position. **15.Bg7 0-0-0.** Another fine move. Black is willing to give back a little material to take the initiative. After White takes the rook Black will have his queen bishop, knight, queen and rook all aiming at White's king, which has no defenders. **16.Bxh8.**

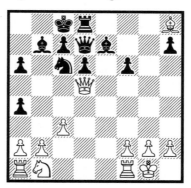

16...Ne5. Now White's queen won't be able to get back to defend the kingside. **17.Qd1 Bf3.** Very powerful, Black wins a tempo on White's queen while not allowing the counterplay White might hope for after, e.g. 17...Qf5 18.Qxa4. **18.gxf3 Qh3.** White has no defence to threats like 19...Nxf3+ and 19...Rg8+, so Reti resigned.

EXCHANGE VARIATION

1.e4   e5
2.Nf3   Nc6
3.Bb5   a6
4.Bxc6 dxc6

The **Exchange Variation**, where White voluntarily gives up the bishop pair in return for damage to the enemy pawn structure, would be a minor footnote if Bobby Fischer hadn't been such a passionate supporter of the line. This is different from all other Spanish lines, and that is perhaps part of its appeal. Black will have to defend accurately for some time, after which a draw is most likely the result.

Since Fischer is the leading Champion exponent of the Exchange Variation, let's see him in action against another World Champion!

(6) FISCHER - SPASSKY
Sveti Stefan (game 9), 1992

1.e4 e5; 2.Nf 3 Nc6; 3.Bb5 a6; 4.Bxc6 dxc6; 5.0–0

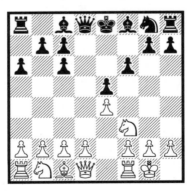

5...f6. This move would be odd in most circumstances, but in the Exchange Spanish it is almost inevitable. **6.d4**. 6.Nxe5 fxe5, 7.Qh5+ Kd7 and despite the exposed position of the Black king, White cannot successfully conclude the attack. **6...exd4; 7.Nxd4 c5.** This lets Black exchange queens. Then, in the endgame, the bishops can be effective. A good plan, but the attack does not end when the queens leave the playing field! **8.Nb3 Qxd1; 9.Rxd1.**

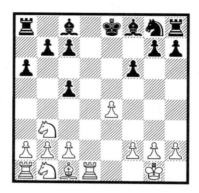

White has a pawn majority on the kingside, and this can be decisive in some endgames. Black has the bishop pair, which can wreak havoc in the middlegame if enough lines are opened. **9...Bg4; 10.f3 Be6.** Black provoked the weakness of the a7-g1 diagonal with this maneuver. **11.Nc3 Bd6; 12.Be3 b6.** Black's clerics are remarkably silent. Yet at the time this game was played, the position was considered quite reasonable. **13.a4.**

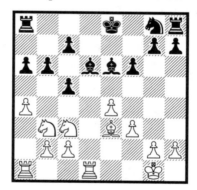

Now, according to Kasparov, Spassky should have played 13...Kf7 with equal chances. The brilliant tactician and theoretician Leonid Shamkovich points out that 13...a5 might also be playable. Shamkovich is probably right, since by allowing the White pawn to reach a5 at the next move Spassky digs his own grave. **13...0-0-0.** The books said this was a fine move, but Fischer proves otherwise. **14.a5 Kb7.**

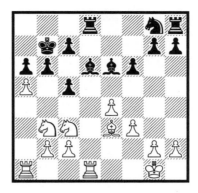

The whole point of the formation with pawn at f6 and bishop at d6 is to prevent the White pawn from reaching e5. Bobby Fischer is not so easily denied! **15.e5!!** The first sign of serious trouble for Black. The pawn cannot be taken. Curiously, this is not the first time this position has been reached. We are still in known territory. **15...Be7.** 15...fxe5; 16.axb6 cxb6; 17.Ne4 Bc7 and White can win material with a small sacrifice. 18.Nbxc5+ bxc5; 19.Nxc5+ Kc8; 20.Rxd8+ Bxd8; 21.Nxe6 is gruesome. **16.Rxd8 Bxd8; 17.Ne4.** An improvement on 17.axb6 cxb6, which had been seen back in 1976.

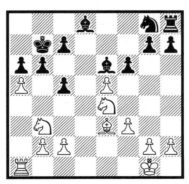

Now Spassky blunders away the game, yet we are still following a game which was over a decade old at the time. Spassky is a creative genius, but has never been known as a particularly hard worker, especially in the opening. **17...Kc6??** 17...Bxb3; 18.cxb3 f5; 19.Rd1 Ne7; 20.Ng5 Nc6; 21.axb6 Bxg5; 22.Bxg5 Kxb6; 23.Rd7 Re8; 24.Rxg7 Rxe5; 25.Rxh7 Re1+; 26.Kf2 Rb1; 27.h4 gave White a substantial advantage in a 1980 game played by Fischer's friend Peter Biyiasas as White. Fischer may have known the game from Biyiasas, or may have read about it in a 1992 book on the opening in which considerable analysis of the position was published, **18.axb6 cxb6.**

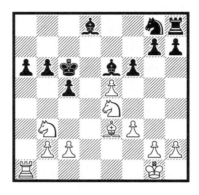

Now the heavily defended pawn at c5 is blown away. **19.Nbxc5! Bc8.** 19...bxc5; 20.Rxa6+ Kd7; 21.Nxc5+ Ke7; 22.Nxe6 g6; 23.Bc5+ Ke8; 24.Ra8 and White wins the bishop. **20.Nxa6 fxe5; 21.Nb4+. White won.**

(7) LASKER - CAPABLANCA
St. Petersburg, 1914

1.e4 e5; 2.Nf3 Nc6; 3.Bb5 a6; 4.Bxc6 dxc6.

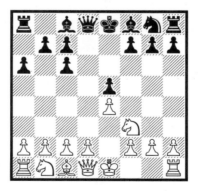

Normally White castles here, but the immediate 5.d4, leading to an early endgame, is very instructive of the basic ideas of the opening. **5.d4 exd4; 6.Qxd4 Qxd4; 7.Nxd4 Bd6.** In the Exchange Variation the bishop pair can be very useful to Black, but White has a pawn majority on the kingside. **8.Nc3 Ne7.** This is a very natural position for the knight, which can move to g6 or c6 as required. At the same time, it is less of a target for White's pieces when it is on e7, compared to the more exposed position on f6. **9.0–0.**

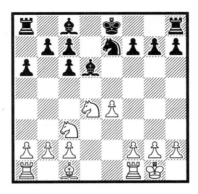

9...0-0. 9...Bd7 Black has the option of castling on either side now; 9...f5; 10.Re1 0-0; 11.e5 Bc5; 12.Nb3 Ba7. Black plans to advance the f-pawn and isolate the pawn at e5. **10.f4.** This creates a weakness on the a7-g1 diagonal. **10...Re8.** A very clever move. Suppose White just "passes" with a move like 11.h3. Then with ...Bc5 Black pins the knight to the king. White must be careful. 10...Bc5; 11.Be3 Re8. Black stands better, since there is the threat of Nd5; 10...f5; 11.e5 Bc5; 12.Be3 Bxd4; 13.Bxd4 Nd5 White has a passed pawn, but a blockade can be set up on the e6-square. **11.Nb3.** 11.h3 Bc5; 12.Be3 Nd5. There are two pins in this position, on the knight at d4 and the bishop at e3. **11...f6.** This is a mistake, creating a weakness. White's threat of advancing the pawn to e5 was not so dangerous. **12.f5.**

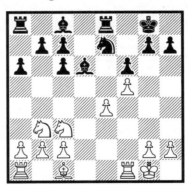

An important move, and a strong one. White concedes control of e5, but takes the e6-square. **12...b6.** An attempt to bring the bishop to a useful diagonal. But that piece would have functioned better as a defender at d7. 12...Bd7; 13.Bf4 Bxf4; 14.Rxf4 Nc8. **13.Bf4 Bb7.** Black should just have captured at f4. **14.Bxd6 cxd6.** The Black pawns on the queenside are weak. **15.Nd4** Capablanca had just overlooked this move. **15...Rad8 16.Ne6.**

This infiltration of the outpost at e6 puts Black in real trouble. **16...Rd7; 17.Rad1 Nc8;** 17...c5; 18.Nd5 Bxd5; 19.exd5 b5 Black will transfer the knight via c8-b6-d7-e5 and will then have a good position, as noted by Capablanca. **18.Rf2 b5; 19.Rfd2 Rde7; 20.b4 Kf7; 21.a3 Ba8.** 21...Rxe6; **22.Kf2 Ra7; 23.g4 h6; 24.Rd3 a5; 25.h4 axb4; 26.axb4 Rae7.** 26...Ra3. Black seizes the open lines and will bring the knight into the game via b6. **27.Kf3 Rg8; 28.Kf4** A serious error. The correct move was 28.Rg3. **28...g6.** Now it is Black's turn to go astray. 28...g5+ was correct. **29.Rg3 g5+.** Too late. **30.Kf3 Nb6; 31.hxg5 hxg5.**

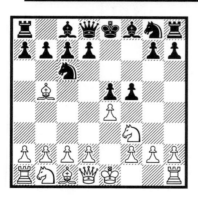

Now White grabs the h-file and the rest is fairly simple. **32.Rh3 Rd7; 33.Kg3 Ke8; 34.Rdh1 Bb7; 35.e5!** A fine move which liberates the d4 square for use by the knight. **35...dxe5; 36.Ne4 Nd5; 37.N6c5 Bc8; 38.Nxd7 Bxd7; 39.Rh7 Rf8; 40.Ra1 Kd8; 41.Ra8+ Bc8; 42.Nc5. White won.**

SCHLIEMANN VARIATION

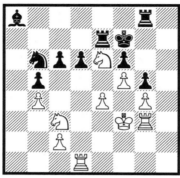

1.e4   e5
2.Nf3 Nc6
3.Bb5 f5

For fearless players, the **Schliemann Variation** is an excellent choice. Periodically refuted, it rises from the ashes like a phoenix, only to be beaten down again for a while. Its precarious status keeps the World Champions away, at least as far as regular use is concerned. It is a great deal of fun to play and is the subject of several monographs by the author, working with Grandmaster Leonid Shamkovich.

(8) FISCHER - MATULOVIC
Herceg Novi (blitz), 1970

1.e4 e5; 2.Nf3 Nc6; 3.Bb5 f5; 4.Nc3. This is the best way to confront the Schliemann, and the choice of champions. White is willing to enter some massive complications. **4...fxe4; 5.Nxe4 d5.**

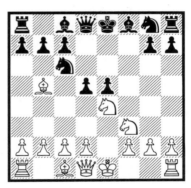

Black has the ideal pawn center, but just for a moment. The pin on the knight at c6 deprives the center of necessary support. **6.Nxe5.** Fischer took every game seriously and he rarely withheld theoretically important moves, even in blitz games. Here he chose the most theoretical variation, unafraid of his opponent's knowledge of the opening. **6...dxe4; 7.Nxc6 Qg5.**

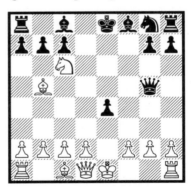

What a wild position after just seven moves! Neither side has much in the way of development, and White's discovered check on the queenside remains a relatively minor threat. **8.Qe2.** This developing move is best, and has the advantage of defending the bishop at b5 and attacking the pawn at e4. **8...Nf6; 9.f4 Qxf4;** 9...Qh4+ is the better move, since the text allows White to complete his development in peace. **10.d4?!** 10.Ne5+! is better, but Black reacts poorly. **10...Qh4+?!** This move is just a waste of time now, and was probably played routinely, counting on the inaccurate play of previous games to be followed in this game. **11.g3 Qh3.**

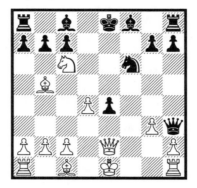

Here Fischer unleashed a powerful novelty: **12.Bg5!** 12.Nxa7+ Bd7; 13.Bxd7+ Qxd7; 14.Nb5 c6; 15.Nc3 Bb4! is good for Black, as demonstrated by Tatai and Zinser: 16.Be3 0–0; 17.0–0 Bxc3; 18.bxc3 b5!; 19.c4 bxc4; 20.Qxc4+ Nd5. **12...a6; 13.Ba4 Bd7; 14.Bxf6 gxf6.** Fischer had this exchange in mind when he played 12.Bg5. White sacrifices material to blow open the kingside. **15.Qxe4+ Kf7.**

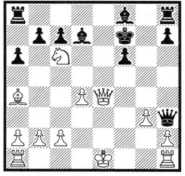

15...Qe6; 16.Qxe6+ Bxe6; 17.0–0! is clearly better for White. **16.Ne5+!** A forcing variation in the romantic style. **16...fxe5; 17.Rf1+ Ke7; 18.Bxd7.**

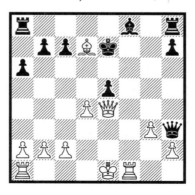

It seems that it took twenty years to determine which capture for Black is more acceptable. **18...Kxd7.** 18...Qxd7 is better. Here White castled in the only game in which the line was played, but in my opinion capturing at e5 with the pawn, giving more scope to the White queen along the fourth rank, makes more sense. Of course in that case White must also worry about the exposed king, so it is easy to understand why castling was played. 19.0-0-0 (19.Qxe5+ is met by 19...Qe6) 19...Qe6; 20.Qxe5 Qxe5; 21.dxe5 gives Black a piece for two pawns, as seen in a 1992 game. **19.Rf7+ Ke8; 20.Rxc7.**

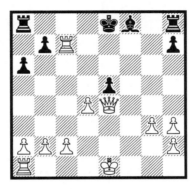

The influence of the rook along the seventh rank is deadly. **20...Bd6; 21.Rxb7.** White has equalized the material without slowing his attack. **21...Rc8; 22.0-0-0.** Finally the White king finds safety. **22...Qxh2; 23.dxe5 Be7.**

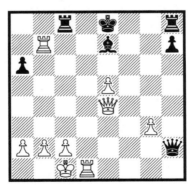

White is down a bishop, but has three pawns and a strong attack. With the next move, Fischer invests another exchange (rook for minor piece) to bring home the point. **24.Rxe7+ Kxe7; 25.Qb7+ Ke6; 26.Qd7+.** The mating hunt is on. **26...Kxe5; 27.Qd5+ Kf6; 28.Rf1+ Kg6; 29.Qf5+ Kh6; 30.Qe6+ Kh5; 31.Rf5+ Kg4; 32.Rf4+ Kxg3; 33.Qg4 mate.**

ITALIAN GAME

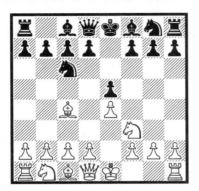

1.e4   e5
2.Nf3   Nc6
3.Bc4

The **Italian Game** is one of the oldest openings in chess and has been analyzed for many centuries. World Champions have tended to prefer the Spanish Game, but the Italian has seen a revival recently, with both Karpov and Kasparov enjoying the White side. Still, it is the Romantic masters, such as Morphy and Steinitz, who are most closely associated with the Italian game. Steinitz, Lasker, Capablanca, Alekhine and Euwe also had experience with these lines.

By placing the bishop at c4, White targets the most vulnerable point in the Black camp, the f7-square, which lies close to the heart of the enemy king. In the 19th century, White usually planned an early, direct assault on the enemy king. As defensive skills improved, however, it became clear that such premature assaults would be easily repelled, and the Italian Game was less frequently seen at the highest levels of competition.

In the middle of the 20th century new ways of handling the White side arose, with a more positional orientation. Instead of launching an early attack, White simply developed all pieces on useful squares, postponing confrontation for later.

This approach was made possible because White controls the center, thanks to the ability to create a pawn chain with pawns at c3 and d4. The ideal pawn center, the goal for White in the Open Game as we discussed earlier, is achieved in stages. The control of the center makes it easy for White to transfer pieces from one side of the board to another, while at the same time limiting the opponent's mobility. White can often afford to sacrifice a pawn or two in order to accelerate the involvement of pieces in the attack.

The Italian Game is effective against weaker opposition, especially players whose defense is not solid. It can also be used against stronger players, but it is unlikely to provide the same benefits as the Spanish Game, because your opponent is likely to beat back any immediate attack and then exploit the weaknesses created during the attack to win by positional means. As with the Spanish Game, an understanding of typical patterns of play is more important than memorization of specific variations. There are almost no traps that White can fall into early in the game.

To prepare to face weaker opposition, study the games of Morphy and Steinitz. If you wish to use the opening in serious play, you should also pay attention to how Kasparov and Karpov handle the White pieces, but remember, except for Morphy and Steinitz, all other World Champions prefer the Spanish Game.

There are three basic variations in the Italian Game. In the **Classical Variation**, Black responds by playing 3...Bc5, and White plans a takeover of the center by advancing a pawn to c3 followed by a pawn advance to d4. Some modern masters take an even quieter method by playing the pawn only to d3, and maneuvering behind closed barriers. The **Evans Gambit** takes a more radical approach, sacrificing a pawn with 4.b4 to lure the Black bishop to b4. Then the advance of the pawn to c3 attacks the bishop, which must retreat, and White is able to plant the pawn at d4 right away. Finally, Black often avoids both of these plans by playing 3...Nf6, the **Two Knights Defense**, which tries to counter the central pressure by attacking the White pawn at e4.

CLASSICAL VARIATION

1.e4   e5
2.Nf3   Nc6
3.Bc4   Bc5
4.c3

In the **Classical Variation**, White attempts to establish the ideal pawn center with 1.e4 e5; 2.Nf3 Nc6; 3.Bc4 Bc5; 4.c3. This can be attempted early in the game, a strategy which is no longer effective since Black has learned how to cope with it, or later, after a preliminary d3 to bring the dark-squared bishop into the game at g5 or e3. The slower path, also known as the Giuoco Pianissimo, has been popular with Anatoly Karpov and several leading Grandmasters.

(9) STEINITZ - VON BARDELEBEN
Hastings, 1895

1.e4 e5; 2.Nf3 Nc6; 3.Bc4 Bc5; 4.c3 Nf6; 5.d4 exd4; 6.cxd4.

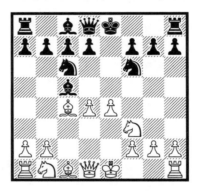

White has established the ideal pawn center and is attacking the Black bishop. **6...Bb4+; 7.Nc3!?** After the safer 7.Bd2 Bxd2+; 8.Nbxd2 d5; 9.exd5 Nxd5 play is about equal. **7...d5!?** After years of study, theorists have found that 7...Nxe4 is best, with the main line being a temporary piece sacrifice: 8.0-0 Bxc3!; 9.d5 , leading to enormous complications. **8.exd5 Nxd5; 9.0-0!**

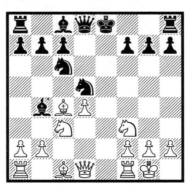

9...Be6. Black cannot take the pawn: 9...Nxc3; 10.bxc3 Bxc3?; 11.Qb3! Bxa1; 12.Bxf7+ Kf8; 13.Ba3+ Ne7; 14.Rxa1 followed by Re1. **10.Bg5 Be7;**

11.Bxd5! Steinitz recognizes that he needs to act fast if he is to achieve any advantage. His attack is based on keeping the Black king stuck in the center. He was justifiably recognized as the founder of modern positional chess, but in his younger days, he was known as 'The Austrian Morphy' for his brilliant attacks. **11...Bxd5; 12.Nxd5 Qxd5; 13.Bxe7 Nxe7; 14.Re1 f6.**

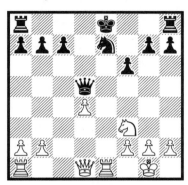

White now needs to maintain his edge in development or Black simply castles by hand with 15...Kf7 and 16...Rhe8, where he will have the better game because of White's isolated pawn on d4. **15.Qe2 Qd7; 16.Rac1!** White might have tried 16.d5 followed by 17.Nd4. **16...c6?** Black's only move was 16...Kf7 to connect the rooks and defend the knight from behind. **17.d5! cxd5; 18.Nd4.** The knight enters the attack with devastating force. **18...Kf7; 19.Ne6 Rhc8; 20.Qg4 g6; 21.Ng5+ Ke8.** Now follows one of the great chess combinations.

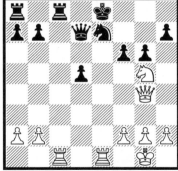

22.Rxe7+! Kf8. 22...Qxe7 loses to 23.Rxc8+ but 22...Kxe7 is not much better: 22...Kxe7; 23.Re1+ Kd6; 24.Qb4+ Kc7; 25.Ne6+ Kb8; 26.Qf4+ Rc7; 27.Nxc7. But after 22...Kf8, it looks as though White is in trouble, because back-rank mate threatens, and in fact all four of White's pieces are about to be captured! Steinitz has seen further. **23.Rf7+! Kg8.**

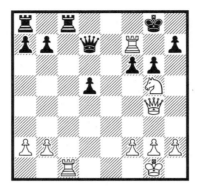

Black still cannot capture the rook: 23...Qxf7; 24.Rxc8+ Rxc8; 25.Qxc8+ Qe8 and White wins. **24.Rg7+!** This monster cannot be killed. **24...Kh8** Black also loses after 24...Kf8, 25.Nxh7+! **25.Rxh7+.** Von Bardeleben resigned here not wanting to provide the pleasure of a beautiful finish. 25...Kg8; 26.Rg7+!

Once again, 26...Kf8; 27.Nh7+ or 26...Qxg7; 27.Rxc8+ lose, so Black must return to h8. But now the queen enters the attack via the opened h-file: 26...Kh8; 27.Qh4+! Kxg7; 28.Qh7+ Kf8; 29.Qh8+ Ke7; 30.Qg7+ Ke8. Black gets mated after 30...Kd6, 31.Qxf6+ Ke7; 32.Qf7+ Kd8; 33.Qf8+ Qe8; 34.Nf7+! Kd7; 35.Qd6 mate.

EVANS GAMBIT

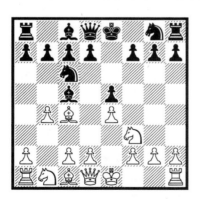

1.e4   e5
2.Nf3 Nc6
3.Bc4 Bc5
4.b4

1.e4 e5; 2.Nf3 Nc6; 3.Bc4 Bc5; 4.b4 is the **Evans Gambit,** a very sharp attacking variation.

Captain Evans' Gambit is enjoying a new round of popularity and is anything but washed up! White sacrifices a pawn for rapid development, as in most gambits. Here, the point is that the bishop on b4 can be attacked by advancing a pawn to c3, and after the bishop retreats, White can advance the d-pawn to d4, setting up the "ideal pawn center".

There are additional weapons at White's disposal. For example, the queen can make good use of the d1-a4 diagonal, and often moves to a4 to put pressure on the a4-e8 diagonal. The bishop at c1 can go to the kingside, but it is often best used at a3, sweeping down the a3-f8 diagonal, or b2, where it lies like a sleeping serpent, only to dart into the kingside after the pawns advance from c3 and d4.

Rapid development combined with control of the center is often sufficient compensation for a pawn. Bobby Fischer and Garry Kasparov have both been seen as White, though only on rare excursions.

(10) FISCHER - FINE
New York, 1963

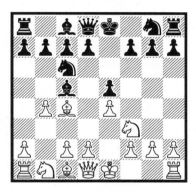

1.e4 e5; 2.Nf3 Nc6; 3.Bc4 Bc5; 4.b4!? Fine, playing Black, was a leading authority on the opening, so the stage was set for an interesting battle. **4...Bxb4; 5.c3 Ba5; 6.d4 exd4.** Fine continues to play sharply. **7.0-0 dxc3?!** It is said that the only way to refute a gambit is to accept it, but this is a bit too much. Black really needs to develop, and even 7...Bb6 is logical, keeping some pressure in the center. **8.Qb3 Qe7; 9.Nxc3.**

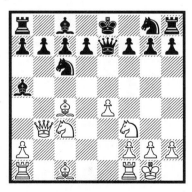

Black must get the queens off the board at all costs, so the correct move is 9...Qb4, even though it gives up the pawn at f7. **9...Nf6?** Black is already struggling but this knight just becomes a target. **10.Nd5!** White grabs the initiative and never lets go. **10...Nxd5; 11.exd5 Ne5.** 11...Nd8? 12.Ba3 d6; 13.Qb5+ Bd7; 14.Qxa5 **12.Nxe5 Qxe5; 13.Bb2 Qg5.**

White must keep up the pressure or else Black's king will escape from the center. **14.h4!** This deflects the enemy queen. **14...Qxh4;** 14...Qg4; 15.Rfe1+! Bxe1; 16.Rxe1+ Kd8; 17.Qe3 Qxh4; 18.g3! Black cannot keep control of e7. **15.Bxg7 Rg8; 16.Rfe1+ Kd8.** Taking the rook leads to the same finish. **17.Qg3!** Black resigned, as there is no way to defend f6.

TWO KNIGHTS

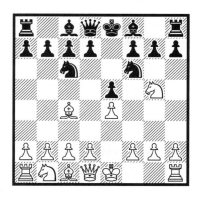

1.e4	e5
2.Nf3	Nc6
3.Bc4	Nf6

The **Two Knights Defense** with 3...Nf6 is generally preferred to the Giuoco Piano lines with 3...Bc5. Black obtains important counterplay by attacking the pawn at e4. Equally crucial, this developing move also helps cover the critical d5-square. The advance of Black's pawn from d7 to d5 is almost always a key part of Black's strategy, and in the most famous cases is the only defense available.

Consider the position after 1.e4 e5; 2.Nf3 Nc6; 3.Bc4 Nf6; 4.Ng5:

This is a position which worries many beginners, because the f7-square is under heavy fire from the combined force of White's bishop and knight. But World Champions realize that this is harmless, because the key defensive move comes to the rescue. Black simply plays 4...d5.

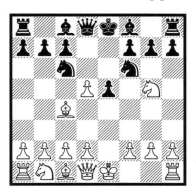

White must capture with the pawn, because if the bishop is used it will be captured by the knight at f6, and then the knight at g5 is under attack, too. Retreating the bishop just gives Black important time to develop. After 5.exd5 we have the following position.

Now Black does not have to recapture the pawn, a strategy which is considered to be rather risky. Instead, Black has traditionally preferred to swing the knight from c6 to a5, attacking the bishop. But the knight can often find itself offside on the a-file, so in the latter half of this century Black has explored the interesting alternative 5...b5!?

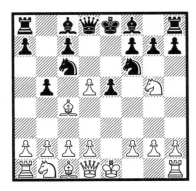

The point is that if White captures the knight at c6, the powerful bishop at c4 falls. At the same time, White does not want to capture at b5, because that would concede the pawn at d5 to the enemy queen.

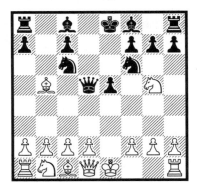

Now the bishop at b5 and the pawn at g2 are both attacked. So this is also not the correct approach for White. Best, according to all theory, is the paradoxical retreat 6.Bf1.

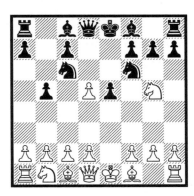

Now it is Black's turn to be careful. If 6...Qxd5? Then 7.Nc3 brings the White army storming into the game. The strangest reply is 6...Nd4 with a complicated and lively game. The upshot of all this is that at World Championship levels the move 4.Ng5 is almost never seen.

Instead, 4.d4 is preferred. After 4...exd4 White has a choice.

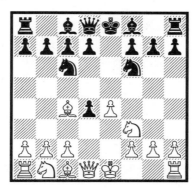

There is no need to regain the pawn right away, since it is much too weak to be maintained by Black. White can either castle or advance the e-pawn and we now enter lines known as the Scotch Gambit because they can also arise from the Scotch via 1.e4 e5; 2.Nf3 Nc6; 3.d4 exd4; 4.Bc4 Nf6 etc.

This is also more common in amateur chess than at professional levels, since Black's resources are generally considered adequate. In fact, in our illustrative game, we'll watch a rare case of a World Champion on the White side, only to be defeated by most brilliant play at the hands of Richard Reti.

(11) EUWE - RETI
Amsterdam (match), 1920

1.e4 e5; 2.Nf3 Nc6; 3.Bc4 Nf6. This is the Two Knights Defense, one of the pathways to the Scotch Gambit. **4.d4 exd4.**

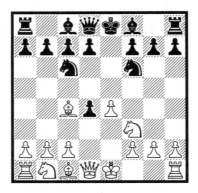

This is not a true gambit, in that Black has no real way of holding on to the material in the long run. White defers the recovery of the pawn, concentrating on rapid development. The main lines are well-established and are seen even in this ancient game. **5.0–0.** White has a sharp alternative in 5.e5, but with careful play Black should be able to equalize. **5...Nxe4.** This is the accepted continuation. The sharp Max Lange Attack with 5...Bc5 is more precarious. **6.Re1.** The pin is not deadly, because the knight cannot be attacked by the pawn. Most of the following moves are forced. **6...d5; 7.Bxd5! Qxd5; 8.Nc3.**

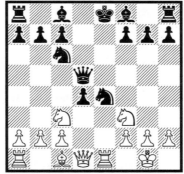

What a collection of pins, ladies, and horses! Both the knight at e4 and the pawn at d4 are pinned, and the queen and knight are both attacked. Yet we mustn't forget that Black has an extra piece, because the White bishop has been sacrificed. **8...Qa5.** Considered best, though 8...Qh5 is an interesting option.

9.Nxd4? When this game was played, the correct plan with 9.Nxe4 was known, but this move had not yet been rejected. In later years Euwe was involved in games with 9.Nxe4, even as Black! In the present game, however, Reti gives the future World Champion a lesson in how 9.Nxd4 is to be handled. Remarkably, the capture was seen even in Grandmaster games in the 1970s! 9.Rxe4+ Be6 10.Nxd4 0-0-0; 11.Be3 Nxd4; 12.Rxd4 Bb4 gives Black a good game; 9.Nxe4! Be6; 10.Neg5 0-0-0; 11.Nxe6 fxe6; 12.Rxe6 Bd6 is the main line these days. **9...Nxd4; 10.Qxd4 f5.**

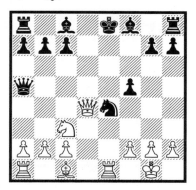

White has nothing but the pin here, and the f-pawn must not advance to f3 because Black would then set up a nasty pin with ...Bc5. **11.Bg5 Qc5.** Over half a century later the Hungarian Grandmaster Josef Pinter discovered that moving the king is stronger. The king is safe at f7 and it is even difficult for White to maintain an equal game. For example, 11...Kf7; 12.Nxe4 fxe4; 13.Qc4+ Kg6; 14.Bf4 Bf5; 15.Bxc7 Qc5, and White is just a piece down. **12.Qd8+ Kf7; 13.Nxe4?!** Euwe failed to find the simple developing move which would have given him sufficient compensation. 13.Rad1 Be6; 14.Qxa8 Nxg5; 15.h4 Ne4; 16.Rxe4 fxe4; 17.Nxe4 was found by Keres. In this position the threat of Ng5+ is strong, and the bishop at f8 is pinned, so despite the extra piece Black faces some problems. **13...fxe4; 14.Rad1.**

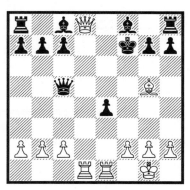

There is no real compensation for the piece. In fact, Reti decides to make a sacrifice of his own. **14...Bd6!!; 15.Qxh8 Qxg5**

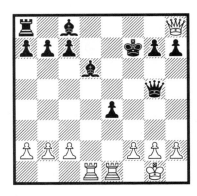

Black has two bishops for the rook, and an attack as well. **16.f4 Qh5; 17.Rxe4**

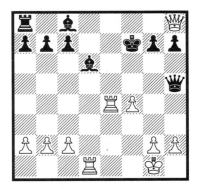

Now a series of combinative blows brings a swift end to the game. **17...Bh3!; 18.Qxa8 Bc5+; 19.Kh1 Bxg2+!!** White is given no opportunity to play Qe8+. **20.Kxg2 Qg4+; 21.Kf1 Qf3+; 22.Ke1 Qf2 mate.**

RUSSIAN GAME

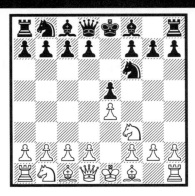

1.e4   e5
2.Nf3   Nf6

The **Russian Game**, also known as the **Petroff Defense**, is a common visitor to the chessboard at all levels of play. To an amateur, the symmetrical nature of the defense makes it fairly easy to play. At the professional level, White is generally considered to hold a very slight advantage in the main lines, which is only natural in a symmetrical position where White gets to move first. Players who are willing to live with this slight disadvantage are quite at home in the Russian Game, which is easy to learn and easy to play, if perhaps a bit boring.

(12) CAPABLANCA - BLACK
New York, 1913

1.e4 e5; 2.Nf3 Nf6; 3.Nxe5 d6; 4.Nf3 Nxe4; 5.d4 d5; 6.Bd3 Bd6.

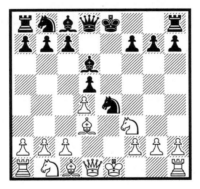

This is the normal defense in the Russian Game. **7.c4.** White begins to undermine the defence of the e4 knight. Usually both sides castle first, but it does not make much of a difference. Unless Black tries to exploit it, as here. **7...Bb4+.** Black forces White to interpose on d2 so he can trade off the exposed knight, but loses a tempo by moving his bishop a second time. Note also that the bishop is *en prise* on b4. **8.Nbd2 0–0; 9.0–0 Re8.**

White, having unpinned his d2 knight, was threatening to take on e4. But the best response was to capture at d2 with the bishop as in a game played the following year between Tarrasch and Marshall, who was a leading exponent of the Black side of the Russian Game. He actually defended this position against Capablanca himself at St. Petersburg 1914, but took with the knight instead and obtained an inferior positon. **10.cxd5 Nf6.** Black wants to recapture with the knight on d5, where it can't be chased by a White pawn. **11.Ne5.**

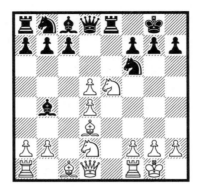

White takes advantage of Black's loss of time to bring his own knight to an agressive square, attacking Black's weakness on f7. **11...Nbd7?** This is a mistake, cutting his queen bishop off from the kingside. **12.Ndf3.** Not only supporting his knight but threatening to go to g5. **12...Nxd5.** This is a blunder: with one White knight already aimed at f7 and the other ready to jump in at e5 or g5 Black should not open the diagonal leading to that square. **13.Nxf7.** Breaking through before Black has a chance to defend the diagonal by ...N7f6 and ...c6 or ...Be6. **13...Kxf7; 14.Ng5+ Kf8.**

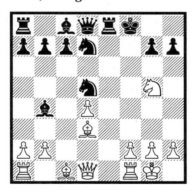

15.Qh5. White has too many threats. Black can't cover the mate on f7 without losing too much material, since the queen is indirectly attacking the knight on d5, e.g. so Black resigned here. 15...Qe7; 16.Nxh7+ Kg8; 17.Qxd5+ Kh8; 18.Qh5. Black is two pawns down and still getting mated. **1–0.**

(13) FISCHER - GHEORGHIU
Buenos Aires, 1970

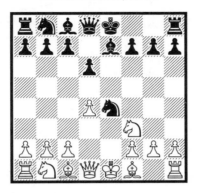

1.e4 e5; 2.Nf3 Nf6; 3.Nxe5 d6; 4.Nf3 Nxe4; 5.d4 Be7. This has failed to catch on as a serious rival to the symmetrical 5...d5, seen in our other illustrative game. **6.Bd3 Nf6; 7.h3**. If White simply castles, then 7...Bg4 is annoying. 7.0–0 Bg4; 8.Re1 0–0; 9.Nbd2 Re8; 10.Nf1 Bf8; 11.Rxe8 Qxe8 brought Black equality in Huebner-Petrosian, Tilburg 1981. **7...0–0; 8.0–0 Re8.** 8...c5 is premature: 9.Nc3 Nc6; 10.Re1 a6; 11.d5 Na7; 12.a4 Bd7; 13.a5 and White was better in Karpov-Smyslov, USSR 1972. **9.c4.**

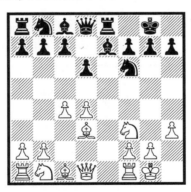

9...Nc6?! This is a poor move, as the knight does not belong on this square. It would be different if Black had an e-pawn headed for e5, but the e-file is vacant. 9...Nbd7; 10.Nc3 Nf8 is very solid, and has been defended by champions, for example 11.d5 Ng6; 12.Re1 Bd7; 13.Bg5 Nh5 was equal in Tal-Smyslov, USSR 1971. **10.Nc3 h6; 11.Re1 Bf8; 12.Rxe8 Qxe8; 13.Bf4 Bd7; 14.Qd2.**

White has a very large advantage. The e-file will be his, and the pawns at c4 and d4 dominate the center. Black's pieces have no scope and there isn't even the hint of a threat from that side of the board. **14...Qc8; 15.d5.** Pointing out that the knight did not belong here. **15...Nb4; 16.Ne4!** A tip that every strong player knows is that exchanging a piece which is not involved in the attack (here, the knight at c3) for one which defends the enemy target (the knight at f6 helps guard the king at g8) works to the advantage of the attacker. **16...Nxe4; 17.Bxe4 Na6.** This knight is a long way from its ruler, who has but a mere cleric for defense. **18.Nd4 Nc5; 19.Bc2 a5.** A typical advance to secure the position of the knight at c5, which can no longer be chased away by the b-pawn. **20.Re1 Qd8; 21.Re3.** The rook is headed to the kingside. **21...b6; 22.Rg3 Kh8; 23.Nf3 Qe7; 24.Qd4 Qf6.** There was no other way to handle the threat of Bxh6.

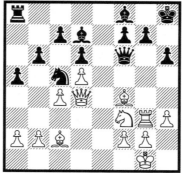

25.Qxf6 gxf6; 26.Nd4. Now Black is positionally lost, and there is still plenty of attacking force to cope with. **26...Re8; 27.Re3 Rb8; 28.b3 b5.** How else could Black try to get some counterplay? **29.cxb5 Bxb5; 30.Nf5.** The rest is simple. **30...Bd7; 31.Nxh6 Rb4; 32.Rg3 Bxh6; 33.Bxh6 Ne4; 34.Bg7+ Kh7; 35.f3.** The knight is pinned and lost, so Black resigned.

KING'S GAMBIT

1.e4 e5
2.f4

The **King's Gambit** begins 1.e4 e5; 2.f4. There was a time, about a hundred years ago, when it dominated the Open Games. As a practical matter, it is a difficult opening to play for White these days, and World Champions avoid it. It is not merely that Black is considered to have adequate resources (see my *Who's Afraid of the King's Gambit*, Chess Enterprises 1991 for details) but that Black has such a wide variety of acceptable defenses.

There are still plenty of things to be discovered in this, one of the most analyzed openings of all. Recently, Black has discovered the strangely effective 2...Nc6; 3.Nf3 (as usual in the King's Gambit 3.fxe5 cannot be played because of 3...Qh4+) and now 3...f5!?

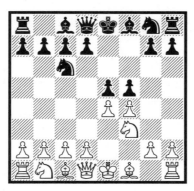

This idea was brought to the attention of the chess world by Tony Miles (see the section on the St. George for more on this creative British Grandmaster) and has been investigated by top analysts. It is too soon to tell if it will be a long-lasting solution to the opening, but it is a further indication that Black's resources seem to be unlimited.

That amateur players fear the King's Gambit is mostly a sign of inadequate defensive skills. If you just keep an eye on White's threats, you'll do just fine. Of course if you don't, the experience can be unpleasant, as we see in our illustrative game.

(14) SPASSKY - SEIRAWAN
Montpellier (Candidates), 1985

1.e4 e5; 2.f4 exf4; 3.Nf3.

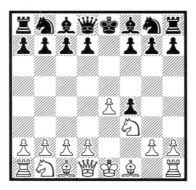

The King's Gambit Accepted is one of the most heavily analyzed openings, with thousands of pages of analysis available. For this reason, Black often tries to find a sideline that won't require too much preparation since the King's Gambit is rarely seen in professional play in modern tournaments.

Boris Spassky has had a long love affair with this romantic gambit, however, and it comes as no surprise when he thrusts the f-pawn forward at move two. Opponents try to prepare refinements, but he never seems to have any difficulty meeting them at the board. **3...Ne7.** An unusual defense. 3...Be7 is very reliable, but placing the knight on that square, even if temporarily, just slows down the development. 3...g5 is the old main line, but it is almost never seen in top competition these days. This is probably due to the enormous amount of preparation required to master all the complications, which does not seem worth the effort when one considers how rare the King's Gambit is. **4.d4 d5.** 4...Ng6 5.h4 forces Black to play 5...h5, with an ugly position. **5.Nc3 dxe4; 6.Nxe4 Ng6; 7.h4!**

Spassky has played this opening before, and was familiar with the appropriate plan for White. **7...Qe7;** 7...Be7; 8.h5 Nh4; 9.Bxf4 gave White a good game in Kuznetsov vs. Bonch Osmolovsky, Moscow 1964. This defense (3...Ne7) is known as the Bonch Osmolovsky Variation. **8.Kf2.**

The White king is treated differently, some might even say disrespectfully, in the King's Gambit. The large amount of breathing room on the kingside keeps it relatively safe. **8...Bg4; 9.h5 Nh4; 10.Bxf4 Nc6; 11.Bb5!** A useful pin, as is typical in the Open Games. White will disrupt the enemy pawn structure. **11...0–0–0; 12.Bxc6! bxc6; 13.Qd3 Nxf3; 14.gxf3.**

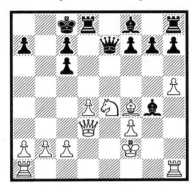

Whose king is safer? White's! **14...Bf5; 15.Qa6+ Kb8; 16.Nc5.** Queen and knight are often a dynamic duo. See how quickly they reach the queenside! **16...Bc8; 17.Qxc6 Rxd4.** There is nothing better, but now Spassky applies his formidable technique. Right now the attack features queen and knight, with assistance from the bishop. Now it is time for the heavy artillery to move into place in the center. **18.Rae1 Rxf4; 19.Qb5+ Ka8; 20.Qc6+ Kb8; 21.Rxe7 Bxe7.**

In terms of material, Black's deficit is minor, and the bishop pair is enough compensation. But the king is still too exposed. It is ironic that the single pawn at f3 provides all the defense the White King needs, while not even the entire Black army can keep the queenside together. **22.Rd1 Rf6; 23.Nd7+ Bxd7; 24.Qxd7 Rd8; 25.Qb5+ Kc8; 26.Rxd8+ Bxd8; 27.Qa4!** There is a direct threat at a7, and an indirect threat at g7 via Qg4+. **27...g5;** 27...Kb8; 28.Qb4+ and White is going to win a pawn.

If the king moves to a8, the key is Qe4+. If c8 is the choice, then Qg4+ works. Finally, if ...Rb6, then Qe8 attacks the bishop and the pawn at f7. **28.Qxa7 Rf4; 29.Qa6+ Kb8; 30.Qd3.** Another pawn falls. **30...Be7; 31.Qxh7 g4; 32.Kg3 White won.**

Black can also decline the gambit with straightforward development, usually via 2...Bc5. It is hard to achieve full equality with this and few top players employ the defense. At amateur levels, however, it is popular.

(15) EUWE - MAROCZY
Amsterdam (4th match game), 1921

1.e4 e5; 2.f4 Bc5. The King's Gambit Declined has been around a long time and fades in and out of popularity. When this game was played, it was, according to Euwe, the standard line.

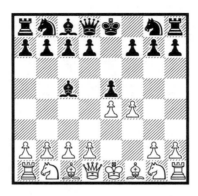

3.Nf3 d6; 4.c3 Euwe was following the fashion of the time, and had Maroczy reacted a little better, would have paid a price for it. But modern thinking supports this move, as well as 4.Nc3. **4...Bg4;** 4...Nf6; 5.d4; (5.Bd3 is an old recommendation. 5...0–0, 6.Bc2 Re8 and White would be in a little trouble, unable to castle and behind in development.) 5...exd4; 6.cxd4 Bb4+; 7.Bd2 Bxd2+; 8.Nbxd2 is better for White, and has been played by female superstar Judith Polgar. **5.fxe5 dxe5; 6.Qa4+ Bd7; 7.Qc2 Qe7; 8.d4.** Finally! The ideal pawn center is established. Black tries to open up some lines but the center holds. **8...exd4; 9.cxd4.**

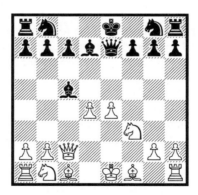

9...Bb4+; 10.Nc3 Bc6. The attempt to use piece pressure to work against the strong center fails because since the king is still at e8, Black cannot effectively use a rook on the e-file. **11.Bd3 Bxc3+?** Black should be developing, not exchanging his only active pieces. **12.bxc3 Bxe4.** A temporary sacrifice, thanks to the pin on the e-file. But the pin only lasts as long as the White king remains in the center. **13.Bxe4 f5; 14.0–0! fxe4; 15.Qb3!** The most precise move, threatening to capture at b7. **15...c5; 16.Ba3 Nf6; 17.Bxc5.** Black just doesn't have time to take the knight. **17...Qf7; 18.c4.**

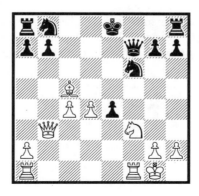

18...b6; 18...exf3; 19.Rae1+ Kd8; 20.Re7 Qxe7; 21.Bxe7+ Kxe7; 22.Qxb7+ Nbd7; 23.Qxf3 is an easy win for White. **19.Ng5 Qd7.** Black has just two defenders, the queen at d7 and knight at f6. Watch one of them disappear! **20.Rxf6!! gxf6; 21.Nxe4.** The threat is now Nxf6+. **21...Qe6; 22.Re1.** Re-establishing the threat, and now Black has no useful defense. **22...bxc5; 23.Nxf6+ Kf7; 24.Qb7+. White won.**

For a counterpoint, let's look at the exciting Falkbeer Countergambit as wielded by Paul Morphy.

(16) SCHULTEN - MORPHY
New York, 1857

1.e4 e5; 2.f4 d5. This is the Falkbeer Countergambit, an aggressive reply to the King's Gambit. **3.exd5 e4.**

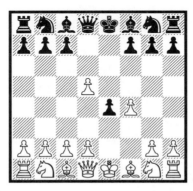

This is the point of the gambit. Just as in the Albin and some variations of the Tarrasch Defense, the advanced pawn creates difficulty in the enemy forecourt. It is hard to develop pieces comfortably. **4.Nc3 Nf6; 5.d3 Bb4.** The battle rages over control of the e4-square. **6.Bd2.** This breaks the pin on the c3-knight, but Black can reinstate it. **6...e3.** It is worth a pawn to deflect the bishop from its defensive duties. **7.Bxe3 0–0; 8.Bd2 Bxc3; 9.bxc3.** Now Black could just recover the pawn, but there are more aggressive paths to investigate. **9...Re8+.**

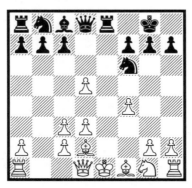

10.Be2. White has two extra pawns, but the pawn structure is a mess and the bishops have no scope. Black now uses the pin on the e-file to add more pressure. **10...Bg4; 11.c4 c6; 12.dxc6 Nxc6.** Black's superior development gives him a clear advantage. **13.Kf1.** White has now abandoned the notion of ever castling. Black would like to keep the pressure on, and invests the exchange to do so. **13...Rxe2; 14.Nxe2.** The knight is now pinned to the queen, and it is easy to pile on more pressure which results in a quick kill. **14...Nd4; 15.Qb1 Bxe2+; 16.Kf2 Ng4+.**

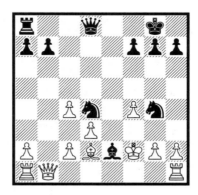

17.Kg1. White's position is so pathetic that the king is nearly checkmated by the minor pieces alone. But to add insult to injury, Morphy finishes with a fine combination by sacrificing a piece. **17...Nf3+; 18.gxf3 Qd4+; 19.Kg2 Qf2+; 20.Kh3 Qxf3+; 21.Kh4.** White resigned without waiting for 21...Nh6, which would be followed by checkmate.

LESS COMMON LINES

There are many other Open Games available to White and Black, and we don't have room to discuss them here. Four examples will suffice to illustrate some of the more important ones.

PHILIDOR DEFENSE

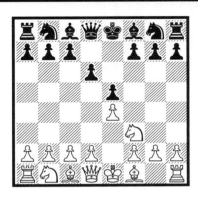

1.e4   e5
2.Nf3   d6

In the **Philidor Defense**, Black locks in the bishop at f8 and remains with a somewhat cramped game. No World Champions has used it seriously as Black, but they have shown the way to play it as White. Here is an excellent example:

(17) MORPHY - DUKE OF BRUNSWICK & COUNT ISOUARD
Paris Opera, 1858

1.e4. This is one of the most famous games in the literature. It was played at the Paris Opera. It didn't take too long for the fat lady to start singing! **1...e5; 2.Nf3 d6.**

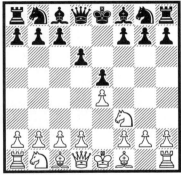

This is the Philidor Defense, a solid opening which nevertheless can provide some attacking chances for Black. **3.d4 Bg4.** This is no longer played. The most promising line is 3...exd4, meeting 4.Nxd4 with 4...g6, or 4.Qxd4 not with 4...Nc6, which allows 5.Bb5, but rather the simple 4...Nf6 or preliminary 4...a6. **4.dxe5 Bxf3; 5.Qxf3 dxe5.** The problem with this position for Black is that White has the bishop pair, a long-term asset. **6.Bc4 Nf6; 7.Qb3 Qe7.**

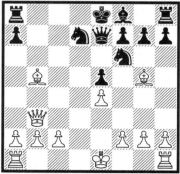

8.Nc3. Given the circumstances of the game, Morphy just didn't feel like capturing the pawn at b7. That would have taken the fun out of the game **8...c6 9.Bg5 b5; 10.Nxb5.** That's more like it. Morphy sacrifices a knight for the b-pawn, instead of capturing it for free at his eighth turn. **10...cxb5; 11.Bxb5+ Nbd7.**

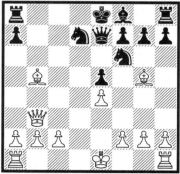

12.0–0–0 Rd8. Both knights are pinned, and Morphy now trades one pin for another. **13.Rxd7 Rxd7; 14.Rd1 Qe6; 15.Bxd7+ Nxd7.** Black has an extra piece, but White checkmates in two moves. **16.Qb8+ Nxb8; 17.Rd8 mate.**

LATVIAN GAMBIT

Given the general ineffectiveness of the King's Gambit for White, you'd think that this reversed King's Gambit structure would be even worse, and it is. Although some strong players have played the **Latvian** for fun, no World Champions have ever used it in an important game.

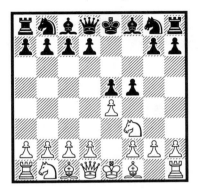

1.e4 e5
2.Nf3 f5

My personal feeling is that after 3.exf5 e4; 4.Ng1 White has a good game. Look at the following diagram:

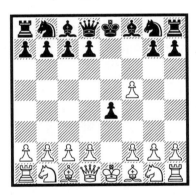

It is easy to see that the pawn at e4 is overextended, and Black's kingside is weak. Nevertheless, this is hardly the most confrontational approach for White. I like it because it is simple and straightforward and about ten minutes worth of study is all that is required to meet this infrequent visitor to the tournament scene. Still, if you have the time and inclination, the main lines are even better for White. For example...

(18) SMYSLOV - KAMYSHOV
Moscow City Championship, 1945

1.e4 e5; 2.Nf3 f5.

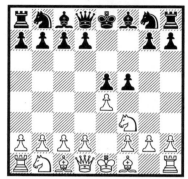

No strong player takes this opening seriously, but one must be prepared to meet it. Don't confuse this with a reversed King's Gambit because it is the e-pawn, rather than the f-pawn, that falls. **3.Nxe5 Qf6; 4.Nc4.** This move dates back to the 18th century, and it is still a good plan. **4...fxe4; 5.Nc3 Qg6?!** 5...Qf7 is Black's best try. Nevertheless, White gets a promising position after 6.d4 Nf6; 7.Ne5 Qe6; 8.Bg5 Bb4; 9.Bc4 with a strong initiative for White. **6.d3 Bb4.** 6...exd3; 7.Bxd3 Qxg2; 8.Qh5+ Kd8; 9.Bg5+ Nf6; 10.Be4 and the Black queen has no escape. **7.Bd2.**

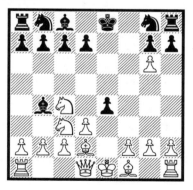

7...Bxc3, 7...exd3 is again a recipe for disaster: 8.Bxd3 Qxg2; 9.Qh5+ Kd8; 10.0-0-0! and Black is in trouble. For example, a correspondence game (Elburg-Michalek) concluded quickly: 10...Nf6; 11.Qh4 Qg4; 12.Qxg4 Nxg4; 13.Rhg1 Nxf2; 14.Rde1 Re8; 15.Bg5+ Be7; 16.Rxe7 Nxd3+. No further moves are given, but it is clear that Black is lost. 17.cxd3 Rxe7; 18.Nd5 Nc6; 19.Nxe7 Nxe7; 20.Re1 and White has an extra piece. **8.Bxc3 d5; 9.Ne5 Qf5; 10.dxe4 Qxe4+; 11.Be2.** White has a huge lead in development, and Black does not dare to take the g-pawn. **11...Nf6;** 11...Qxg2; 12.Bf3 Qg5; 13.Qxd5 Qe7; 14.0-0-0 c6; 15.Bh5+ g6; 16.Nxg6 cxd5 (16...hxg6 17.Bxg6+ Kf8 18.Qf3+ wins on the spot.)

17.Nxe7+ Kxe7; 18.Bxh8 and Black will lose. **12.0–0 c6.** Black is trying to support the center, but is hopelessly behind in development. **13.Bh5+ Kf8; 14.Re1 Qh4.**

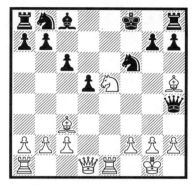

Now Smyslov finishes with a very cute move. **15.Bg6! Na6.** Obviously the bishop could not be captured because White would recapture with the knight, setting up a family fork. **16.Qe2** The mating plan is to move the knight and then sacrifice the queen at e8 to create a mating net. **16...Bh3; 17.Nf3.** Black resigned because Black cannot save the queen and stop White from playing Qe7+ at the same time. **White won.**

VIENNA GAME

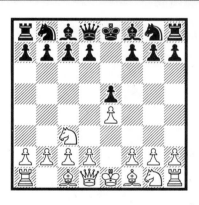

1.e4   e5
2.Nc3

The **Vienna Game**, like many of the Open Games, was a more popular opening at the turn of the last century than it is now. It has seen many swashbuckling adventures, and one variation is a real monster: the Frankenstein-Dracula Variation which arises after 1.e4 e5; 2.Nc3 Nf6; 3.Bc4 Nxe4; 4.Qh5 Nd6; 5.Bb3 Nc6; 6.Nb5 g6; 7.Qf3 f5; 8.Qd5 Qe7; 9.Nxc7+ Kd8; 10.Nxa8.

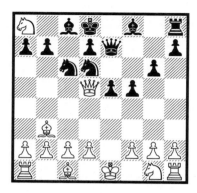

This is such a wild position that strong players tend to avoid it on principle. After all, one tiny piece of home-analysis can turn the tables. It is a lot of fun for amateurs, however.

No recent World Champion has played the Vienna with great consistency, but Steinitz, Alekhine, Spassky and Fischer found it an acceptable alternative to the Spanish Game. There are some interesting games that have involved the World Champions. Here is one of them.

(19) STEINITZ - LASKER
London, 1899

1.e4 e5; 2.Nc3.

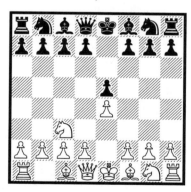

This is the Vienna Game. Although White usually prefers the more aggressive 2.Nf3, which attacks the pawn at e5, this opening also has merits. The e-pawn is defended and it is difficult for a Black pawn to advance to d5. **2...Nf6; 3.f4.**

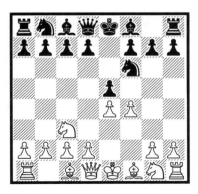

This highly entertaining defense is rarely encountered, however, because Black has an easier route to equality with 5...Be7. **3...d5; 4.d3.**

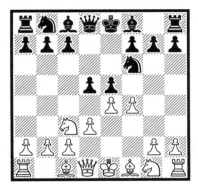

Typical Steinitz – a quiet prelude to a melee. **4...Nc6; 5.fxe5 Nxe5; 6.d4 Ng6.** A fairly active plan for Black. **7.exd5.** This is more effective than advancing the pawn to e5. White now has a greater presence in the center of the board. **7...Nxd5; 8.Nxd5 Qxd5; 9.Nf3 Bg4; 10.Be2 0-0-0.**

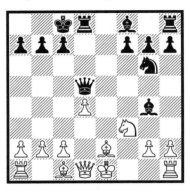

Play has proceeded logically. Black can be more than satisfied with the position, since the pawn at d4 is weak and White has not yet castled, so Black has excellent prospects of taking over the initiative. **11.c3 Bd6; 12.0–0 Rhe8!** A good player always brings all of the pieces into the attack. **13.h3 Bd7.** Black does not want to exchange pieces, because a kingside attack is planned. **14.Ng5?!** Premature. Continuing development with 14.Bd2 was indicated. **14...Nh4; 15.Nf3.**

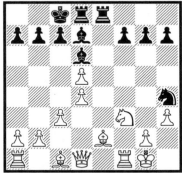

Black's pieces are in position, so the time is now! **15...Nxg2!** A demolition sacrifice, which rips open the kingside. **16.Kxg2 Bxh3+; 17.Kf2 f6!**

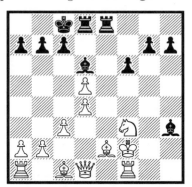

Patience is one of the hardest chess skills to acquire. The White king is exposed, and the bishop at c1 and rook at a1 are not likely to be able to assist in the defense. Lasker makes sure that White will not blunt the attack by sticking the knight at e5, and prepares a kingside pawn assault. Taking the rook at f1 would have been pointless. **18.Rg1 g5; 19.Bxg5.** White has no real choice but to return the piece, since otherwise the g-pawn would be rammed down his throat. **19...fxg5; 20.Rxg5 Qe6; 21.Qd3 Bf4.**

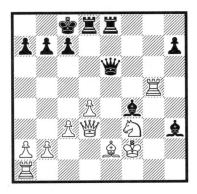

The Black bishops are just too much, and White's game collapses. **22.Rh1 Bxg5; 23.Nxg5 Qf6+; 24.Bf3 Bf5!; 25.Nxh7 Qg6!; 26.Qb5 c6; 27.Qa5 Re7; 28.Rh5 Bg4; 29.Rg5 Qc2+; 30.Kg3 Bxf3. Black won.**

BISHOP'S OPENING

The **Bishop's Opening** arises on 1.e4 e5; 2.Bc4 and usually it leads into positions from the Italian Game, for example after 2...Nf6; 3.d3 Nc6; 4.Nf3. There are independent paths, however, such as the brutally direct 3.d4!?

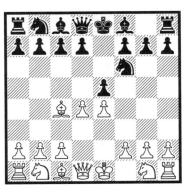

1.e4   e5
2.Bc4 Nf6
3.d4!?

You won't find the move 3.d4 in the repertoire of World Champions however. As usual, attempt by White to overpower the Black camp immediately are not usually effective, and theoreticians have worked out the lines which give Black equality.

(20) ALEKHINE - RETHY
Munich, 1941

1.e4 e5; 2.Bc4.

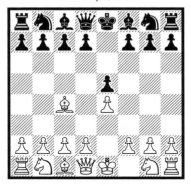

There is nothing wrong with this move, which will usually transpose to one of the other Open Games. In this case we see a hybrid between the Vienna and the Bishop's Opening, an approach very popular with classical masters. **2...Nf6; 3.d3** (4.d4 exd4, 5.Nf3 is a gambit with a rather dubious reputation.) **Nc6; 4.Nc3 Be7.** Both sides are playing it safe, but now White opens up the game. **5.f4 d6; 6.Nf3 Bg4; 7.0–0 Nd4?**

Black is too impressed by the pin on the knight at f3. Simply castling would have been wiser. Given that a World Champion was playing White, one would have thought Black might have shown a little more respect. If this move was effective, Alekhine wouldn't have allowed it. **8.fxe5 Bxf3; 9.gxf3 dxe5.**

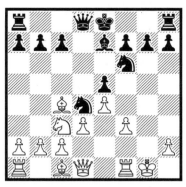

At first it looks as though Black's plan has succeeded, since the White king looks vulnerable. But none of Black's pieces are in a position to exploit it, and so the advantage of the bishop pair is significant. Alekhine now renews the pressure on the center and threatens to open up some lines in the center while Black's king has not yet found shelter. **10.f4! Bd6; 11.Be3 Nc6; 12.d4!** The pressure is unrelenting. White is clearly better. **12...exd4; 13.Bxd4 Nxd4; 14.Qxd4 Qe7.**

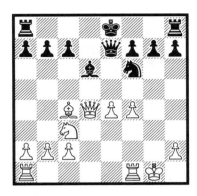

Black has survived immediate destruction and is close to castling. There is a serious threat of ...Bc5. For all that, however, White owns the center and threatens a nasty fork at e5. **15.Kh1 Bc5; 16.Qd3 Rd8; 17.Qe2.** After a few retreats, White is ready to bounce back. Meanwhile, Black is getting nervous. With queenside castling no longer an option, and an open g-file discouraging kingside castling, Black tries a reckless and wrongheaded attack. **17...h5?** Hoping to sink the knight at g4 and cause some damage in concert with the bishop at c5. **18.Rf3! Bd4; 19.e5 Bxc3; 20.bxc3.**

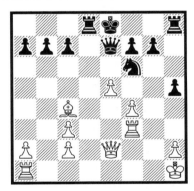

White's pawn structure is a mess, but that does not matter. Black's pieces have no coordination, and things aren't going to get any better. **20...Nd5; 21.Rg1 Kf8; 22.f5!** The White pawns control all the important squares. **22...f6.** This prevents the further advance of the f-pawn but effectively locks the h8-Rook out of the game. **23.e6.**

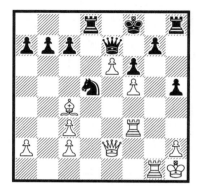

Black must have felt like a boxer awaiting the knockout punch, knowing it is just a matter of time before his head hits the canvas. **23...h4; 24.Qe4 c6; 25.Rd1 g5; 26.Rfd3!** The *en passant* capture would have been irrelevant. **26...Kg7; 27.Bxd5 cxd5; 28.Rxd5 Rxd5; 29.Qxd5.** Now suddenly the pawn structure decisively favors White,. **29...Rc8; 30.Qd7 Re8; 31.Qa4 Rd8; 32.Rxd8.** Black resigned. If the rook is captured then Qd7+ ends it all. **1–0.**

8. SEMI-OPEN GAMES

INTRODUCTION

When Black replies to 1.e4 with a move other than 1...e5, we have a **Semi-Open Game**. In these cases Black delays a central confrontation until later in the game. The most classical of the Semi-Open Games involve an early ...d5 by Black. Although the Semi-Open Games were once only a rare visitor to serious chess, they now dominate the repertoires of most top players.

One of the great appeals of the Semi-Open Games is that they lead to unbalanced positions and tend toward fewer draws than the Open Games. We'll see the exciting directions these openings lead to in the following pages.

OVERVIEW

The most popular Semi-Open Game is the **Sicilian Defense** where Black plays 1...c5.

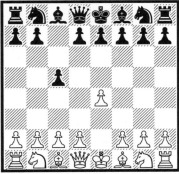

This move discourages the immediate occupation of the center with 2.d4, which is only seen as a gambit, the Smith-Morra Gambit (1.e4 c5; 2.d4 cxd4; 3.c3), since after 2...cxd4; 3.Qxd4?! Nc6, Black develops with tempo and takes over the initiative.

The only serious alternative in the 19ᵗʰ century was the **French Defense** with 1...e6.

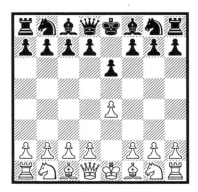

This solid opening allows White to build the ideal center with 2.d4, only to force its destruction with 1...d5. The downside, one which has kept many strong players away from the defense, is the very limited scope of the bishop at c8, which often remains an ineffective spectator, locked in behind a wall of pawns.

The Caro-Kann Defense, 1...c6, allows the bishop to emerge from c8, and is a much more spacious opening in general. It has always been respectable, and would be more popular if not for holding a somewhat drawish reputation.

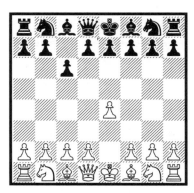

In fact, the opening can be played for a win, because usually the game comes down to a complicated ending with chances for both sides. Good endgame technique is required in the Caro-Kann.

In the **Pirc and Modern Defenses**, Black plays an early ...g6 and ...Bg7. On the first move, both 1...d6 and 1...g6 are played.

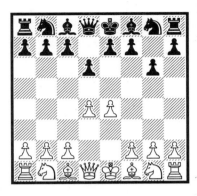

In the Pirc, the knight is developed at f6, but in the Modern Defenses, Black prefers to keep the diagonal clear and either develops the knight at e7 or h6, or else delays it until very late in the opening. These are highly transpositional openings and rely more on a feel for the position than on strict memorization of well-worked out lines.

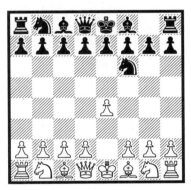

Alekhine's radical 1...Nf6, long known as the **Alekhine Defense**, allows White to overwhelm the center with 2.e5 Nd5, 3.d4; with c4 and even f4 to follow. It has a counter-punching nature, and White must be careful not to overextend. The increase in defensive skills during the 20th century has made the opening more respectable, but no World Champion, even Alekhine, relied on it for many important encounters.

The remaining defenses never figured prominently in the repertoires of the World Champions but are sometimes seen even at the highest levels. These include the **Scandinavian Defense** (1...d5), the Nimzowitsch Defense (1...Nc6) and the St. George Defense (1...a6). Other moves are almost never seen in serious chess and will receive only a brief mention.

WORLD CHAMPION OPENINGS

As the following chart shows, the relative role of the Semi-Open Games have been part of the repertoires of most World Champions.

Of course you should keep in mind that the Semi-Open Games were much rarer in the 19ᵗʰ Century and played a much smaller role in the repertoires of the World Champions. Take another look at the chart earlier, and you will see how the Open Games dominated earlier play.

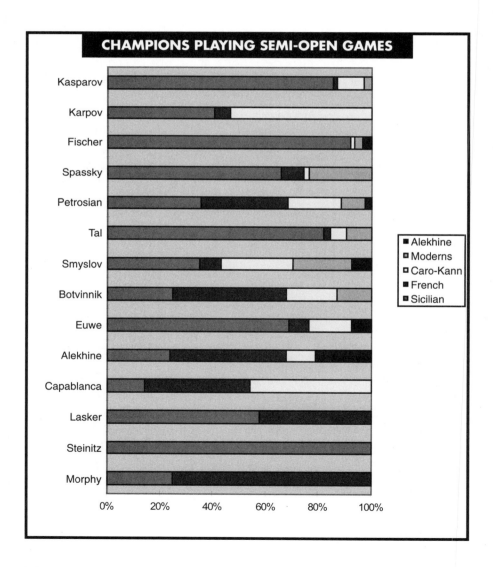

CHAMPIONS PLAYING SEMI-OPEN GAMES

Legend:
- Alekhine
- Moderns
- Caro-Kann
- French
- Sicilian

The most striking shared characteristic of the Semi-Open Games is Black's willingness to accept a more limited degree of mobility. White is generally allowed at least a small advantage in the center, and control of the central squares makes it more difficult for Black's pieces to cross the middle of the board. White almost never has a pawn on either e3 or d3, so those squares can be used to transfer pieces.

Black, on the other hand, frequently has a pawn on either e6 or d6, and sometimes both. In most cases, White has firm control over the e4 square, another important pivot point, if unoccupied, or home to a powerful central pawn.

Unlike the Open Games, the Semi-Open Games do not share typical formations. On the contrary, even within each of the Semi-Open Games there is a tremendous diversity in the structures which arise in the many different subvariations.

We'll look at the Sicilian Defenses first.

SICILIAN DEFENSE

When Black chooses the **Sicilian Defense**, it is clear that White is in for a battle to the death. The Sicilian is the sharpest defense, because after 1.e4 c5 the symmetry is already broken, but the battle for the center is not conceded.

The main idea for Black in almost all of the Sicilian Defenses is to play ...d5. This will not come right away, and the pawn often sits on d6 until the middlegame is underway. Normally, White plays 2.Nf3 and then 3.d4. After Black captures on d4 with the pawn at c5, the c-file can be used by Black.

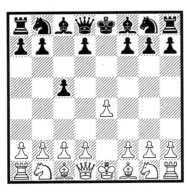

1.e4   c5

Often, pressure will be built with ...g6, ...Bg7 or (...Be7, ...Bf6), ...Rc8 and ...Qa5, with all of Black's forces concentrated at c3.

Otherwise, there is little to unify the diverse Sicilians. Much depends on which formation Black adopts, and even then, White will have many important decisions to face, such as which side to castle on. These days most of these questions are more or less settled, and as a result anyone wanting to play the Sicilian had better be prepared to learn a lot of theory. In the Dragon or Najdorf Variations, among the most studied, it often pays to be prepared all the way up to move 25!

There are quite a number of individual Sicilian Defenses, but there are half a dozen which stand out in the championship repertoire, all of which start 1.e4 c5; 2.Nf3.

The dangerous **Dragon Variation** is the head of a family of related lines where Black fianchettoes the bishop at g7. Usually it is reached via 2...d6; 3.d4 cxd4; 4.Nxd4 Nf6; 5.Nc3 g6. White normally castles queenside and launches a pawnstorm on the kingside, while Black aims everything at the White king. No World Champion has made a career out of it, but Kasparov adopted it in his 1995 PCA title defense to good effect.

The nasty **Najdorf Variation** sees Black plant a pawn at a6, both to keep out enemy knights and also to prepare to launch a queenside attack with ...b5. After 2...d6; 3.d4 cxd4; 4.Nxd4 Nf6; 5.Nc3 a6. White has many options, but none have been effective enough to discourage top players from using it. Kasparov and Fischer are its best known champion exponents.

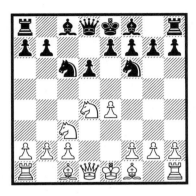

The **Classical Variation** begins 2...d6; 3.d4 cxd4; 4.Nxd4 Nf6; 5.Nc3 Nc6; or 2...Nc6; 3.d4 cxd4; 4.Nxd4 Nf6; 5.Nc3 d6. This is most directly confronted by 6.Bg5, the Richter-Rauzer Attack, where Black usually replies 6...e6 so that if White captures at f6, Black can recapture with the queen.

For some reason, this opening is almost exclusively seen in top-level competition. It leads to longer, more positional struggles than the Najdorf or Dragon. If those openings are the Tchaikovsky and Wagner of the Sicilians, we might look at the Classical as belonging stylistically to Schubert.

The **Scheveningen Variation**, named for a town in Holland, combines ...e6 with ...d6, instead of the ...Nc6/...d6 combination of the Classical. The pawn at e6 can serve as a critical point, being attacked by White as the gateway to Black's position. White can continue with simple development or go for broke on the kingside with the dangerous Keres Attack, which begins 2...d6; 3.d4 cxd4; 4.Nxd4 Nf6; 5.Nc3 e6; 6.g4.

Often Black plays the Scheveningen Sicilian defensively, trying to create impregnable barriers. A *hedgehog* position, where Black's jagged pawn formation keeps the enemy at bay, is often the result. The opening requires a combination of finesse and brutality, and brings to mind the music of Beethoven.

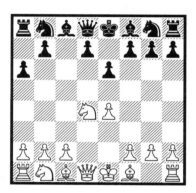

Black does not have to play an early ...d6 at all. The **Kan Variation** 2...e6; 3.d4 cxd4; 4.Nxd4 a6 has long been popular, with the pawns serving to patrol the important squares at b5, d5 and f5. The play can transpose to the Najdorf or Scheveningen, but usually either ends up in a hedgehog or follows its own path. The weaknesses of the dark squares at b6 and d6 is indisputable, but does not deter players from adopting the Black side. The bad bishop at c8 give the variation a French flavor, so perhaps Berlioz would be the appropriate musical metaphor.

Finally, we have the structurally odd variations with an early ...e5, most prominently the **Lasker-Pelikan Variation**, named after our World Champion and an important player of the post-World War II era. After 2...Nc6; 3.d4 cxd4; 4.Nxd4 Nf6; 5.Nc3 e5 there is a glaring hole at d5, and the battle will be waged primarily on the light squares. White has an advantage in space, but Black will be able to create counterplay on the light squares with ...b5 and ...f5. The variation has recently become fully respectable and has a following among many top players. There is some dissonance in the structure, and yet some very impressive romantic games have arisen.

DRAGON VARIATION

1.e4	c5
2.Nf3	d6
3.d4	cxd4
4.Nxd4	Nf6
5.Nc3	g6

The mighty **Dragon** is a favorite of professional and amateur alike. Black stations the bishop at g7 to influence the long diagonal stretching from a1 to h8. A rook slides to c8, putting pressure on the entire c-file. A knight at f6 keeps an eye on e4. The Black king is surrounded by defenders on the kingside. The Dragon is so logical that it would appear to be a solution to all of Black's problems in the opening.

The picture is not quite so rosy, however. In the main line, known as the Yugoslav Attack, White sends the king to the queenside and can launch a vicious pawn storm along the h-file and g-file. World Champions have tended to prefer the White side, because it is fairly easy to play, though it is not, as Bobby Fischer once claimed, a mere matter of tossing in a few sacrifices followed by checkmate.

Instead, the Dragon leads a precarious life. Each variation is critical, and new moves can quickly wipe out a decade of accepted wisdom. This helps to explain why the World Champions are by and large reluctant to face the dangers associated with defending the Dragon. One well-prepared novelty can lead to positions in which mate is inevitable. An amateur or low ranked professional can study at home and find one key move which, when played at the board, leaves the champion with no defense.

Despite this, Garry Kasparov shocked the chess world in 1995 by choosing the Dragon against challenger Viswanathan Anand, and his patronage is likely to create new enthusiasm for the Black side. Still, playing the Dragon requires a tremendous investment of time and energy because many of the variations have been worked out to depths of 25 or 30 moves. One recent book on the Dragon concentrated only on one subvariation beginning at move ten, but still ran over 300 pages of dense text!

(21) ANAND - KASPAROV
PCA World Championship (game 11), 1995

1.e4 c5; 2.Nf3 d6; 3.d4 cxd4; 4.Nxd4 Nf6; 5.Nc3 g6! Kasparov adopts the Dragon for the first time in tournament play. It is an excellent match strategy, because it is almost inconceivable that Anand had expected this. Kasparov had plenty of knowledge of Anand's strategy against the Dragon. The tongue of the serpent is the bishop at g7, which can lash out all the way across the board to inflict serious damage. **6.Be3.** Vishy chooses the most testing continuation after some reflection. **6...Bg7; 7.f3.** This sets up the Yugoslav formation, which is one of the most popular methods of greeting the Dragon. **7...0–0; 8.Qd2 Nc6.**

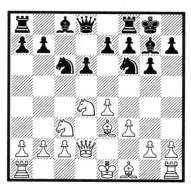

9.Bc4. Anand does not chicken out. He walks right down the ramp of theory, which has been worked out in some cases to well past move 30 and consumes hundreds of pages in the literature.

9...Bd7; 10.0–0–0. 10.h4 usually transposes to the main line, as seen in the game Schiller - Herbst, from the 1986 Pan American Intercollegiate Championship. 10...Rc8; 11.Bb3 h5; 12.0–0–0 Ne5; 13.Bh6 Bxh6; 14.Qxh6 Rxc3; 15.bxc3 Qa5; 16.Kb1! Rc8; 17.g4 Nc4; 18.gxh5 Qxc3; 19.Bxc4 Rxc4; 20.Rd3. This move was known from analysis by Sapi and Schneider, who were much too optimistic in their evaluation for White. 20...Qb4+; 21.Nb3 Nxh5; 22.Qg5. This was my choice. 22.Rd5 and 22.Rg1 have also been seen. 22...Nf6; 23.Rhd1 Rc5; 24.Qe3 a5; 25.Qe1 Qb6; 26.Kc1 Re5; 27.Qc3 Be6. The theoreticians commenting on this game helpfully supplied the evaluation of "unclear" to this position. **28.Rd4 Qa7; 29.Ra4 b6; 30.Re1.** White's position is fairly solid, but the formation is purely defensive. **30...Qd7; 31.Rd4 a4.** Now the game enters another maniacal phase. **32.f4 Rh5; 33.Nd2 Rc5; 34.Qb2 Qc6.** Black has the initiative, but the White pawns are also ready to advance. The game was eventually drawn, and remains one of the most critical lines in the Yugoslav Attack.

10...Ne5; 11.Bb3 Rc8; 12.h4 h5. This is the Soltis Variation, worked out in the 1970s by Andy Soltis. It was the subject of a recent book containing over 300 pages devoted exclusively to analysis of the line. **13.Kb1.** An example of the latter approach is seen (via transposition) in the note to move 10. **13...Nc4; 14.Bxc4 Rxc4; 15.Nde2 b5; 16.Bh6 Qa5.** Nothing new so far. Former U.S. Champion Patrick Wolff, one of Anand's seconds, helped develop this line. 16...b4; 17.Bxg7 Kxg7; 18.Nd5 Nxd5; 19.exd5 Qa5; 20.b3 Rc5; 21.g4! gave White a strong attack in Wolff-Georgiev, Biel 1993. **17.Bxg7!?** This was a footnote in the reference books. **17...Kxg7; 18.Nf4 Rfc8; 19.Ncd5.** The game has quieted down and takes on a positional character. **19...Qxd2; 20.Rxd2.**

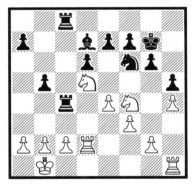

With this move Anand declined Kasparov's offer of a draw. **20...Nxd5; 21.Nxd5 Kf8; 22.Re1 Rb8; 23.b3 Rc5; 24.Nf4 Rbc8.** Both sides are quietly improving their positions. **25.Kb2 a5; 26.a3 Kg7; 27.Nd5 Be6.**

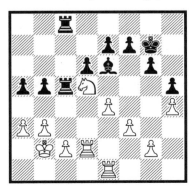

28.b4?. Anand slips up. Equality could have been preserved: 28.Nxe7 Re8; 29.Nd5 Bxd5; 30.b4 axb4; 31.axb4 Rc4; 32.Rxd5 Rxb4+; 33.Kc1 f5; 34.Rxd6 fxe4; 35.Kd2 with a level position. **28...axb4; 29.axb4 Rc4.** Now 30.Nxe7 would leave White with excellent drawing prospects, but Anand overlooks Kasparov's deep mating threat. **30.Nb6?? Rxb4+; 31.Ka3 Rxc2.** White resigned. It was a terrible blow for Anand, who missed several chances.

NAJDORF VARIATION

Although the **Najdorf Variation** (pronounced Nye-dorf), named for the great Polish-Argentinean Grandmaster Miguel Najdorf, has been studied as extensively as the Dragon, there seems to be more room for originality and as a result it has been the favored Sicilian among the World Champions. The basic formation is characterized by pawns at d6 and a6. The e-pawn can be stationed at e6 or e5, depending on White's choice of formation.

1.e4	c5
2.Nf3	d6
3.d4	cxd4
4.Nxd4	Nf6
5.Nc3	a6

Black plans to attack on the queenside with an early ...b5. Then White has to worry about the further advance of the pawn to b4, because then the knight must move and the pawn at e4 can be left without defense. Here, too, castling on opposite wings is typical, with the Black king headed kingside and the White king moving to the queenside. This allows both sides to launch uninhibited attacks.

Bobby Fischer and Garry Kasparov have been the leading advocates of the Najdorf at the World Championship level. Both have built their careers on the defense, but have been equally effective on the White side of the opening. The Najdorf is relatively young, being virtually unknown until after the Second World War, and this has allowed top players to carry out investigations in a wide range of variations.

White can adopt any of several popular plans. The sharpest line is 6.Bg5, which leads to lines which have a particularly wild character. After 6...e6 7.f4 Black can play the "standard" 7...Be7, the exciting but suspect Polugayevsky Variation with 7...b5, or the absolutely inscrutable Poisoned Pawn Variation in which Black goes pawn hunting with 7...Qb6, 8.Qd2 Qxb2 and then remains on the defensive for the rest of the game. This bold choice is preferred by both Fischer and Kasparov.

The Sozin Attack with 6.Bc4 was a powerful weapon in the arsenal of Bobby Fischer, so much so that it is often called the Fischer Attack. In the 1993 PCA title match, challenger Nigel Short employed it effectively against Kasparov. The Sozin can be reached from several different Sicilian variations, so it is appealing to White.

Other moves are likely to transpose to the Scheveningen Variation (below) after Black plays ...e6, and are not considered major threats to the Najdorf. When White plays slowly, Black can develop in comfort with ...Be7, ...Nbd7 (or ...Nc6), ...Qc7 and kingside castling.

(22) FISCHER - GELLER
Monte Carlo, 1967

1.e4 c5; 2.Nf3 d6; 3.d4 cxd4; 4.Nxd4 Nf6; 5.Nc3 a6; 6.Bg5 e6; 7.f4 Qb6.

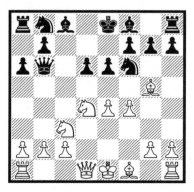

This is the wild Poisoned Pawn Variation, Fischer's specialty as Black. Here is one game where he shows how to handle the White side. Even though he lost, he completely outplayed his opponent in the opening. **8.Qd2 Qxb2; 9.Rb1.** There is one worthy alternative: 9.Nb3 Qa3; 10.Bxf6 gxf6; 11.Be2 h5; 12.0–0 Nd7; 13.Kh1 h4! and Black threatens to advance to h3. 14.h3 Be7; 15.Rad1 b6; 16.Qe3 Bb7; 17.f5 Rc8; 18.fxe6 fxe6; 19.Bg4 Qb2! gave Black excellent counterplay in a contest between Nigel Short and Garry Kasparov, played at the 1995 tournament in Riga.

9...Qa3; 10.f5. White has also thoroughly investigated 10.Be2. **10...Nc6.** Black must get some pieces off the board, in order to be prepared to handle the fierce White attack against the king, which is stranded in the center. **11.fxe6 fxe6; 12.Nxc6 bxc6; 13.e5 Nd5.**

13...dxe5; 14.Bxf6 gxf6; 15.Ne4 is also exciting. Black can capture the pawn at a2 or play more conservatively with a developing move. For example 15...Be7; 16.Be2 h5; 17.Rb3 Qa4; 18.Nxf6+ (18.c4 f5; 19.0-0 fxe4; 20.Qc3 Bc5+; 21.Kh1 Rf8; 22.Bxh5+ Kd8; 23.Rd1+ Bd4; 24.Rxd4+ exd4; 25.Qxd4+ Bd7; 26.Qb6+ Ke7; 27.Qc5+ Kf6; 28.Qd4+ e5; 29.Qxd7 was agreed drawn in Gorky-Spassky, USSR 1968.). 18...Bxf6; 19.c4 Ra7; 20.0-0 Be7; 21.Rb8 Rc7 22.Qd3 Bc5+; 23.Kh1 Ke7; 24.Qg6 Kd6; 25.Rd1+ Bd4; 26.Rxd4+ exd4 27.Qg3+ e5; 28.c5+ Kd5; 29.Bf3+ e4; 30.Qg5+ Kc4; 31.Qc1+ Kd5; 32.Qg5+ was also drawn, in Kasparov-Rashkovsky, USSR 1979.

Kasparov played this theoretically important game before he even earned his Grandmaster title. These days only the very best players in the world dare to "discuss" this variation with him at the board! **14.Nxd5 cxd5.**

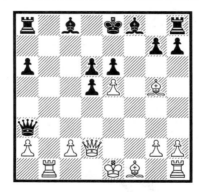

15.Be2 dxe5; 16.0-0 Bc5+ 16...Ra7, defending along the second rank, is now considered more reliable. 17.c4 Qc5+; 18.Kh1 d4; 19.Bh5+ g6; 20.Bd1 Be7; 21.Ba4+. This effective bishop journey has been seen in many games. The end of opening theory is still well beyond the horizon. 21...Kd8; 22.Rf7 h6; 23.Bxh6 e4. This position has been reached in dozens of games. White seems to get the upper hand on 24.Be3! e5; 25.Bg5 e3; 26.Bxe3 although the verdict is still out on 26...Rb7; 27.Re1 Be6; 28.Rg7 Kc8; 29.Bf2 Qb4; 30.Qd1 with a very messy position. **17.Kh1 Rf8; 18.c4.** It is normal for White to try to break up Black's central pawn mass. **18...Rxf1+; 19.Rxf1 Bb7.**

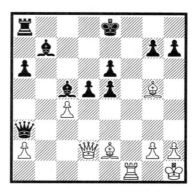

This is where Fischer fell. **20.Bg4?** 20.Qc2! e4, 21.Bg4 gave Tal a good position as White against Bogdanovic at Budva 1967. **20...dxc4; 21.Bxe6 Qd3; 22.Qe1 Be4!** A fine move from the Soviet star and Najdorf specialist. The lines are closed, the Black king is safe, and White is simply two pawns down. **23.Bg4 Rb8; 24.Bd1 Kd7; 25.Rf7+ Ke6. Black won.**

The more traditional lines are no less exciting. Instead of embarking on a wild excursion to pick up a pawn, Black can quickly mobilize and expand with pawns on the queenside, anticipating White's castling there. We see that strategy at work in the following game.

(23) SPASSKY - ELISKASES
Mar del Plata, 1960

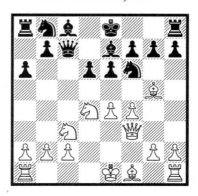

1.e4 c5; 2.Nf3 d6; 3.d4 cxd4; 4.Nxd4 Nf6; 5.Nc3 a6; 6.Bg5 e6; 7.f4 Be7; 8.Qf3 Qc7. This is the main line of the Najdorf. White will attack on the kingside, whether or not Black castles there. **9.0–0–0 Nbd7; 10.g4 b5; 11.Bxf6 Nxf6.** Recently the capture with the pawn has been revived, but it is likely to be a temporary phenomenon. **12.g5 Nd7; 13.a3.** Later 13.f5!? would become the primary choice. This remains a viable alternative, and a popular choice.

13...Bb7? An obvious move, but not best. 13...Rb8 is the main line. Black keeps the b-file open for operations. 14.h4 b4; 15.axb4 Rxb4; 16.Bh3 0-0 is one main line. Bobby Fischer, in a game against Minic from Zagreb 1970, demonstrated that 17.Nf5 Nc5!; 18.Nxe7 Qxe7 is fine for Black. But White can get the advantage by sacrificial means. 17.Nxe6 fxe6; 18.Bxe6+ Kh8; 19.Nd5 and Black is in serious trouble. **14.Rg1.**

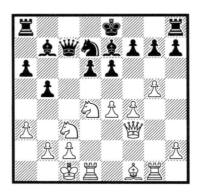

14.Bh3 is more promising. Tal used it successfully against Gligoric at Moscow 1963: 14...0-0-0; 15.Bxe6! fxe6; 16.Nxe6 Qc4; 17.Nd5 Bxd5; 18.exd5 Kb7; 19.b3 Qc8; 20.Rd3 Nb6; 21.Rc3 Qd7; 22.Rc7+ Qxc7; 23.Nxc7 Kxc7; 24.Qc3+ gave him a significant advantage. **14...g6.** A good alternative is 14...d5!; 15.exd5 Nb6 as played by Fischer against O'Kelly at the 1960 Olympiad in Leipzig. **15.Bh3 0-0-0?** This is a serious error. 15...Nc5!; 16.Qe3 Qb6 is assessed as equal by John Nunn, one of the world's leading theoreticians. **16.Bxe6!** This small sacrifice leads to an overwhelming position. **16...fxe6; 17.Nxe6 Qb6; 18.Nxd8 Rxd8; 19.Qh3.**

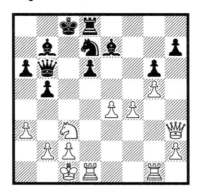

Black has two bishops for a rook, but White has two extra pawns, a pin on the knight at d7 and an attack at h7. Black must try to get an attack going very quickly. **19...b4; 20.axb4 d5; 21.Nxd5 Bxd5; 22.exd5 Bxb4.** The White king still has two healthy defenders, and three extra pawns are just too much of an advantage. **23.Rg3 Re8; 24.d6!** This keeps the Black pieces from getting coordinated. **24...Qc6; 25.Qxh7 Qe4; 26.Kb1 Rf8; 27.Rgd3!** White takes control of d4.

27...Rxf4. 27...Bc5; 28.Rc3 Qxf4 would have led to immediate disaster after 29.Rxc5+! Nxc5; 30.Qc7 mate **28.Rd4 Qe5; 29.Rxf4 Qxf4; 30.Qxg6** As pieces leave the board, White's advantage grows and the defense becomes more an exercise in futility. **30...Qe5; 31.Qg8+ Kb7; 32.Qd8 Qb5; 33.Qc7+ Ka8; 34.g6 Ba3; 35.Qc3 Bc5; 36.g7.** Black resigned.

The move 6.Bg5 used to dominate the scene, but in recent years 6.Bc4 has become more popular.

(24) SHORT - KASPAROV
PCA World Championsip (16), 1993

1.e4 c5; 2.Nf3 d6; 3.d4 cxd4; 4.Nxd4 Nf6; 5.Nc3 a6; 6.Bc4. The Sozin attack was featured in the 1993 PCA World Championship match, and many contributions to the theory of the opening were made during this event. **6...e6; 7.Bb3 b5.**

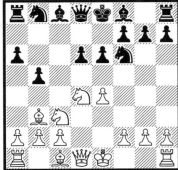

Black has other plans, including bringing the knight from b8 to either d7 or c6, but this is Kasparov's choice. **8.0–0 Be7.** 8...Bb7 is a promising alternative. 9.f4 Nc6; 10.Nxc6 Bxc6; 11.f5 e5; 12.Qd3 Be7; 13.Bg5 Qb6+; 14.Kh1 0–0; 15.Bxf6 Bxf6; 16.Bd5 secured the d5-square, and the advantage, for White in Fischer-Gadia, Mar del Plata 1960. Black should play 9...b4, 10.Na4 Bxe4 with a reasonable game. **9.Qf3.** White has a number of alternative plans. 9.f4 0–0; 10.f5 b4; 11.Nce2 e5; 12.Nf3 Bb7 and White couldn't take advantage of the d5-square, so Black was better in Fischer-Smyslov, Yugoslavia (Candidates Tournament) 1959.

9...Qc7; 10.Qg3! The weakness at g7 is now a target. **10...Nc6.** 10...Nbd7 is probably the best move, for example 11.Re1 Nc5, 12.Nf5 and Black dare not take the knight, because then after Qxg7 the pawn at f7 is in danger. **11.Nxc6.** This exchange is still the recommended path. **11...Qxc6; 12.Re1.** 12.f3 is an interesting alternative which may promise a slight advantage to White. **12...Bb7.** This is acknowledged as the best plan, putting more pressure at e4. **13.a3**

Rd8; 14.f3. 14.Qxg7 is just too risky.

Short later demonstrated the power of the attack with the following variation. 14.Qxg7 Rg8; 15.Qh6 d5; 16.exd5 Nxd5; 17.Bxd5 Rxd5; 18.Ne4 Rd1; 19.Rxd1 Qxe4; 20.f3 Rxg2+; 21.Kxg2 Qxf3+; 22.Kg1 Qg2 mate.

14...0-0; 15.Bh6 Ne8; 16.Kh1. Short's improvement over a previous game which saw 16.Ne2. The move is usefull because it prevents annoying checks on the a7-g1 diagonal. **16...Kh8; 17.Bg5 Bxg5; 18.Qxg5 Nf6; 19.Rad1 Rd7; 20.Rd3 Rfd8; 21.Red1 Qc5; 22.Qe3 Kg8; 23.Kg1 Kf8.** Black can be satisfied with this position. **24.Qf2 Ba8; 25.Ne2.**

Short said later that he was too embarrassed to offer a draw here. Kasparov's next move is a major error, and the exchange of queens should have led to a draw. **25...g6?; 26.Nd4 Qe5.** Black can't play 26...e5 because of 27.Rc3!, e.g., 27...Qa7; 28.Nc6 Qxf2+; 29.Kxf2 Rc8; 30.Nxe5 Rxc3; 31.Nxd7+ Nxd7; 32.bxc3. **27.Re1 g5; 28.c3 Kg7; 29.Bc2 Rg8; 30.Nb3 Kf8; 31.Rd4 Ke7; 32.a4!**

Black has strong queenside play and a much better bishop. **32...h5; 33.axb5 axb5; 34.Rb4 h4; 35.Nd4 g4; 36.Rxb5 d5; 37.Qxh4 Qh5; 38.Nf5+.** Kasparov resigned here. Play might have continued: 38...exf5; 39.exf5+ Kf8; 40.Qxf6 Bb7; 41.Rxb7 Rxb7; 42.Qd8+ Kg7; 43.f6+ Kh8; 44.Qxg8+ Kxg8; 45.Re8 mate.

SCHEVENINGEN VARIATION

The **Scheveningen Variation** (skven-ing-en is the typical English pronunciation) has been played by most of the modern World Champions, and Kasparov, Spassky and Tal frequently played the Black side. It is very similar to the Najdorf in most of the typical lines.

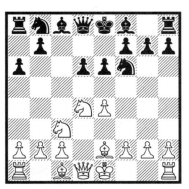

1.e4	c5
2.Nf3	d6
3.d4	cxd4
4.Nxd4	Nf6
5.Nc3	e6
6.Be2	a6

Note that this is a Najdorf with ...e6 for Black and Be2 for White. Neither move is obligatory, but this is the normal formation. Technically, the Scheveningen arises after 1.e4 c5; 2.Nf3 d6; 3.d4 cxd4; 4.Nxd4

Nf6; 5.Nc3 e6, but in fact this move order is rather rare because White then has the option of launching the dreaded Keres Attack with 6.g4, a radical move but one which puts a lot of pressure on the kingside.

So in modern chess the Scheveningen is more commonly reached via the Najdorf (1.e4 c5; 2.Nf3 d6; 3.d4 cxd4; 4.Nxd4 Nf6; 5.Nc3 a6; 6.Be2 e6) or Classical (1.e4 c5; 2.Nf3 Nc6; 3.d4 cxd4; 4.Nxd4 Nf6; 5.Nc3 d6; 6.Be2 a6) variations.

Unlike the Najdorf and Dragon, where Black aims for rapid queenside attacks, the Scheveningen is quieter and slower. Black often sets up a *hedgehog* formation with ...b6; ...Bb7; ...Qc7; ...Be7 and kingside castling. The hedgehog gets its name from the defensive characteristics of the position. If White presses too hard the little critter can inflict painful damage, and the endgames in particular are often favorable to Black.

The Scheveningen:
Black's target position

One factor which further differentiates the Scheveningen from the Sicilians previously discussed is the almost independent nature of White and Black moves. In the above diagram, this is Black's target position. The transpositional possibilities are enormous, and while it is certainly not true that each side can adopt almost any order of moves, there is a great deal of flexibility.

Each side chooses a target formation and develops pieces to achieve that formation. White's options in relation to black's setup include the English Attack, which resembles the Yugoslav Attack of the Dragon with f3, Be3, Qd2, queenside castling and a kingside pawn storm. Alternatively, White can play more positionally, castling kingside and trying to exploit the weakened dark squares on Black's queenside. White will in any case try to maintain a strong grip on the center of the board and Black will try to undermine it.

(25) SMYSLOV - RUDAKOVSKY
Soviet Championship, 1945

1.e4 c5; 2.Nf3 e6; 3.d4 cxd4; 4.Nxd4 Nf6; 5.Nc3 d6; 6.Be2 Be7. The Scheveningen features the "small center" for Black, with the pawns at d6 and e6 keeping the enemy pieces at bay. **7.0–0 0–0; 8.Be3 Nc6; 9.f4 Qc7.**

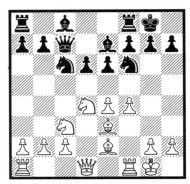

This is a Modern handling of the Scheveningen Variation, where Black delays the advance of the a-pawn to a6. Lines with an early ...a6 are known as the Classical Lines. Ironically, for the past couple of decades the classical approach has come to dominate, but that is mostly due to the fact that many Scheveningens are reached from the Najdorf move order 1.e4 c5; 2.Nf3 d6; 3.d4 cxd4; 4.Nxd4 Nf6; 5.Nc3 a6, avoiding the Keres Attack..

In either approach, both sides develop quickly and castle kingside. White enjoys a bit more space but the Black position is very solid. **10.Qe1.** The queen often shifts to this square, from which it can leap to h4 and participate in a kingside attack. **10...Nxd4.** It is common to exchange knights at d4. Here Black has the added advantage that this can be followed by a strong thrust in the center.

11.Bxd4 e5! Although this creates some holes at d5 and f5, it gives the bishop at c8 some breathing room. **12.Be3 Be6;** 12...exf4; 13.Bxf4 is also possible, but Black should not get greedy. 13...Qb6+; 14.Kh1 Qxb2?; 15.Qg3 Kh8; 16.e5 dxe5; 17.Bxe5 and White threatens to play Nd5! **13.f5 Bc4; 14.Bxc4 Qxc4.** Black has eliminated the light-squared bishops but the kingside belongs to White.

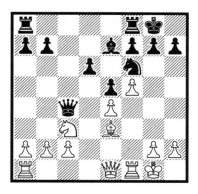

15.Bg5 Rfe8; 16.Bxf6 Bxf6. In exchanging bishop for knight, White counts on the tremendous outpost at d5 to bring home the point. **17.Nd5 Bd8; 18.c3 b5; 19.b3 Qc5+; 20.Kh1 Rc8.** Black has no targets. White can now freely pursue the enemy king. **21.Rf3 Kh8.**

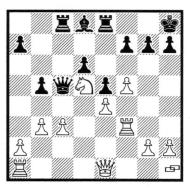

22.f6! The barriers start to fall. **22...gxf6; 23.Qh4 Rg8; 24.Nxf6 Rg7; 25.Rg3 Bxf6; 26.Qxf6.** Black resigned. White will bring the rook at a1, which has not yet moved, into the game with devastating effect. The game might have concluded 26...Rcg8; 27.Rxg7 Rxg7; 28.Rd1 Qxc3; 29.h4 Qc7; 30.Rxd6.

Now let's turn to the one approach for White which most Scheveningen players find so annoying that they seek transposiitonal move orders to avoid it.

(26) KARPOV - HORT
Moscow, 1971

1.e4 c5; 2.Nf3 d6; 3.d4 cxd4; 4.Nxd4 Nf6; 5.Nc3 e6; 6.g4.

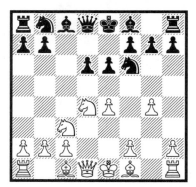

This is the much-feared Keres Attack, the greatest dis-incentive to Black's move order. It is by no means clear that White has a guaranteed advantage, but the results overwhelmingly favor the first player. So even Kasparov, who loves to defend the Scheveningen, often arrives via a Najdorf route to avoid the Keres.

6...Nc6. There are two significant alternatives in 6...e5 and 6...h6. Let's consider a few examples from a recent tournament where top stars were compelled to begin each game with the Sicilian Defense. It was held in Buenos Aires, and greatly enriched the theory of the opening. 6...e5; 7.Bb5+ Bd7; 8.Bxd7+ Qxd7; 9.Nf5 h5; 10.Bg5 Nh7; 11.Bd2 hxg4; 12.Qxg4 g6; 13.Ne3 Qxg4; 14.Nxg4 led to an eventual draw in the game between Ljubojevic, one of the stars of the 1970s, and young Judith Polgar, the most accomplished female chessplayer ever. 6...h6 is also very popular.

7.h4 (7.g5 hxg5; 8.Bxg5 Nc6; 9.Bg2 Bd7; 10.Nb3 a6 ;11.Qe2 Qc7; 12.0-0-0 0-0-0; 13.h4 Kb8; 14.h5 Be7; 15.f4 was seen in Polgar's game against 1994 World Championship candidate Valery Salov, who surprised her with 15...Ng8! a new move with a lot of venom. The game continued 16.Nd4 Bf6; 17.Nf3 Nge7; 18.Bxf6 gxf6; 19.Qd2 and now a remarkable defensive maneuver should have led to an advantage for Black, even though White gained a pawn with 19...Rh6; 20.Qxd6 Qxd6; 21.Rxd6 Kc7; 22.e5 and here 22...Rg8 would have given Black a slight advantage.).

7...Be7; 8.Be3 Nc6; 9.Bb5 Bd7 was introduced by Salov in his game against Shirov. 10.Qe2 h5; 11.gxh5 Nxh5; 12.0-0-0 Qc7 and Black had a promising position, with no real weaknesses, while the pawn at h4 is stopped in its track. **7.g5.**

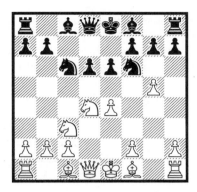

7...Nd7; 8.Be3 a6 9.f4. White's advancing pawns look menacing, but there is not much piece action to support the kingside attack yet. **9...Be7; 10.Rg1 Nxd4.** Hort, one of the top stars of the 1960s and 1970s played this reluctantly, since it concedes the center to White, who now has better control of e5. Therefore Black will have to occupy that square while he can. **11.Qxd4.**

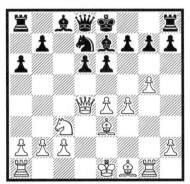

11...e5!; 12.Qd2 exf4; 13.Bxf4 Ne5. Black has executed his plan to take over the e5-square, but has had to accept a weak d6 pawn in return.

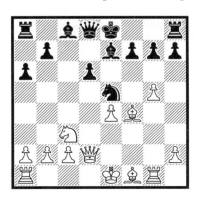

14.Be2 Be6; 15.Nd5! White correctly establishes a blockade at d5. If he had castled first, then Black would have been able to thwart this plan with 15...Qa5! **15...Bxd5; 16.exd5.** A difficult choice. Generally, one uses a piece to blockade a pawn, but here the weakness at d6 would have a counterpart at e4. Karpov's choice also gives more scope to his light-squared bishop. **16...Ng6.** Hort tries to mix it up.

The threat is the capture at f4 followed by Qa5+. **17.Be3 h6?!** This is an error of judgment. Black reasoned that White would not capture, because that would result in a displacement of his king. But with the d-file sealed, the White king will rest comfortably at d1. **18.gxh6 Bh4+; 19.Kd1 gxh6; 20.Bxh6.**

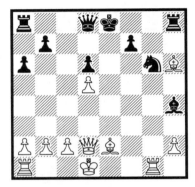

Nevermind White's insignificant extra pawn at c2. The question is, where should the Bh4 be posted? **20...Bf6; 21.c3 Be5.** This is clearly a good square for the bishop, and there is a serious threat here of kingside infiltration with 22...Qh4,e.g ; 23.Bg5 Qb6; 24.Be3 Qc7. But Karpov, recognizing the danger, puts a stop to Black's plans. **22.Rg4! Qf6?!**

Despite White's advantages (bishop pair, open lines in the center), Hort should have taken the opportunity to restore the material balance with 22...Bxh2. Instead, he chose to play for complications. **23.h4!** A strong positional move, saving and advancing the h-pawn. It is based on the tactical point that 23...Nxh4? would be countered by 24.Bg7. **23...Qf5; 24.Rb4.** This rook performs the double duty of protecting the fourth rank and attacking on the queenside. **24...Bf6; 25.h5 Ne7.** Not 25...Ne5?, which drops a piece to 27.Rf4! **26.Rf4.** 26.Rxb7?? Rxh6!; 27.Qxh6 Qxd5+ picks up the Rb7. **26...Qe5.**

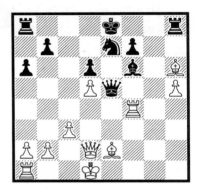

Black still hasn't castled, and will not be allowed to do so! **27.Rf3! Nxd5; 28.Rd3 Rxh6.** No better was 28...Ne7 19.Bf4!. **29.Rxd5!** White had to avoid the tactical trick 29.Qxh6 Bg5 when 30...Ne3+ would have been very powerful. **29...Qe4.**

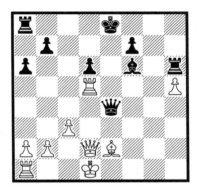

Keep your eye on the White rook, currently residing at d5. **30.Rd3! Qh1+.** The threat of Re3, combined with pressure at h6, forces Black to take this desperate measure. He was in time pressure as well. **31.Kc2 Qxa1; 32.Qxh6 Be5; 33.Qg5.** Hort ran out of time, but that just brought a merciful end to the game. **White won.**

CLASSICAL VARIATION

The **Classical Variation** is one of the old...
It often transposes into othe...
are characteristically classic...   ...xd4;
4.Nxd4 Nf6; 5.Nc3 d6 we re...

1.e4	c5
2.Nf3	Nc6
3.d4	cxd4
4.Nxd4	Nf6
5.Nc3	d6

If White plays 6.Bc4, then play usually transposes to the Sozin Attack, while on 6.Be2, the normal reaction is to switch to the Scheveningen with 6...e6, though 6...e5, the Boleslavsky Variation, is sometimes seen. But the real test of the line is the Richter-Rauzer Attack with 6.Bg5. This leads to very complex play, so much so that it is rarely seen in amateur games.

The Richter-Rauzer can host typical Sicilian fireworks, since here, too, opposite wing castling is normal, but more often pieces are exchanged early in the middlegame and the result depends on the subtle evaluation of strong and weak squares.

A typical line is 6.Bg5 e6; 7.Qd2 Be7; 8.0-0-0 0-0; 9.f4 h6; 10.Bh4 e5; 11.Nf5 Bxf5; 12.exf5, with an unbalanced pawn structure. Good endgame technique is required in such structures, and this perhaps helps to explain why weaker players tend to avoid it. After all, handling complex endgames is much more difficult than calculating tactical variations.

Mikhail Botvinnik liked to employ this defense as an alternative to his favorite French. The other World Champions were more comfortable on the White side.

(27) TAL - KLIAVINS
Riga (Latvian Teams Championship), 1958

1.e4 c5; 2.Nf3 Nc6; 3.d4 cxd4;4. Nxd4 Nf6; 5.Nc3 d6; 6.Bg5 e6; 7.Qd2.

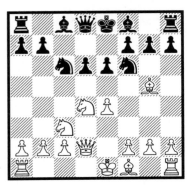

The Richter-Rauzer paths divide here. The Classical lines follow the simple plan of ...Be7 and kingside castling. The most common variations use an immediate ...a6. Many Black defenders adopt both strategies, as well as other moves such as 6...Bd7. **7...a6; 8.0–0–0 Bd7.** Black can also play 8...h6 here.

9.f4. Here there are two plans. Black can either continue with development or provoke the bishop at g5. **9...h6.** 9...Be7; 10.Nf3 b5; 11.Bxf6 gxf6; 12.Kb1 Qb6; 13.Bd3 is a typical line. Now Black should castle queenside. Karpov demonstrated the risk of premature queenside action against Timman at Skopje 1976 13...b4?!; 14.Ne2 a5; 15.f5 a4; 16.Nf4 Qc5; 17.Be2 Rb8; 18.fxe6 fxe6; 19.Ne1 and the knight was ready to re-emerge at d3. **10.Bh4.**

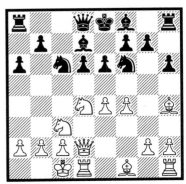

Black has tried three moves here. The most interesting is the immediate capture of the pawn at e4, which we explore in this game. **10...Nxe4.** 10...g5; 11.fxg5 Ng4 pins the g-pawn to the bishop. 12.Nf3! Be7 allows White to play the vigorous 13.g6! after which Black is in trouble; 10...Be7; 11.Nf3 b5; 12.e5 dxe5; 13.fxe5 Nd5 is a complicated position which awaits judgment in the tournament arena. **11.Qe1! Nf6.** 11...Nxc3 loses to 12.Bxd8 Nxd1; 13.Bb6.

12.Nf5 Qa5; 13.Nxd6+ Bxd6; 14.Rxd6.

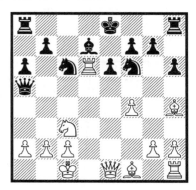

Now Black should have simply castled queenside, but instead adopts an artificial and ineffective plan. **14...Ne7.** 14...0-0-0; 15.Rd1 Qc7; 16.Qf2 was a bit better for White in Spassky-Rabar, Goteborg (Interzonal) 1955. **15.Rd1 Ng6.** 15...Nf5, 16.Bxf6 gxf6 allows White to attack with 17.g4. **16.Ne4 Qxe1; 17.Nd6+ Ke7.** 17...Kf8; 18.Bxe1 Nxf4; 19.Bd2 N4d5; 20.Nxb7 gives White an extra pawn. **18.Bxe1 Nd5; 19.Nxb7 Ngxf4; 20.g3 Ng6; 21.Bg2 Rhb8.** If 21...Bc6, Tal has the strong reply 22.Rxd5!, which frees the b4-square for use by the bishop. **22.Rxd5!**

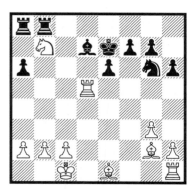

Anyway! To Tal, such sacrifices were almost child's play. **22...Bc6.** 22...Rxb7? would lose to 23.Rxd7+ Rxd7; 24.Bxa8; 22...exd5; 23.Bb4+ Ke8; 24.Re1+ Be6; 25.Bxd5 is equally deadly. **23.Bb4+ Ke8; 24.Rd8+ Rxd8; 25.Bxc6+. 1-0.**

KAN VARIATION

The **Kan Variation**, also called the **Kan Sicilian**, is unrelated to the Caro-Kann, and is named after a Soviet theoretician who developed a unique strategy for Black based on a formation with ...e6 and ...a6. Naturally this defense can transpose to other Sicilians including the Najdorf and Scheveningen, but usually when Black plays 1.e4 c5; 2.Nf3 e6; 3.d4 cxd4; 4.Nxd4 a6, the idea is to play with greater originality.

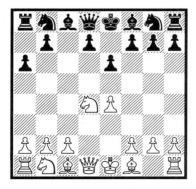

1.e4	c5
2.Nf3	e6
3.d4	cxd4
4.Nxd4	a6

Indeed, even now there is no consensus regarding the three major Sicilian Defenses with an early ...e6: the pure Kan, the Paulsen with an early ...Nc6, and the Taimanov with both ...Nc6 and ...Qc7. There are plenty of other strategies available too, where Black plays ...Bc5 or sets up a hedgehog formation. So the keyword for the Kan is flexibility.

As with all Sicilians, Black will attempt to advance ...d5 as soon as it is safely playable. By not playing ...d6, Black can achieve this in one move rather than two. In addition, a queen at c7 can be joined by a bishop at d6, creating a battery against h2. Since both sides usually castle kingside, this can be a surprisingly effective strategy. Black can add fuel to the fire with ...h5 and ...Ng4.

At first, the Kan failed to attract the attention of top players because it seemed that with 5.c4 White could more or less permanently discourage ...d5.

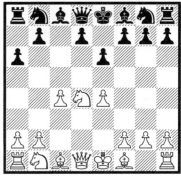

This version of the Maroczy Bind eventually proved to be ineffective, however, because Black was able to create counterplay after 5...Nf6; 6.Nc3 Nc6 or even 6...Bb4.

In the 1950s and 1960s the opening became more fashionable, and even now there is much fertile territory for exploration. The World Champions have not taken a strong interest in the Black side, but this is mostly due to the fact that they choose other move orders to reach similar positions, such as the hedgehog formations. In general, they seem to be more comfortable with the small center approach of ...e6 and ...d6, and don't fully trust the position without ...d6 because of the weak dark squares at e5 and c5.

In addition, the flexible nature of the opening means that the theory of the line is less clear and less focused, an advantage to lower-ranked players but not of much use to the top professionals.

(28) SMYSLOV - SPASSKY
Moscow vs. Leningrad, 1959

1.e4 c5; 2.Nf3 e6; 3.d4 cxd4; 4.Nxd4 a6; 5.c4.

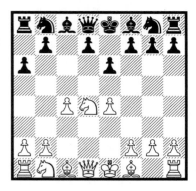

Setting up the bind is not such a common strategy these days, as Black has better resources than we see in this game. **5...Nc6.** Spassky leaves the well-known paths of 5...Nf6. A third option, perhaps best, is to station the queen at c7. For example 5...Qc7; 6.a3 Nf6; 7.Nc3 Nc6; 8.Be3 Be7; 9.Rc1 Ne5; 10.Be2 Ng6; 11.0-0 b6; 12.f4 0-0; 13.b4 Bb7 with a balanced game in Torre-Karpov, Bad Lauterberg 1977. **6.Nc3 Bc5.** The bishop nudges the horse backwards, and then sets up a pin. **7.Nb3 Bb4; 8.Bd3 Nge7; 9.0-0 0-0.**

Both sides have been developing, but now Black adopts a typical plan for this type of formation. He captures on c3, and then advances his d-pawn. But his artificial position (Ne7) helps White. **10.Qc2 Bxc3; 11.Qxc3.**

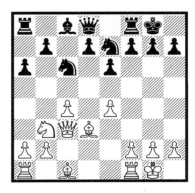

Black can now get in the ...d5 break, which is usually the goal of the Sicilian. Spassky was willing to give up the minor exchange (bishop for knight) in order to get this in. Had he seen what was coming at move 16, he might have adopted a different strategy. **11...d5; 12.Be3 dxc4; 13.Bxc4 Qc7; 14.Rac1 Rd8; 15.f4 Bd7.**

Black seems ready to claim equality, after Ra8-c8. But the weakness of the dark squares on the queenside give White an inviting target for the Be3. **16.Qe1!** White transfers his queen to f2, where it will not only support the g1–a7 diagonal, but also gives more impetus to an advance of the f-pawn, since f7 is no longer guarded by the Black rook. **16...b6.** 16...b5; 17.Be2 Be8; 18.Qf2 Rab8; 19.Nc5 exploits the dark squares in a different way. **17.Qf2 Rab8; 18.f5! Qc8.**

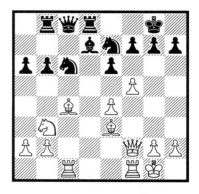

Examining this diagram we see that the pressure point is e6, and the next few moves are aimed directly at the target. They prove to be the last moves! **19.Nd4! Nxd4.** 19...e5 opens a line, but more importantly allows White to advance the f-pawn further with 20.Nxc6 Nxc6 21.Bd5. Also good for White is 19...exf5; 20.exf5 b5; 21.f6! **20.Bxd4 Nc6; 21.fxe6 Bxe6; 22.Bxe6.**

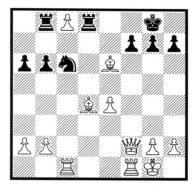

Black resigned, because mate is inevitable after 22...Qxe6; 23.Rxc6 Qxc6; 24.Qxf7+.

There is a related but somewhat more conservative approach seen in the following game.

(29) KASPAROV - KENGIS
Riga (Tal Memorial), 1995

1.e4 c5; 2.Nf3 e6; 3.d4 cxd4; 4.Nxd4 Nc6; 5.Nc3 Qc7. This is the Paulsen Variation of the Sicilian. Black develops slowly but creates a formation that is hard to crack. **6.Be2 a6; 7.0–0 Nf6.**

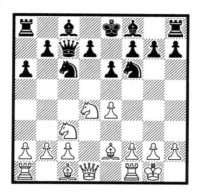

8.Kh1. White plays this move so that the f-pawn can advance. **8...Nxd4; 9.Qxd4 Bc5.** The exchange of knights allows the bishop to develop with tempo. Black should follow this with ...b5 and ...Bb7. **10.Qd3 h5?!** This is premature. Black should first play ...b5 and ...Bb7, and only then begin the kingside assault, as Ivanchuk demonstrated against Anand at the Buenos Aires Thematic Tournament, 1994. **11.Bg5!?** How real is the threat to capture the knight? Not very substantial, since that would only open another line to the White kingside. **11...b5; 12.f4.**

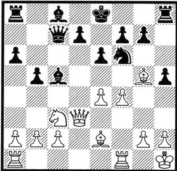

12...Bb7. Black fails to appreciate the danger. There is a White pawn at f4 and that means that the e5-square is under White's control. **13.e5! Nd5.** 13...Ng4 can be met by 14.Bf3!, since 14...Nf2+ fails to 15.Rxf2 Bxf2; 16.Bxb7 Qxb7; 17.Ne4 as pointed out by Dolmatov. **14.Nxd5 Bxd5, 15.a4.** 15.Bf3 would have been more to the point. **15...Qc6; 16.Bf3 Bxf3; 17.Rxf3.** White's forces are in place, and if Black castles anytime soon, the sacrificial move Bf6! is in the offing. **17...bxa4; 18.f5 Rb8; 19.Raf1 0-0?** This is an invitation that will not be refused!

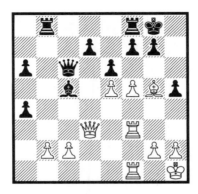

20.Bf6! The bishop can be sacrificed, as the heavy artillery remains aimed at the enemy king. **20...Qb5.** If Black accepts the offer with 20...gxf6 then 21.Rg3+ is followed by Qe2 and mate is inevitable. **21.Rg3 g6.** If Black captures the queen at d3, then White wins with a typical motif: 21...Qxd3; 22.Rxg7+ Kh8; 23.Rg5+ Kh7; 24.Rxh5+ Kg8; 25.Rh8 mate. **22.Qd1 exf5; 23.Rxf5 Rb6; 24.Qxh5.** Checkmate cannot be prevented. **White won.**

LASKER-PELIKAN VARIATION

There are a cluster of Sicilian Defenses which involve an early ...e5 by Black, but the most respectable of these is the **Lasker-Pelikan**. All of these systems have an obvious drawback, a big gaping hole at d5. Black has almost no chance of ever achieving the "Sicilian break" with ...d5. For this reason it has not been a big favorite either of the World Champions or of theoreticians. That evaluation is changing, however.

1.e4	c5
2.Nf3	Nc6
3.d4	cxd4
4.Nxd4	Nf6
5.Nc3	e5

This ancient line was derided by early theoreticians, but that judgment was influenced greatly by the inadequate defensive technique of the time. Lasker resurrected the opening in his 1910 match against Schlechter, and it surfaced from time to time in later games. However, it was clear that Lasker, and the World Champions following, did not really trust it.

In the 1970s, Russian Evgeny Sveshnikov brought the opening back to the tournament repertoire, though it would be another decade or so before it began to be taken seriously. Only in the 1990s, with several top players using it regularly, has the defense achieved full respectability.

The hole at d5 is serious, but Black has found ways of creating counterplay on both flanks, with ...b5 and ...f5 flying in the face of the White forces. The normal line is 6.Ndb5 d6; 7.Bg5 a6; 8.Na3 b5, known as the Chelyabinsk or Sveshnikov Variation. White can now play 9.Nd5 or postpone it slightly with 9.Bxf6 gxf6, 10.Nd5. The knight retains its powerful post at d5, but Black can operate against it by playing ...f5 and capturing the supporting pawn at e4.

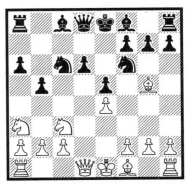

Even so, the World Champions have not been attracted to these "anti-positional" systems and prefer to play the White side. In any case, the Lasker-Pelikan and other systems with ...e5 are not popular with World Champions.

(30) FISCHER - SOLTIS
Manhattan Chess Club (Blitz), 1971

1.e4 c5; 2.Nf3 Nc6; 3.Nc3 Nf6; 4.d4 cxd4; 5.Nxd4 e5; 6.Ndb5 d6;7.Bg5 a6.

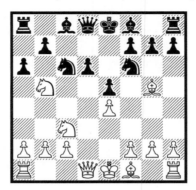

Now 8.Na3 b5 would lead to the well-developed Sveshnikov Variation, but Fischer slides off the main line of theory by interpolating the capture at f6. **8.Bxf6.** 8.Na3 b5; 9.Bxf6 gxf6; 10.Nd5 Bg7; 11.c3 f5 is the main line now, and is getting a workout with Vladimir Kramnik, the latest superstar, stubbornly defending the Black side.

For example, a recent game at Novgorod 1995 against former World Championship challenger Nigel Short, continued 12.exf5 Bxf5; 13.Nc2 Be6; 14.g3 0-0; 15.Bg2 Rb8; 16.0-0 Qd7 when Short unveiled 17.a4! and obtained an advantage. **8...gxf6; 9.Na3 f5.** This is the approved response. **10.Bc4 Bg7?** 10...Ra7! is a very strange looking move, but it turns out that it is best. In fact, according to Sveshnikov, who owns a great deal of Lasker-Pelikan territory, it was known even to Russian school children, and discovered by a very young Anatoly Karpov! The point is that Black is going to play ...b5 anyway, and then Qh5 won't threaten the f7 square.

11.Qh5! Even in blitz games, Fischer never held back on the theoretical surprises, as we will also see in the Fischer-Matulovic game. Here he springs a new move on New York Post columnist Grandmaster Andy Soltis. 11.0-0 0-0; 12.Bd5 f4; 13.Nc4 Nd4 led to complicated play in Tsikelashvili -Timoshenko, Vladimir 1966, with which the well-read Soltis may have been familiar. **11...0-0; 12.exf5 Nd4; 13.Bd3.** Black's problem is the defense of the king. White has bishop and queen aimed at h7, and Black can't get his pieces to the kingside quickly. **13...f6; 14.Be4 Rb8; 15.Nd5.**

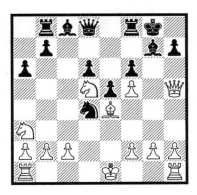

The key drawback to the Lasker-Pelikan is that it concedes this important square to White. **15...Qa5+; 16.c3 Rf7; 17.g4 Bd7; 18.0-0.** Now the knight at d4 is actually threatened. **18...Ne2+; 19.Kh1 Bc6; 20.Rad1!** Fischer keeps control of his prized possession—the d5-square. **20...Nf4.** This looks strong, but it has a flaw.

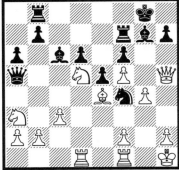

21.Nxf4! Bxe4+; 22.f3 Bc6; 23.Ne6. The knight has found a home in an even better neighborhood. **23...d5.** Black is ordinarily delighted to see this advance achieved, but here it is irrelevant, as the g-pawn just keeps trucking along. **24.g5!; Be8 25.g6.** Black resigned, for good reason.

FRENCH DEFENSE

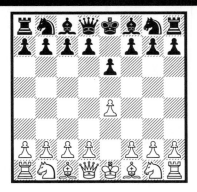

1.e4   e6

The **French Defense** is an opening which most players either love or hate. With the very first move Black tells the bishop at c8 that it is going to be a long time before that piece will play an active role in the game, at least on the kingside. White will be granted an advantage in the center and an advantage in space. Why then, should anyone want to play it as Black, especially such distinguished players as World Champions Botvinnik and Petrosian?

The answer lies in the solid nature of the defense, and the ease with which over-ambitious play by White can be punished. Most games continue 2.d4 d5 (Black can slide into the St. George Defense with 2...a6 instead) when White is faced with a serious decision: what to do about the vulnerable pawn at e4?

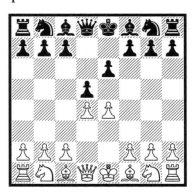

In general, the most principled reply is to defend the pawn while developing a piece, and there are two possibilities here for the knight at b1. In the Classical and Winawer Variations, White chooses 3.Nc3. The **Classical** approach is to respond 3...Nf6, also developing a knight, but the dominant line has been **Winawer's** 3...Bb4, which pins the knight at c3 and threatens to capture it. In the **Tarrasch Variation**, White plays 3.Nd2, which temporarily blocks the bishop at c1 but which does not allow the pin at b4 because on 3...Bb4?! White can reply simply 4.c3!

Of course White can also advance or exchange the e-pawn.

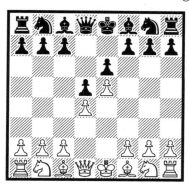

The **Advance Variation** 3.e5 locks in the enemy bishop at c8 and secures an advantage in space, but Black can obtain counterplay with 3...c5 followed by ...Nc6 and ...Qb6 with a lot of pressure at d4, and can also attack the pawn chain with ...f6, which is a typical French strategy.

As with most symmetrical lines, the exchange at d5 does not achieve anything.

After 3.exd5 exd5 Black can comfortably develop all of the army, and this strategy is rarely adopted by White. Other rare approaches by White are 2.d3; 2.Qe2, 2.f4 and even 2.Bb5!?; which prevents ...d5 by pinning the d-pawn, and can lead to a silly draw after 2...Qg5; 3.Bf1 Qd8; 4.Bb5 etc.

CLASSICAL VARIATION

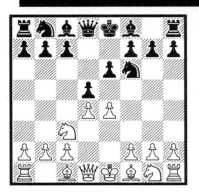

1.e4   e6
2.d4   d5
3.Nc3 Nf6

The **Classical Variation** is one of the oldest chess openings, and it is enjoying a renaissance with world championship challenger Nigel Short leading the charge. While the World Champions have always been up to the challenge, for a long time mere mortals did not dare to adopt these passive lines. In the 1990s, however, several new resources have been found for Black, and the MacCutcheon Variation, where Black meets the standard 4.Bg5 with the exciting 4...Bb4!? has renewed interest on the part of Francophiles.

Black suffers from the usual French bad bishop, locked in at c8, but counterplay is often present in the center. When the White pawn advances to e5, as is usually the case, Black will try to undermine the d4-e5 chain by playing ...c5 and, eventually, attack it with ...f6.

(31) KASPAROV - SHORT
Amsterdam (Euwe Memorial), 1994

1.e4 e6; 2.d4 d5; 3.Nc3 Nf6.

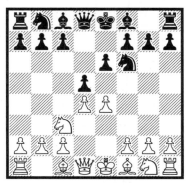

Now White can play 4.Bg5, which allows either a pure Classical with 4...Be7 or a MacCutcheon with 4...Bb4. Often White avoids both by putting the question to the knight immediately with 4.e5. **4.e5.** The old Steinitz Variation is enjoying renewed popularity as well. **4...Nfd7; 5.f4 c5; 6.Nf3 Nc6.** This is the normal continuation. The battle rages for control of the d-pawn. **7.Be3 cxd4.**

The alternative is 7...Qb6 which can be met by 8.Qd2 The pawn sacrifice offered by this move has rarely been tested in the tournament arena. I was quite surprised when young Grandmaster Gabriel Schwartzman accepted it against me at the 1994 United States Open. The game was very exciting, and shows how the inspiration derived from the Kasparov game we are examining can be translated effectively into a similar plan.

My game continued 8...Qxb2; 9.Rb1 Qa3; 10.dxc5. This was my own idea. I decided to eliminate the dark-squared bishops and use Kasparov's attacking formation on the kingside. 10...Bxc5; 11.Bxc5 Qxc5; 12.Bd3 a6; 13.h4 Nb6; 14.Rh3! Nc4; 15.Bxc4 Qxc4; 16.a3! This is a very important move. I had to free the knight from the need to hang around at c3 just to defend the poor pawn. 16...b5; 17.Ne2 Bd7; 18.Nfd4! This eliminates the enemy knight, and I have a decent endgame even without the pawn, because Black is left with a very bad bishop.

18...Nxd4; 19.Nxd4 Rc8; 20.Rbb3! There are two points to this move. One is to be ready to transfer to the kingside at a moment's notice, and the other, more subtle, will be revealed shortly. 20...0-0, 21.Rhg3 f6. Standard French counterplay. 22.f5!? I hadn't worked out all the tactics here. But I had a great deal of confidence and had seen some pleasant long variations, beginning at move 27!

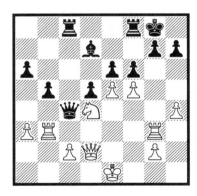

22...exf5. This fell in with my plans. But what about the alternative? Could I have held the position following: (22...fxe5; 23.Qh6 Rf7; 24.Rb4 Qc5!; 25.fxe6 Re7!; 26.exd7 exd4+; 27.Kf1 Rf8+; 28.Kg1 d3+; 29.Kh2 Kh8!; 29...dxc2? allows 30.Rbg4! with devastating threats at g7! 30.Qf4! Rxd7; 31.Qg4 Rdf7; 32.cxd3 Qc1. It might not have been easy, but neither would it have been a simple matter to find all these moves at the board!) 23.Rbc3! A critical preparatory move before the real attack begins. 23...Qa4; 24.Qh6 Rf7; 25.exf6 g6; 26.Rxg6+

hxg6; 27.Qxg6+ I had already worked out the rest of the game, and didn't bother to look for any alternative plans. 27...Kf8; 28.Qh6+ Ke8; 29.Qh8+ Rf8; 30.Re3+ Kd8; 31.Qxf8+ Kc7; 32.Qc5+ Kb8; 33.Qd6+ Rc7; 34.Rc3 Qa5; 35.Qxc7+ and my opponent resigned. This was one of the biggest upsets of the Open. Now back to our Kasparov game

8.Nxd4 Bc5; 9.Qd2 0–0; 10.0–0–0 a6; 11.h4

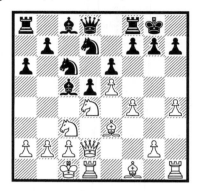

The point of this move is to provide a route to the third rank for the rook. In the game cited at move seven we saw this idea at work. **11...Nxd4; 12.Bxd4 b5; 13.Rh3 b4; 14.Na4 Bxd4; 15.Qxd4 f6.** This was an original idea, but 15...Qa5 would have been a better choice. **16.Qxb4 fxe5; 17.Qd6!** 17.fxe5 Nxe5 gives Black fewer headaches. **17...Qf6.**

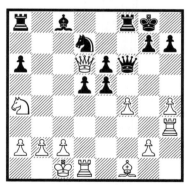

Now Kasparov plays a brilliant and unexpected move. **18.f5!!** The pawn cannot be captured. **18...Qh6+.** 18...exf5; 19.Qxd5+ Kh8; 20.Qxa8 wins a rook; 18...Qxf5; 19.Rf3 Qg4; 20.Rxf8+ Nxf8; 21.Nb6 Bb7; 22.Nxa8 Bxa8; 23.Bxa6 Qxg2; 24.Rf1 and Black can resign. **19.Kb1 Rxf5.** The pawn is gone, but another file is open! Against 19...Nf6 White could try 20.fxe6. **20.Rf3 Rxf3; 21.gxf3 Qf6; 22.Bh3 Kf7.** There was little choice, as Kasparov pointed out that 22...Nf8; 23.Nb6 Qxf3 loses to 24.Rf1 Qxh3; 25.Rxf8 mate. **23.c4.**

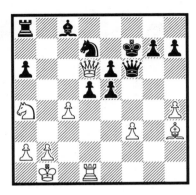

Here Short might have been better off with 23...d4, keeping the d-file closed. **23...dxc4; 24.Nc3 Qe7; 25.Qc6 Rb8; 26.Ne4 Nb6!** Short finds the only defense, but Kasparov still has a huge advantage. 26...Nf8 defends the e-pawn but White wins with 27.Nd6+ Kg8; 28.Nxc8 Qb4; 29.Bxe6+ Kh8; 30.b3! as given by Kasparov. After 30...cxb3; 31.Bxb3 Black has no more attack. **27.Ng5+ Kg8; 28.Qe4 g6; 29.Qxe5 Rb7; 30.Rd6.**

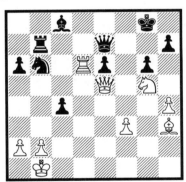

The e-pawn is doomed. **30...c3; 31.Bxe6+ Bxe6; 32.Rxe6.** Black resigned. Kasparov provided the following convincing conclusion: 32...Nc4; 33.Qxc3 Na3+; 34.Kc1 Qd7; 35.Rc6 and the threat of Rc8+ is fatal. **White won.**

WINAWER VARIATION

1.e4   e6
2.d4   d5
3.Nc3   Bb4

The **Winawer** is the sharpest variation of the French, and from Botvinnik's time to quite recently it dominated the French arena. It leads to very complex play, an example of which is the French Poisoned Pawn Variation. 1.e4 e6; 2.d4 d5; 3.Nc3 Bb4; 4.e5 c5; 5.a3 Bxc3+; 6.bxc3 Ne7; 7.Qg4 Qc7; 8.Qxg7 Rg8; 9.Qxh7 cxd4 and here White has a choice.

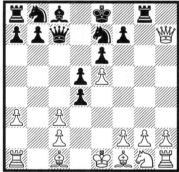

Both 10.Kd1 and 10.Ne2 are common. In either case White has problems developing, but Black still has that bad bishop at c8. The evaluation of these positions remains controversial. In any case, thorough knowledge of the many well-analyzed variations is essential to playing the Winawer effectively as Black or White.

(32) TAL - BOTVINNIK
World Championship (12), 1961

1.e4 e6; 2.d4 d5; 3.Nc3 Bb4.

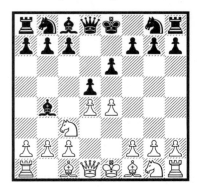

The Winawer is the most deeply investigated variation of the French. As such, it attracts players who enjoy the challenge of exploring hundreds of lines, looking for improvements which can deliver a full point against a less well-prepared opponent. **4.e5 c5; 5.a3 Bxc3+; 6.bxc3 Qc7.**

This is the most complex, yet at the same time, one of the most common continuations. With the main alternative, 6...Ne7, Black offers a pair of pawns on the kingside, but sees great counterplay in the center. Often, neither king enjoys the safety of a castled position. The text gives Black one additional option, which is explored in this game. **7.Qg4 f5.** This is possible because Black chose 6...Qc7 rather than 6...Ne7.

Now the g-pawn is protected. The price Black pays is that ...f6 is no longer an option, so the White center is easier to maintain. 7...Ne7 is more popular. After 8.Qxg7 Rg8, 9.Qxh7 cxd4 White chooses between 10.Kd1 and 10.Ne2, each aimed at addressing the threat of ...Qxc3+. **8.Qg3 Ne7.** Black does not have to offer the g-pawn here. 8...cxd4; 9.cxd4 Ne7 (9...Qxc2; 10.Bd2 lets White take over the c-file with Rc1.) 10.Bd2 0–0; 11.Bd3 b6; 12.Ne2 Rf7 was seen in Diez del Corral-Petrosian, Palma de Mallorca 1969, where Petrosian pointed out that 13.h4! would have given White a small advantage. **9.Qxg7 Rg8; 10.Qxh7 cxd4; 11.Kd1.**

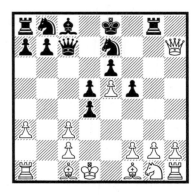

White must do something about the pressure on the c-file. The king is relatively safe, since Black has only the queen to attack with. If Black is able to marshall more attacking power, however, things can become dangerous. **11...Bd7.** 11...Nbc6;12.Nf3 Nxe5; 13.Bg5 N7g6 was played in Gligoric-Petrosian at the 1959 Candidates tournament, but Euwe discovered that 14.Bf6! is overpowering, so this line has been retired. **12.Qh5+ Kd8.** 12...Ng6; 13.Ne2 d3; 14.cxd3 Ba4+; 15.Ke1 Qxe5; 16.Bg5 Nc6; 17.d4 Qc7; 18.h4 gave Tal a clear advantage in the first game of the 1960 title match against Botvinnik. **13.Nf3 Qxc3; 14.Ra2 Nbc6; 15.Rb2 Kc7; 16.Rb5!**

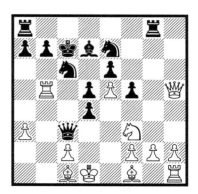

This move controls important squares at a5 and c5. **16...Rh8.** Tal now sacrifices the queen, noting the miserable position of Black's queen. Nevertheless, the less flashy 17.Qg5! would have been wiser, objectively **17.Qxh8 Rxh8; 18.Bb2 Qxf3+; 19.gxf3 Ng6?.** What would Tal have done if Botvinnik had found 19...Rh4!; for example 20.f4 Ng6; (20...Rxf4; 21.h4 Nxe5; 22.Rb3 Ng4; 23.Ke1 Ba4; 24.Rg3 Bxc2; 25.Be2! d3; 26.Bxg4 Rxg4; 27.Rxg4 fxg4; 28.Kd2 is given in the classic work on the Winawer by John Moles.) 21.Bc1 Nxf4; 22.Bxf4 Rxf4; 23.h4 Nxe5 with the deadly threat of ...Ng4, which White cannot meet because the rook at b5 is attacked.

Now it is interesting to note that in the authoritative 1993 monograph on the main lines of the Winawer by Viktor Korchnoi, the analysis ends here with the opinion that Black stands much better. But Moles had already published the following analysis in his 1975 book! 24.Rb3 Ng4; 25.Ke1 Nxf2; (25...Be8; 26.h5 Nxf2; 27.h6! Nxh1; 28.h7 Rh4; 29.Rh3 winning.) 26.Rg1 Ng4; 27.h5 Be8; 28.Rh3 Re4+; 29.Be2! and White wins. The moral of the story: don't ignore older sources of information—they may contain nuggets overlooked in more recent works! **20.h4 Ngxe5; 21.h5 Nf7; 22.f4.**

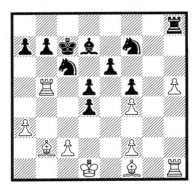

White has too many assets here. There is the extra exchange, of course, and a powerful passed pawn. In addition, the bishop pair can be used effectively. Finally, it is hard to see how Black's pawn mass can be activated. **22...Nd6; 23.Rb3 Ne4; 24.Ke1 Rh6; 25.Be2 Be8; 26.Rd3.** White has to trade the pawn at h5 for the one at d4. **26...Nf6; 27.Bxd4 Nxd4; 28.Rxd4 Bxh5; 29.Rd3!** The awkward position of the rook at h6 is exploited. A deadly pin is threatened. **29...Rh7; 30.Rdh3 Bg6.** This is the only way to release the pressure, but the exchange of rooks accentuates White's advantage.

31.Rxh7+ Nxh7; 32.Rh6 Nf8; 33.Rh8 Nd7; 34.Rg8 Bf7; 35.Rg7. White has effectively improved his position. The e-pawn will be his reward. **35...Be8; 36.Re7 Kd8; 37.Rxe6 Bf7; 38.Rh6 Ke7; 39.Bd3 Be6.** Now it is the turn of the f-pawn. **40.Rh5 Nf6; 41.Rg5.** There was no point in continuing since the adjournment point was reached and if 41...Ne4, then 42.Rh5 leads to a winning position. **White won.**

The theory-dependent nature of the opening has led many players, including World Champions to prefer the quieter streams of the Tarrasch Variation.

TARRASCH VARIATION

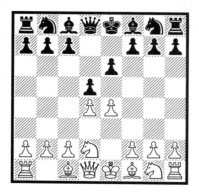

1.e4	e6
2.d4	d5
3.Nd2	

In the **Tarrasch Variation**, White stations the knight at d2 rather than c3. Black is no longer able to pin it as in the Winawer or MacCutcheon Variations, because against ...Bb4 White can always play c3. The Tarrasch Variation has a quite different nature than the Classical or Winawer. Often positions arise which see one side or the other accept an isolated d-pawn, an important structural feature which determines the flow of the game.

Tal used the Tarrasch Variation effectively as White, winning many impressive games. It is a good choice for beginners and experts alike, because it is fairly simple to play. One thing to keep in mind, however, is that Black has a choice of several acceptable plans, including 3...Nf6, 3...c5 and 3...a6. Guimard's anti-positional 3...Nc6!? is also sometimes seen, even though it temporarily blocks the advance of the c-pawn.

(33) KARPOV - UHLMANN
Madrid, 1973

1.e4 e6; 2.d4 d5; 3.Nd2 c5.

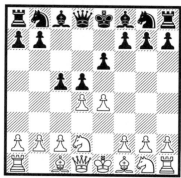

This remains one of the most popular defenses to the Tarrasch. **4.exd5 exd5.** Black can also capture with the queen. **5.Ngf3 Nc6; 6.Bb5 Bd6; 7.dxc5 Bxc5.** Tarrasch, who developed this approach for White, loved isolated pawns. He was disappointed to discover that Black would have that "luxury" in his own pet line. On the other hand, most strong players consider the isolated pawn a slight weakness unless accompanied by a strong intitiative or good piece play, so many players have favored the White side. **8.0–0 Nge7; 9.Nb3 Bd6.**

In positions with an isolated d-pawn White has two main objectives: the blockade of the isolated pawn and the elimination of Black's dark-squared bishop. **10.Bg5!** This move directly implements White's plan by transferring the bishop to a post from which it can reach the h2-g8 diagonal (via h4 to g3). **10...0–0; 11.Bh4 Bg4; 12.Be2 Bh5?!** The superior 12...Re8! had already been introduced by Uhlmann, but he was probably afraid of a prepared innovation. **13.Re1 Qb6; 14.Nfd4!**

Black must now do something about the bishop at h5. **14...Bg6.** If Black had exchanged bishops, the isolated pawn would have less protection. Uhlmann decides that the bishop may be of use at e4, since any eventual f2-f3 will weaken the a7-g1 diagonal. **15.c3 Rfe8; 16.Bf1!** Karpov realizes that this is the best square for the bishop, since on f3 it could be attacked by Nc6-e5. As we will see, the control of the e-file plays an important role in the remainder of the game. **16...Be4; 17.Bg3!.** Now that all of White's pieces have been properly positioned, the exchange of bishops is appropriate. **17...Bxg3; 18.hxg3.**

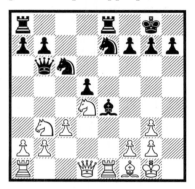

The cluster of pawns in front of the king creates an insurmountable protective barrier. **18...a5!?** The weakening of b5 is probably more significant than Black's mild initiative, but perhaps the move was played without taking into consideration White's potential sacrifice of the b-pawn. **19.a4 Nxd4; 20.Nxd4!** Karpov correctly maintains the blockade with the piece, since if 20...Qxb2 then 21.Nb5! threatens both 22.Nc7 and 22.Re2. **20...Nc6; 21.Bb5!** The pin encourages Black's rook to leave the e-file. Probably 21...Bg6 would have been best here. **21...Red8?!; 22.g4!** A very clever move, the point of which is to create threats of trapping the enemy bishop should it retreat to g6 (with f2-f4-f5). **22...Nxd4.** Now White gets a superior endgame. **23.Qxd4 Qxd4; 24.cxd4 Rac8.** 24...Kf8 would not have prevented infiltration by the White rooks: 25.Re2 Rac8; 26.f3 Bg6; 27.Rae1 Rc7??; 28.Re8+ Rxe8; 29.Rxe8 mate. **25.f3 Bg6.**

26.Re7. The immediate objective has been achieved. After the doubling of rooks on the e-file, Karpov illustrates his famous endgame technique. **26...b6; 27.Rae1 h6; 28.Rb7 Rd6; 29.Ree7 h5; 30.gxh5 Bxh5; 31.g4 Bg6; 32.f4 Rc1+; 33.Kf2 Rc2+; 34.Ke3 Be4; 35.Rxf7 Rg6; 36.g5 Kh7; 37.Rfe7 Rxb2; 38.Be8! Rb3+; 39.Ke2 Rb2+; 40.Ke1 Rd6; 41.Rxg7+ Kh8; 42.Rge7. White won.**

ADVANCE VARIATION

1.e4	e6
2.d4	d5
3.e5	

The **Advance Variation** with 3.e5 appeals to many amateur players because it leads to an advantage in space and is easy to play. At Championship level, however, it has been terribly ineffective, and only a few top professionals have been found on the White side. In typical French fashion Black will try to undermine the White pawn chain, starting with pressure at d4 via 3...c5.

As Black, Botvinnik and Petrosian have demonstrated that this system is not difficult to play. By studying their games, French fans can eliminate the Advance Variation from their worry list. Still, one must be well prepared, as there are some sharp lines and White can achieve good results against unprepared opponents, as the next game shows.

(34) TAL - NEI
Soviet Union, 1958

1.e4 e6; 2.d4 d5; 3.e5 c5; 4.c3 Nc6; 5.Nf3.

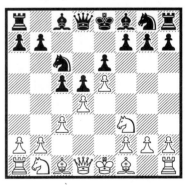

The Advance Variation is rarely used by top players, because it leads to a very fixed pawn structure, and Black's source of counterplay is a no-brainer: attack key points along the b2-e5 pawn chain.

5...Qb6; 6.Bd3. This is the Milner-Barry Gambit, a fun line which was developed by the late Sir Stuart Milner-Barry, one of the most important figures on the British chess scene. **6...cxd4; 7.cxd4 Bd7.** This move is intended to set up the threat of capturing at d4, which would have led to disaster if played immediately. 7...Nxd4??; 8.Nxd4 Qxd4; 9.Bb5+ picks up the Black queen. **8.0–0 Nxd4; 9.Nxd4.** There are alternatives, but this is the most testing continuation. **9...Qxd4; 10.Nc3.**

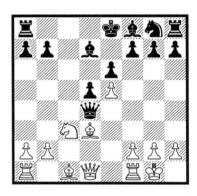

The position is more complicated than it seems. Even the American theoretician and devoted Francophile John Watson is unsure how Black should continue. He has great faith in the plan adopted by Nei in this game, and indeed, it has become the main line. **10...Qxe5.** Black can also try 10...a6 and 10...Ne7.

There is plenty of terra incognita to explore. **11.Re1 Qd6?!.** 11...Qb8; 12.Nxd5 Bd6; 13.Qg4 Kf8; 14.Bd2 h5; 15.Qh3 Bc6 is now the normal continuation. Watson has played it several times, and his conclusion is that after 16.Ne3 Nf6; 17.Nc4 Be7; 18.Bc3 and now 18...Ng4!, an original idea which has not yet been tested, Black stands well. In fact, he sums up: "The whole 10...Qxe5 line favors Black, in my opinion."

12.Nb5. Returning to our game, we see what happens when Black tries to hold on to the d-pawn. **12...Qb8; 13.Qf3 Bd6.** Black is hoping that White will be satisfied to trade the knight for the good bishop, but White has greater ambitions. **14.Qxd5! Bxh2+.** This pawn does not matter. The clerics can fatten themselves on pawns, but their monarch will pay the bill. **15.Kh1 Bc6; 16.Qg5!** This move is credited to Pachman, but as we see, it had already been played in a game. **16...Nf6; 17.f4!** Tal is patient. The g-pawn will be captured, but only at the appropriate moment. **17...h6.** Forcing matters, but there was nothing better. **18.Qxg7 Rg8.**

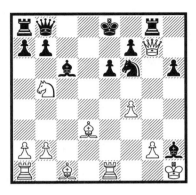

Perhaps Black was hoping that White would settle for the knight at f6. **19.Rxe6+!!** A brilliant finish, typical of Tal. **19...fxe6; 20.Bg6+ Kd8 21.Qxf6+.** This game is not in the *Complete Games of Mikhail Tal*, and that is truly a pity, because it is quite elegant. **White won.**

CARO-KANN DEFENSE

1.e4 c6

In the **Caro-Kann Defense**, Black will advance the d-pawn to d5 on the second move, confronting the White pawn at e4. Unlike the French, the Caro-Kann does not force Black's bishop to sit idly at c8. Instead, it has an open highway to the kingside, and is usually developed quite early in the game.

Even though players often castle on opposite wings, the Caro-Kann cannot be defeated by direct attacks in most cases. The Black position can usually absorb whatever White throws at it, and endgame play is typical. This is why World Champions have often employed the defense, since their superior endgame technique can bring home many tournament points.

The main lines of the opening follow 1.e4 c6; 2.d4 d5; 3.Nc3 dxe4; 4.Nxe4, though the **Advance Variation** (3.e5) and **Panov Attack** (3.exd4 cxd5, 4.c4) are very popular alternatives these days. After 3.Nc3 dxe4, 4.Nxe4, Black has a choice of four different systems. The **Classical Variation** system with 4...Bf5 dominated the opening until the late 1980s, when World Champion Anatoly Karpov turned 4...Nd7, the **Karpov Variation**, into the main line. The systems with 4...Nf6 are not seen in top level play because of the damage White can inflict on the pawn structure with 5.Nxf6+.

In addition to Karpov, the Caro-Kann holds strong appeal for Vasily Smyslov. It seems that in most cases, players who enjoy the Caro-Kann also like to defend the Open Games, especially the Spanish. Once again, Karpov takes the lead in these safe lines.

CLASSICAL VARIATION

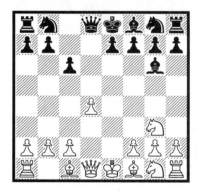

1.e4	c6
2.d4	d5
3.Nc3	dxe4
4.Nxe4	Bf5
5.Ng3	Bg6

The **Classical Variation** has been a popular opening for most of this century. The bishop is developed on the kingside so that after an eventual ...e6 it can remain a factor in the game. In fact, White usually plays an early Bd3 to exchange light-squared bishops. Typically, White enjoys a small advantage in space, but Black's position is very solid. Both sides have chances in the endgames, which often feature knights galloping all over the board.

Play typically continues 6.h4 h6; 7.Nf3 Nd7; 8.h5 Bh7; 9.Bd3 Bxd3; 10.Qxd3 e6; 11.Bd2 Ngf6; 12.O-O-O.

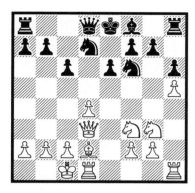

Now Black can choose between playing ...Qc7 with queenside castling, or ....Be7 with kingside castling. In either case, it is very hard for White to establish a serious advantage. Until quite recently this was the main line of the Caro-Kann, but Anatoly Karpov, who we'll look at after the following game, has brought a different plan to the forefront.

(35) SPASSKY - BOTVINNIK
USSR Teams, 1966

1.e4 c6; 2.d4 d5; 3.Nc3 dxe4; 4.Nxe4 Bf5.

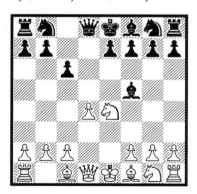

In the Classical Variation, Black quickly develops the queenside pieces, usually intending to castle in that direction. **5.Ng3 Bg6; 6.h4.** The threat of 7.h5 must be met, so Black has to weaken the kingside. **6...h6; 7.Nf3 Nd7; 8.h5 Bh7; 9.Bd3.** There is no better use for this bishop than to eliminate its opposite number, leaving the kingside weak. **9...Bxd3; 10.Qxd3 Ngf6; 11.Bd2 Qc7; 12.0–0–0 0–0–0.**

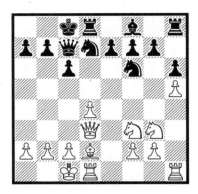

This is the normal continuation. Now White wants to find a way to get to the pawn at f7, and the logical way is by getting a knight to e5. If Black captures, then White's pawns at e5 and h5 will cramp the kingside. **13.Qe2 e6; 14.Ne5 Nxe5; 15.dxe5 Nd5; 16.f4.** Mission accomplished. Black will have a permanent disadvantage in space on the kingside. On the other hand, in a knight endgame, the White pawns will fall like ripe apples. **16...c5.**

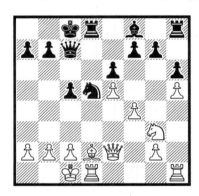

This threatens 17...c4, so White's hand is forced. **17.c4 Nb4; 18.Bxb4.** 18.Kb1 was recommended by Botvinnik. 18...Be7, 19.Bc3 was appended by Kasparov, who notes that sooner or later the knight will retreat to c6, citing resemblance to Parma-Barcza, Kapfenburg 1970. But there are perhaps some significant differences. 19...Kb8; 20.Ne4 Rxd1+; 21.Rxd1 Rd8 and the position remains unclear. **18...Rxd1+; 19.Rxd1 cxb4.** Now, as Botvinnik noted, the White king will have difficulty finding shelter, and Black will have counterplay in any queen endgame. **20.Ne4 Be7; 21.Nd6+ Kb8.**

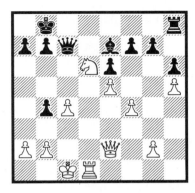

This is a "critical position" which has been the subject of much discussion. Critical positions are often found in messy openings, but sometimes also in games like these, where there is a sense that one player needs to play with absolute precision. **22.Nxf7.** 22.g3 was claimed by Boleslavsky to secure an advantage for White, but Kasparov has shown that this is an optimistic evaluation.

22...f6; 23.exf6 Bxd6; 24.fxg7 Re8; 25.Qg4 (Boleslavsky) 25...Qxc4+; 26.Kb1 Qe4+!; 27.Ka1 Rg8; 28.Rxd6 Rxg7 with chances for both sides, according to Kasparov. But I would prefer to be Black here. **22...Rf8; 23.Nd6 Rxf4; 24.g3 Rf8; 25.Qg4 Qd7!** 26.Kb1; 26.Qxg7? loses to 26...Bg5+. **26...Bg5;** 26...Rf2 is refuted by 27.Qxg7 Qa4; 28.Rc1! **27.Nb5 Rf1!**

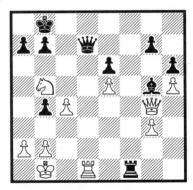

Black already has sufficient counterplay. **28.Kc2.** White has to settle for a pawn-down ending here, hoping that his knight will be able to outmaneuver the enemy bishop. Against Botvinnik, this is wishful thinking! 28.Rxf1 loses instantly to 28...Qd3+. **28...Rxd1; 29.Qxd1 Qxd1+; 30.Kxd1 Be3!** Botvinnik wastes no time in limiting the scope of the knight. **31.Ke2.** 31.b3 Bf2; 32.g4 Bc5 dominates the knight completely. Botvinnik gives the following line: 33.Ke2 a6; 34.Nd6 Bxd6; 35.exd6 b6; 36.Kd3 Kb7; 37.Ke4 Kc6; 38.Ke5 Kd7 and White loses the d-pawn and the game. **31...Bc1; 32.b3 Bb2!; 33.Nd6 Bxe5; 34.Ne4**

Kc7; 35.g4.

The endgame has now taken shape. Black must find a way to open up some lines so that his king can take an active role. To do so, he will temporarily sacrifice a pawn at b5. 35.Nc5 Bxg3 36.Nxe6+ Kd6 37.Nxg7 Ke5 38.Ne8 Ke6 and the knight gets trapped. **35...Kc6; 36.Kd3 b5; 37.cxb5+ Kd5!** Better than 37...Kxb5; 38.Nd2 Kc6; 39.Ne4!. **38.g5?!** 38.Ke3 Bc7; 39.Kf3! Kd4; 40.Nf2 Kc3; 41.Ke2 Kb2; 42.Kd3 Kxa2; 43.Kc2 would have been a better drawing plan, as Spassky later demonstrated, because the Black king would not be able to play any role, and the knight could establish a blockade on the light squares. **38...hxg5; 39.Nxg5 Bf4; 40.Ne4 Bh6.**

As Botvinnik noted, the key here is for the bishop to occupy a post where it can both control e3, to stop harassing checks, and also defend the pawn at b4. **41.Nf2 Bg5; 42.Ng4 Bf4; 43.Nf2 Bd6; 44.Ng4.** 44.Ne4 Bc7!; 45.Nf2 Bb6; 46.Ne4 Ke5; 47.Nd2 Kf4; 48.Kc4 Ke3; 49.Nf1+ Ke2; 50.Ng3+ Kf3; 51.Nf1 Bc7! guarantees victory for Black, according to Botvinnik. **44...Bc5; 45.h6 gxh6; 46.Nxh6.**

The kingside pawns have been eliminated, but this means that Black can concentrate his attention on advancing his passed pawn, which also limits White's ability to maneuver. **46...e5; 47.Nf5 e4+; 48.Ke2 Ke5; 49.Nh4 Kd4; 50.Nf5+ Kd5; 51.Nh6 Be7; 52.Ng4 Bg5; 53.Nf2 Kd4; 54.Nd1 Bc1; 55.Nf2 Kd5; 56.Ng4 Bg5; 57.Nf2 Bf6; 58.Ng4 Bd4; 59.Nh2 Bc5; 60.Nf1 Kd4; 61.Nd2 Bb6.**

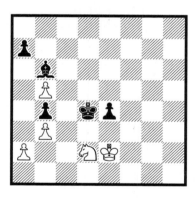

62.Nc4? This natural move throws the game away. 62.Nf1 Kc3; 63.Ng3 Kb2; 64.Kd1! Kxa2; 65.Kc2 e3; 66.Ne2 would have drawn, in similar fashion to the alternative discussed at move 38. **62...Kc3; 63.Kd1 Bd4!** Black wants to maneuver his king to d3. **64.Ke2 e3; 65.Na5 Kb2; 66.Nc6 Bc5; 67.Ne5 Kxa2; 68.Nd3 Be7** and White resigned because his b-pawn falls and then Black's b-pawn marches on.

KARPOV VARIATION

With 4...Nd7, instead of 4...Bf5, the **Karpov Variation**, a very different picture emerges. The bishop at c8 does not enter the game quickly, because it is blocked by the knight.

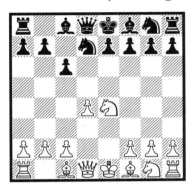

1.e4	c6
2.d4	d5
3.Nc3	dxe4
4.Nxe4	Nd7

The point of the strange-looking move is to be able to develop the knight from g8 to f6. If Black does this without preparation, then White will exchange knights and cripple Black's pawn structure. Some players are willing to live with the doubled pawns that result, but not top stars.

White now has several choices. 5.Bc4 and 5.Nf3 lead to what used to be the main lines, but in the late 1980s a plan with an immediate 5.Ng5 suddenly emerged from obscurity to gain equal status. Play usually continues 5...Ngf6, 6.Bd3 and now Black has tried many plans, usually falling just short of equality but with a sound game. Anatoly Karpov has been at the forefront of the defenders of this system from the Black side.

(36) KAMSKY - KARPOV
Dortmund, 1993

1.e4 c6; 2.d4 d5; 3.Nd2 dxe4; 4.Nxe4 Nd7. This is the Filip-Flohr-Petrosian-Smyslov-Karpov Variation! That gives some idea of the appeal of this quiet move to positional players. Black uses this awkwardly placed knight to prepare Ng8-f6, when a White capture will not cause Black to double the kingside pawns. **5.Ng5.**

This is the most aggressive reply and the one which is most often seen these days. Strangely, it was considered a minor option as recently as a decade ago. 5.Bc4 Ngf6; 6.Ng5 e6; 7.Qe2 Nb6 is the other main line. Karpov got a good position with it against Topalov at Belgrade 1995: 8.Bd3 h6; 9.N5f3 c5; 10.dxc5 Bxc5; 11.Ne5 Nbd7; 12.Ngf3 Qc7; 13.Bf4 Bb4+; 14.Nd2 Bxd2+; 15.Kxd2 0–0; 16.Rhd1 Nc5; 17.Ke1 Nd5; 18.Bg3 Nxd3+; 19.Rxd3 b5; 20.a4 Ba6! **5...Ngf6; 6.Bd3 e6; 7.N1f3 Bd6.**

Black has several options here, and 7...h6 and 7...Be7 are often seen. But this is the most ambitious move. **8.Qe2.** White often plays this before deciding which side to castle to. **8...h6; 9.Ne4.** The removal of a pair of knights is not pleasant for White, but retreating with 9.Nh3 allows Black to attack with 9...g5. 9.Nxe6 fxe6, 10.Bg6+ Ke7 is fine for Black. **9...Nxe4; 10.Qxe4 Nf6; 11.Qh4.** Usually the queen retreats to e2, which is a somewhat safer post. Kamsky is going all-out for the win. **11...Ke7.**

This move had been prepared by Karpov years in advance of this game.. Black's forces are well-placed, and Karpov can contemplate a kingside attack. **12.Ne5** White sacrifices a pawn, hoping to build an attack against the exposed Black king. **12...Bxe5; 13.dxe5 Qa5+; 14.c3 Qxe5+; 15.Be3.** In return for the pawn White has the bishop pair and some potential for an attack against the Black king. **15...b6; 16.0–0–0 g5; 17.Qa4 c5; 18.Rhe1 Bd7!** The Black pawns keep the bishop on e3 at bay, and there are no discoveries to be feared.

19.Qa3 Rhd8; 20.g3 Qc7. Overprotecting c5 against any sacrificial possibilities. **21.Bd4 Be8; 22.Kb1 Rd5.** A good move, but Karpov remarked that 22...Bc6 might be even stronger. **23.f4 Rad8; 24.Bc2 R5d6; 25.Bxf6+ Kxf6; 26.fxg5+ hxg5; 27.Rxd6 Rxd6.** Many pieces have left the board, and White has less to show for the investment of a pawn. **28.c4 Ke7; 29.Qe3 f6; 30.h4 gxh4.**

Kamsky's offer of a draw was politely refused. For Karpov, a pawn is a major advantage! **31.gxh4 Qd7; 32.Qh6 e5?** Karpov was drifting into time pressure, and missed the simple 32...Rd2!, 33.Rf1 Qd4! which would have quickly put an end to the game. **33.h5 Qg4; 34.Qh7+ Kd8; 35.h6 Rd2; 36.Qf5 Qxf5.**

37.Bxf5 Bd7? A serious time pressure blunder. Kamsky could now play 38.Kc1! after which Karpov admitted that Black would be fighting for the draw, despite the extra pawn. The rook would have to retreat along the d-file, to prevent White from playing Rd1, and then the h-pawn would be hard to stop. **38.Bg6?** Kamsky returns the favor and misses his chance. **38...Rh2.** The h-pawn will no longer be a problem, and can be captured eventually. **39.h7 Ke7; 40.Bd3 Be6; 41.Rg1 f5; 42.Rg7+ Kf6; 43.Rxa7 e4!**

White's piece are competely out of play, and the material balance is unimportant. **44.Be2 f4; 45.b3 f3; 46.Bd1 Bf5; 47.Kc1 Bxh7; 48.Rb7 Ke5; 49.Rxb6 Rxa2. Black won.**

ADVANCE VARIATION

Unlike the French, the Caro-Kann can be effectively challenged by the advance of the e-pawn to e5 — the **Advance Variation**. This weapon was used by Mikhail Tal in his Championship challenge against Mikhail Botvinnik. In the 1980s, Dutchman John van der Wiel revived the opening and brought it to more than mere respectability. In the 1990s it has become a real thorn in the side of the Caro-Kann, though resources have been found which keep Black's game playable.

After 3.e5 Bf5 White can choose from a huge array of plans, all of which are playable. PCA 1993 World Championship challenger Nigel Short has shown the hidden talents of 4.Nc3, while the wild lines with 4.Nc3 e6 5.g4 are fully established in the repertoires of top stars.

(37) TAL - BOTVINNIK
World Championship (8), 1961

1.e4 c6; 2.d4 d5; 3.e5 c5. Tal doesn't always get enough respect for his contributions to opening theory. There are plenty of variations named after other World Champions but Tal's contributions are usually refinements of existing theory. Here, however, he takes Botvinnik's 3...c5, then still considered respectable, and buries it. Botvinnik switched to 3...Bf5 in the next game! **4.dxc5.**

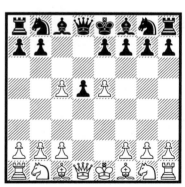

This variation was considered playable for Black until this game, and then fell into disfavor, until 1993, when former American Champion Yasser Seirawan wrote a monograph on the Advance Variation in which he evaluated the move as leading to an equal game. Few authorities agree with him, however. **4...e6.** One thing is certain: if this line is playable for Black, it must be with the development of the knight to c6, not this move. 4...Nc6; 5.Bb5 (5.Nf3 is a reasonable alternative for White.) 5...e6; 6.Be3 Nge7; 7.Nf3 Nf5; 8.Bd4 Nfxd4; 9.Qxd4 Qa5+; 10.Nc3 Qxb5; 11.Nxb5 Nxd4 is Seirawan's preferred line. After 12.Nbxd4 Bxc5, Black stood better in Westerinen-Arkell, London (Watson Farley Williams) 1988.

5.Qg4 Nc6? This is the obvious square for the knight, but it is the wrong one. In fact, in the sixth game of the match Botvinnik had equalized with 5...Nd7; 6.Nf3 Ne7; 7.Bg5 h6; 8.Bxe7 Qxe7; 9.Nc3 Qxc5; 10.0-0-0 a6; 11.Kb1 Nb6 and the game held chances for both sides. Nevertheless, Botvinnik did not return to it in the next game, instead abandoning 3...c5 altogether. **6.Nf3 Qc7; 7.Bb5 Bd7; 8.Bxc6 Qxc6.** 8...Bxc6, 9.0-0 and Black won't get the pawn back. **9.Be3 Nh6.**

When a World Champion has to play a move like this, you know that something has gone very wrong. As every beginner knows, placing a knight at h6 just invites White to capture it with the bishop and inflict massive damage on the Black pawn structure. Botvinnik must have figured that he wasn't going to castle in that direction anyway. **10.Bxh6 gxh6; 11.Nbd2 Qxc5; 12.c4!**

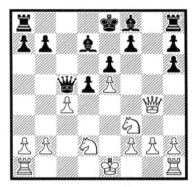

The lines to the enemy king won't stay closed for long, so Black must hustle his king to the queenside. **12...0-0-0; 13.0-0 Kb8; 14.Rfd1 Qb6; 15.Qh4.**

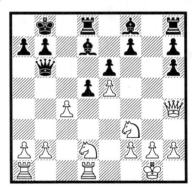

It is clear that White has the advantage, because Black's bishops are ineffective and there are just too many holes in the position. **15...a5** Black wants to play...Bc5 and ...Rg8 to create an attack on the enemy king. **16.Rac1 Rg8; 17.Nb3 a4.** 17...Rc8; 18.cxd5 Rxc1; 19.Nxc1 exd5; 20.Rxd5 would give White a dominating position. **18.c5 Qc7; 19.Nbd4** White's knights are worth more than the enemy bishops. Black does not dare to go pawn grabbing. **19...Rc8.** 19...Bxc5; 20.b4! axb3; 21.Nxb3 b6; 22.a4 h5 (intending...Rg4); 23.a5 Rg4; 24.Qxh5 Rdg8; 25.axb6 Rxg2+; 26.Kh1 and White wins a piece. **20.b4 axb3; 21.axb3 Qd8; 22.Qxd8 Rxd8.**

The queens are gone, but White is effectively a pawn up, since the h-pawns are weak and doubled. **23.b4 Rg4; 24.b5 Rc8; 25.c6!** The pawns fly forward and crack open the enemy position. White is now winning. **25...Be8.** 25...bxc6; 26.bxc6 Be8; 27.Rb1+ Kc7; 28.Rb7+ Kd8; 29.Rc1 Rc7; 30.Nb5 Rxb7; 31.cxb7 and the pawn promotes. **26.Rc2 Bg7; 27.Ra1 Bxe5; 28.Nxe5 Rxd4.**

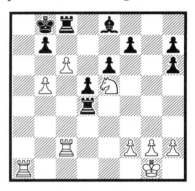

29.Nd7+! and Botvinnik resigned, because of **29...Bxd7.** 29...Kc7; 30.b6+ Kd8; 31.cxb7; **30.cxd7 Rd8; 31.Rc8+! Rxc8; 32.Ra8+!! White won.**

PANOV ATTACK

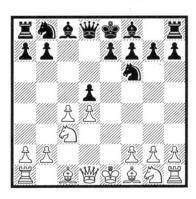

1.e4	c6
2.d4	d5
3.exd5	c:d5
4.c4	Nf6
5.Nc3	

The **Panov Attack** is a highly transpositional opening which can be reached from the Caro-Kann, Nimzoindian, Queen's Gambit, even the Sicilian! It is traditionally considered part of Caro-Kann territory, because, from the Caro-Kann, the game can reach any of the positions belonging to the Panov, where other move orders allow only limited transpositions. In the Caro-Kann, the move order is 1.e4 c6; 2.d4 d5; 3.exd5 cxd5; 4.c4, usually followed by 4...Nf6 and 5.Nc3.

Black has three basic approaches:

| **5...g6** | **5...Nc6** | **5...e6** |

The first two are firmly in Caro-Kann territory, but 5...e6, the most popular move, leads to positions that can be reached from many openings.

Most of the World Champions have experience on one or both sides of the Panov, especially the Nimzoindian lines which follow 5...e6 6.Nf3 Bb4. One side or the other will often quickly obtain an isolated d-pawn, as is the case, for example, in the common line 7.cxd5 Nxd5.

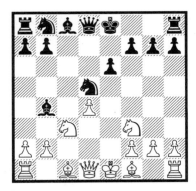

Now White's pawn at d4 is isolated. This is not necessarily a weakness. Some great chessplayers, such as Siegbert Tarrasch, loved to play these kinds of positions. We'll look at this theme in more detail when we deal with the Tarrasch Defense to the Queen's Gambit.

The Panov Attack is also known as the Panov-Botvinnik Attack, because World Champion Botvinnik used it so effectively, though he was also successful on the Black side! Your author has also enjoyed playing both sides of this exciting opening.

(38) ALEKHINE - BARATZ
Paris, 1933

1.e4 c6; 2.d4 d5; 3.exd5 cxd5; 4.c4. This is the famous Panov Attack. In the present game we will examine the strategy where Black steers the game into the deep waters of the Nimzoindian. **4...e6.** 4...Nf6 is considered slightly more accurate. **5.Nc3 Nf6; 6.Nf3 Bb4.** This position can be reached by 1.d4 Nf6; 2.c4 e6; 3.Nc3 Bb4; 4.e3 c5; 5.Nf3 cxd4; 6.exd4 d5 and other transpositions are available.

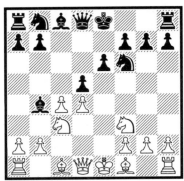

7.Bd3 dxc4. Now that the White bishop has moved, this capture is appropriate. **8.Bxc4 0–0; 9.0–0 b6.** This is one of the most common formations for Black. The crucial element is the isolated d-pawn at d4. It is a little weak, but controls important squares. Black can try to blockade it with a knight, but that strategy is not as effective here as in the lines with ...Be7 (instead of ...Bb4) because in those lines the bishop can redeploy at f6, with effective pressure at d4. For that reason one often finds the bishop retreating to e7, usually in reaction to a White advance of the a-pawn to a3. **10.Bg5 Bb7; 11.Rc1 Nc6; 12.Qd3.**

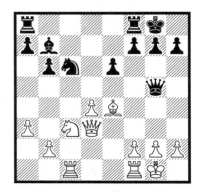

This is one method of setting up the battery of queen and bishop on the b1–h7 diagonal. The bishop will retreat to c2 via b3. Alternatively White can place the queen at b1, and let the bishop head the battery from d3. **12...Be7; 13.a3 Nd5.** The blockade is in place. **14.Bxd5 Bxg5.** Karpov prefers to capture with the pawn here. **15.Nxg5 Qxg5; 16.Be4.**

White has more control of the center and pressure on both light-squared long diagonals, with particular concentration at c6. **16...g6;** 16...Rfd8!; 17.f4 Qf6;18.d5 gives White a strong initiative. **17.Qb5! Qxb5; 18.Nxb5 Na5.** There wasn't much choice, though this leads to an inferior position. 18...Rac8 would have been met by 19.Nd6 and White should win. **19.Bxb7 Nxb7; 20.Rc7.** We have a classic example of the devastating power of an invasion of the 7th rank.

20...Rfb8. 20...Na5; 21.Nxa7 Nc4; 22.Rxc4 Rxa7; 23.Rb4 is clearly better for White, who has an extra pawn. **21.Re1!** Alekhine cleverly prepares to open up the e-file and bring a second rook to the 7th rank. The prosaic 21.Rc1 would have been less effective. **21...a6; 22.Nc3 Nd6; 23.d5!**

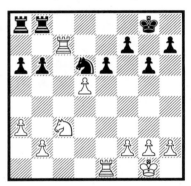

An important advance. Even though this seems to lead to simplification, the passive positions of the Black rooks gives White a big advantage. **23...Ne8; 24.Rc6 exd5; 25.Nxd5.**

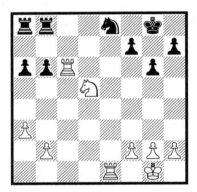

Now White wins material by force. **25...b5; 26.Nb6 Rxb6.** 26...Ra7; 27.Nc8! is a cute win for White. **27.Rxb6 Kf8; 28.Rc1 Ra7; 29.Rb8** Black could have, and should have resigned here, especially since White was the reigning World Champion! **29...Re7; 30.Kf1 Re6; 31.Re1 Ke7; 32.Rxe6+ fxe6; 33.Rb7+ Kd6; 34.Rxh7 Kd5; 35.Rh6 Nd6; 36.Rxg6 a5; 37.h4 Nf5; 38.h5. White won.**

Black does not have to transpose to the Nimzoindian lines. Instead, the bishop can be developed more conservatively at e7.

(39) BOTVINNIK - KONSTANTINOPOLSKY
Sverdlovsk, 1943

1.e4 c6; 2.d4 d5; 3.exd5 cxd5; 4.c4 Nf6; 5.Nc3 e6; 6.Nf3 Be7. This is the alternative to the Nimzoindian plan with ...Bb4. It is obviously available more easily from the Caro-Kann move order, since the Nimzoindian is defined by an early ...Bb4.

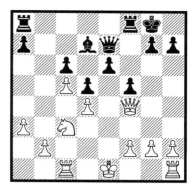

7.Bg5 0–0; 8.Rc1. The pawn can advance to c5 either now or later. **8...Nc6; 9.c5.** This move order has the advantage of avoiding an immediate b6 by Black. The idea is a straightforward pawn storm on the queenside. **9...Ne4.** 9...b6 fails to 10.Bb5! **10.Bxe7 Qxe7; 11.Be2.** This is the proper square for the bishop at this point, even though it will move again in a few moves. Black threatened e5, and so the e-file should be kept protected. **11...Bd7; 12.a3 f5?** A serious and instructive positional error. Although this central formation does work for Black in many positions, it fails here because the e5-square is protected only by a very vulnerable knight. 12...f6 ;13.b4 Nxc3; 14.Rxc3 a6; 15.0–0 Rfd8 and Black prepares the advance of the e-pawn, according to Botvinnik.

13.Bb5! Changed circumstances demand a rethinking of the placement of one's pieces. It is a consequence of the excessive advance of the Black f-pawn that the e5 square is now weak, so its defender at c6 must be removed. **13...Ng5.** Black responds logically, trying to prevent the occupation of e5. **14.Bxc6 Nxf3+; 15.Qxf3 bxc6; 16.Qf4!**

The mighty queen functions as a lowly blockader. More importantly, however, it controls a whole pile of dark squares.. **16...Rae8; 17.0–0 e5.** Otherwise Qe5 and Re1 will secure the outpost forever. **18.Qxe5 Qxe5; 19.dxe5 Rxe5; 20.f4!** This blockades the pawn at f5 and leaves Black with a very bad bishop. **20...Re7; 21.Rfe1.** White can win easily if the rooks can be removed from the board. The knight is much better than the bishop, which has no room to maneuver. In addition, the king can now enter the game.

21...Rfe8; 22.Rxe7 Rxe7; 23.Kf2 Kf7; 24.Rd1 Re8; 25.Rd2! The e2-square will be used for the confrontation on the e-file. **25...h6; 26.Re2 Rb8;** 26...Rxe2+; 27.Nxe2 d4; 28.Nxd4 and the king cannot get to the critical f5-square. **27.Ke3 Rb3; 28.Kd4 Kf6; 29.Na2!** The idea is to play Nc1 and then b3. **29...Rb8; 30.b4.**

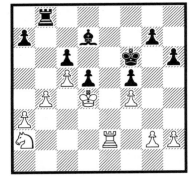

30...g5. There was nothing to be done about the queenside, so Black tries to open another front. 30...a5; 31.bxa5 Ra8; 32.Nc3 Rxa5; 33.a4. **31.g3 gxf4; 32.gxf4 a6; 33.Nc3 Rg8!** The best chance in a bad position. The White pawns were going to break through anyway. **34.a4 Rg4; 35.Rf2 Be6; 36.b5 axb5; 37.axb5! cxb5; 38.Nxb5 Rg1; 39.Nc3.** The c-pawn is now a runner. **39...Kf7; 40.Rb2 Rf1; 41.Ne2 Re1; 42.Ke5!** Black cannot avoid zugzwang and a loss of further material. **42...d4; 43.Kxd4 Kg6; 44.Nc3 Kh5; 45.Re2 Rxe2; 46.Nxe2 Kg4; 47.Ke5 Bc8; 48.Nd4 h5.**

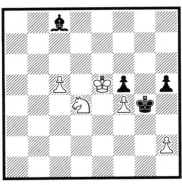

49.Nxf5! Bd7; 50.Ng7 Ba4; 51.f5 Kg5; 52.Ne6+. White won.

Here is an example of an alternative plan for Black.

(40) TAL - BRONSTEIN
USSR Championship, 1971

1.e4 c6; 2.c4 d5; 3.exd5 cxd5; 4.d4. Tal turned to the Panov Attack shortly after his 1961 match with Botvinnik. **4...Nf6; 5.Nc3 Nc6.**

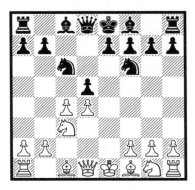

This is the messiest line in the Panov Attack, where Black has introduced many strange ideas in an attempt to throw White off stride. **6.Bg5 Bg4.** Alternatives include 6...Qa5 and 6...Be6, both of which lead to very complicated positions. **7.Be2!** Simple and strong. 7.f3 Be6, 8.c5 is also good. **7...Bxe2.** 7...Be6; 8.Bf3 and the pressure on the center is unbearable. **8.Ngxe2 dxc4.** As usual, this capture entails a great degree of risk, because White gets to plant a pawn at d5. **9.d5 Ne5; 10.0–0.**

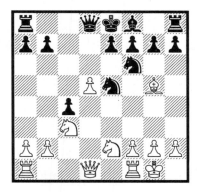

Already the Black position is awkward. Bronstein would like to play 10...e6 but he can't: **10...h6.** 10...g6; 11.d6! exd6; 12.Bxf6 Qxf6; 13.Nd5 Qd8; 14.Qa4+ is overwhelming; 10...e6; 11.Bxf6 Qxf6; 12.Qa4+ Nd7; 13.dxe6 Qxe6; 14.Rad1 and the pin is excruciating. **11.Bf4 Ng6; 12.Qa4+ Qd7; 13.Qxc4.** White has regained his pawn with a clearly better position.

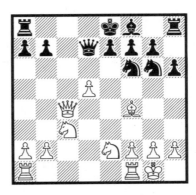

13...Rc8; 14.Qb3 e5!? Bronstein realizes the desperate nature of his position and tries a radical move to upset the game. 14...Nxf4; 15.Nxf4 g5; 16.Ne6!! fxe6; 17.dxe6 Qc6; 18.Rac1 and Black's problems have no satisfactory resolution, except, perhaps, falling on his sword. **15.dxe6 Qxe6; 16.Qxb7 Bc5; 17.Nd4!** A classic case of a king staying too long in the center. **17...Bxd4.** 17...Qd7; 18.Rfe1+ Ne7; 19.Qxd7+ Nxd7; 20.Nf5 Kf8; 21.Nxe7 Bxe7; 22.Nb5 and White has enough to win.

18.Rae1 0–0. 18...Be5; 19.Bxe5 0–0 doesn't quite work: 20.Bxf6 Qxf6; 21.Qxa7 and Black can't cope with the queenside pawns. **19.Rxe6 fxe6; 20.Bd6.** There is not enough compensation for the queen. **20...Rfd8; 21.Bc7 Rf8; 22.Nb5!** A strong move which leaves the bishop with no good landing site. **22...Be5; 23.Bxe5 Nxe5; 24.Qxa7 Nd5; 25.Qd4 Ng6; 26.h4 Ngf4; 27.Qe4.** Black resigned, since the queenside pawns are ready to roll and the e-pawn is a weakling.

PIRC AND MODERN DEFENSES

1.e4   g6
2.d4   d6

In the **Pirc** and **Modern** lines, Black plays a very early ...g6 and allows White to dominate the center. This hypermodern approach has never held much appeal to World Champions though there are plenty of professionals who rely on them. It might seem strange that the fianchetto of the bishop at g7 is very popular against 1.d4, but not against 1.e4. The reason for this is quite simple: the fianchetto structure is more effective when White has a pawn at c4, because the pawn cannot be used at c3 to support the center.

The Pirc and Modern differ fundamentally in the role of the knight at g8. In the Pirc, it makes an early appearance at f6, while in the Modern, it almost never goes to f6, and often stays home for a long time. The Pirc is considered more conservative, but also offers fewer winning chances to Black.

In any case, the World Champions have been devastatingly effective on the White side of these openings. We examine three games where quite different strategies are employed. The first game shows a double fianchetto by Black. In the remaining two games, the strategies are set by White. In the Classical line White follows in the tradition of the Semi-Open Games by developing a knight at c3, leaving the c-pawn at c2. In the second, we see White head for the Indian games by advancing the pawn to c4 before developing the knight.

(41) STEINITZ - MONGREDIEN
London, 1863

1.e4 g6; 2.d4 Bg7.

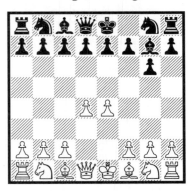

Once rejected as bizarre, the Modern Defense is now quite respectable. World Champions have not taken to it, by and large, however. **3.c3 b6**. This is a bit too much, and the double-fianchetto is no longer seen. Steinitz acts with appropriate restraint and achieves a good position. **4.Be3 Bb7; 5.Nd2.** The problem with Black's approach at that time is that it acted as if White were not a participant in the game. Here Steinitz erects a solid center with plenty of support, and he does not overextend, so Black has no targets. **5...d6; 6.Ngf3 e5.**

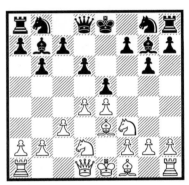

7.dxe5! Steinitz resolutely avoids advances which might provide targets for Black's pieces. 7.d5 c6 8.c4 Ne7 9.Be2 f5 gives Black good counterplay. **7...dxe5; 8.Bc4 Ne7; 9.Qe2.** This is a good move, which clears the d1–square for a rook. **9...0–0; 10.h4! Nd7.** The general rule is that one reacts to flank activity with a counterthrust in the center, but here Black has nothing to do in the middle of the board. **11.h5 Nf6; 12.hxg6! Nxg6.** 12...hxg6 would lose a pawn to 13.Nxe5 **13.0–0–0 c5?!** Black does not appreciate the danger he is in on the kingside. **14.Ng5 a6.** Black wants to drive back the enemy bishop, but has no time for such luxuries. **15.Nxh7! Nxh7**

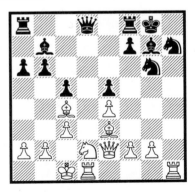

Having sacrificed a knight, White now shows that the fireworks are just beginning. **16.Rxh7!! Kxh7; 17.Qh5+ Kg8; 18.Rh1.** 18.Qxg6 Qf6! **18...Re8.** The only way to avoid mate at h7. **19.Qxg6 Qf6.**

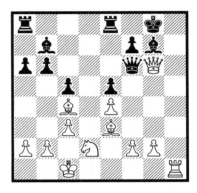

At first it is not easy to see how the attack will continue, but Steinitz has worked it all out. **20.Bxf7+.** Now that the rook has been displaced from f8, this brings the game to a close. **20...Qxf7; 21.Rh8+! Kxh8; 22.Qxf7.** Black resigned. After 22...Bc6, 23.Qc7 wins even more material.

(42) FISCHER - SUTTLES
United States Championship, 1965

1.e4 g6; 2.d4 Bg7; 3.Nc3 d6; 4.Be3 c6; 5.Qd2.

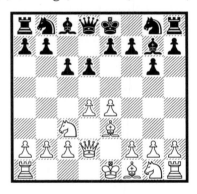

White has adopted a common formation against the Modern Defense. True to Fischer's style, he can't wait to get an attack going on the kingside, so he aims at h6 and dreams about shoving the h-pawn down the file. That isn't so easy to accomplish against one of the best Modern Defense specialists in history. **5...Nd7; 6.f4.** 6.Nf3 is also good, for example 6...b5; 7.Bd3 a6; 8.a4 Bb7; 9.0–0 Qc7 and as rising star Michael Adams of England demonstrated against Dunnington at Hastings 1995, White gets an advantage by capturing at b5.

6...Ngf6. Now the game is more of a Pirc, but clearly Suttles wasn't going to develop the knight by placing it on the vulnerable h6 square. **7.Nf3 0–0, 8.h3 b5.** This advance is an integral part of the Modern strategy. Often Black has exclusive control of the queenside while White operates on the other wing, but Fischer keep his eye fixed on the a-file. **9.Bd3 Nb6; 10.b3 a5; 11.0–0 b4; 12.Ne2.**

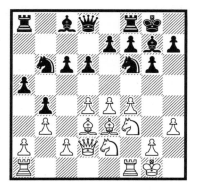

Fischer has established such a strong center, it almost seems that he was trying to make a point against his hypermodern opponent! Objectively, White has a sizable advantage. Suttles, of course, would argue that point. So it is up to Fischer to take this position and find a way to win. This is not so simple, and his strategies are well worth studying. **12...d5; 13.e5 Ne4.** Retreating wasn't worth considering. White is not going to give up the bishop at d3 for the knight at e4, because later ...Ba6 would grab the a6-f1 diagonal. **14.Qe1 f5; 15.a3.** Fischer needs some open lines. There is nothing happening on the kingside, so he turns to the queenside. **15...bxa3; 16.Rxa3 a4; 17.Qa1 Ba6; 18.Bxa6 Rxa6**.

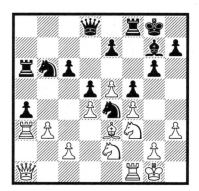

White has pressure on the queenside. Black's bishop seems to be locked out of play but that can later be remedied by ...e6 and ...Bf8. **19.Nc3 Qc7; 20.Ne1.** The start of a journey to c5. The knight covers a lot of distance in a small amount of time. **20...Rfa8; 21.Nd3 R6a7; 22.Qb2 e6; 23.Nc5 Bf8; 24.Rfa1**.

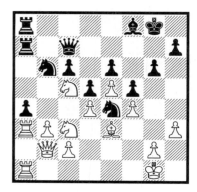

Fischer has simply mounted all the pressure on the a-file, and the pawn is now ready to drop. **24...Kf7; 25.N3xa4 Nxa4; 26.bxa4 Bxc5; 27.dxc5.** Black can do nothing but squirm as White begins to make real progress. And Fischer was famous for enjoying the sight! **27...Kg8; 28.Rb3 Qa5; 29.Kh2 h5; 30.Rb8+ Rxb8; 31.Qxb8+ Kh7; 32.Rb1 Qxa4; 33.Qf8 Rg7; 34.Rb8 g5; 35.Qh8+ Kg6; 36.Qe8+ Rf7; 37.Rb7. White won.**

(43) BOTVINNIK - SUTTLES
Belgrade, 1969

1.d4 g6; 2.e4 Bg7; 3.c4 d6; 4.Nc3. Black can opt out of the Modern Defense here by playing 4..Nf6, leading to the King's Indian, but Suttles was a major contributor to the theory of the Modern and usually went his own way. One approach he liked was to play an early ...Nc6, to tempt the White d-pawn forward and open up the h8-a1 diagonal. **4...e5.**

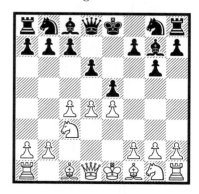

The advantage of holding back the knight at g8 is that the bishop at g7 has a more direct influence on the dark squares in the center. **5.Nge2.** Botvinnik didn't mind falling in with Suttles scheme. In fact, he wrote that he probably should have played d5 immediately! **5...Nc6; 6.d5 Nce7; 7.f3 f5**. This move is at the heart of Black's strategy. The pressure will build at e4, because Black can follow with ...Nf6. **8.Be3.** Black must now consider the consequences of 8...Nf6 9.Qd2 with the threat of a kingside attack involving Bh6. So Suttles decides to eliminate the bishop. Botvinnik noted that the exchange deprives the kingside of an important defender, which may be significant if Black castles in that direction. **8...Bh6; 9.Bxh6 Nxh6; 10.Qd2 Nf7**. Suttles often likes to configure his horses this way. **11.g3**. Keeping an eye on the f4-square. **11...0–0; 12.Bg2 c6; 13.0–0 cxd5; 14.cxd5 Qb6+; 15.Kh1 Bd7; 16.Rae1**.

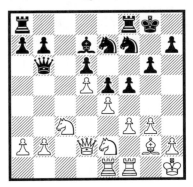

Both sides have played logically. The weakness at d6 is not significant as long as the barrier at e5 and f5 stays intact, but Botvinnik formulates a plan to undermine it. **16...Kg7; 17.f4! Rae8; 18.Nc1!** A cunning move, even if Botvinnik says so himself. One point is that if Black captures at f4, then the knight can get to the d4-square via b3, while additional breathing room on the e- and f-files adds to the pressure on Black's position. **18...exf4; 19.gxf4 fxe4; 20.Nxe4 Nf5**.

Unfortunately there is no direct attack here, since 21.Qc3+ is parried by 21...Qd4. Nevertheless, Black is really starting to miss that dark-squared bishop! **21.Nb3 Rc8; 22.Bh3 Ng3+; 23.hxg3 Bxh3 24.Nd4**. Black's light squares are so weak that he cannot afford to take the rook.

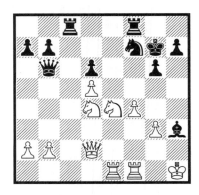

24...Rfe8. 24...Bxf1; 25.Ne6+ wins, for example 25...Kh8; (25...Kg8; 26.Nf6+ Kh8;27.Nd7) 26.Nxf8 Bh3; (26...Rxf8; 27.Qc3+ Kg8; 28.Nf6+ Kg7; 29.Ne8+ Kh6; 30.Qg7+ Kh5; 31.Nf6 mate; 26...Bb5; 27.a4 Bxa4; 28.b3 Qxb3; 29.Qd4+ Kg8; 30.Ne6) 27.Ne6 is much better for White. **25.Rf3 Rc4; 26.Rd3 Qb4; 27.b3 Qxd2; 28.Rxd2**. The endgame is still clearly better for White. **28...Rc7; 29.Rde2 Bg4;** 29...Rce7; 30.Nxd6 Rxe2; 31.Nxe8+ Rxe8; 32.Rxe8 and White wins. **30.Re3 Bf5?.** This fails to address the threat. Botvinnik recommended 30...Bd7. **31.Nxd6 Nxd6; 32.Nxf5+ gxf5; 33.Rxe8 Nxe8; 34.Rxe8**.

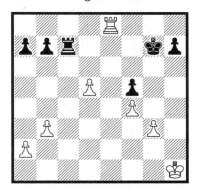

This endgame is not a simple win, because the pawns at d5, g3 and a2 are all possible targets. Botvinnik clarifies the position by exchanging the pawn at d5 for the one at h7. **34...Kg6; 35.Re2 Rc1+; 36.Kg2 Rd1; 37.Re6+ Kf7; 38.Rd6 Ke7; 39.Rh6 Rxd5; 40.Rxh7+ Kd6; 41.Kh3.** Now the plan is clear. White will establish a passed pawn on the kingside and promote it. The remainder of the game is a magnificent display of endgame technique by Botvinnik. **41...Ra5; 42.Kh4 b5; 43.Kg5 Rxa2; 44.Kxf5 a5; 45.g4 Ra3; 46.Ra7 Kc5; 47.g5 Kb6; 48.Ra8 Rxb3; 49.g6 Rg3; 50.Kf6 b4; 51.g7 Kb5; 52.g8Q Rxg8; 53.Rxg8. White won.**

ALEKHINE DEFENSE

The **Alekhine Defense** is one of the few major openings to bear the name of a World Champion, in this case Alexander Alekhine. Yet Alekhine only played it on rare occasions, and used it less than two dozen times. This provocative opening begins 1.e4 Nf6 and invites White to directly attack the knight with 2.e5.

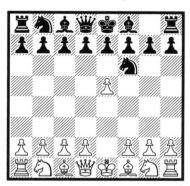

1.e4 Nf6

The knight usually moves to d5, where it can be further harassed by White pawns. It is reasonable to ask why any sane chessplayer would want to defend the position, after, say 2...Nd5; 3.d4 d6; 4.c4 Nb6 ;5.f4, the dreaded Four Pawn Attack.

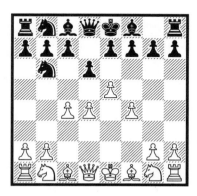

The answer is that after 5...dxe5, 6.fxe5 Black can sooner or later obtain counterplay either with ...c5 or ...f6, nipping away at the White pawn mass. For this reason, World Champions prefer the quieter lines with 4.Nf3, satisfied to simply maintain an advantage in space. Anatoly Karpov has been particularly effective with this approach.

(44) KARPOV - ALBURT
Malta (Olympiad), 1980

1.e4 Nf6; 2.e5 Nd5; 3.d4 d6; 4.Nf3 Bg4.

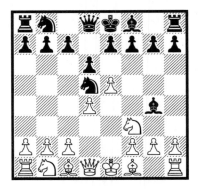

This is the Modern Variation of the Alekhine Defense. It leads to a small but persistent advantage for White, and Black has been turning to alternatives such as former U.S. Champion Lev Alburt's pet line with 4...g6, which he perhaps should have adopted for this important encounter.

5.Be2 Nc6. This is a divergence from the main line with 5...e6; 6.0–0 Be7; 7.c4 Nb6; 8.Nc3 0–0; 9.Be3 d5; 10.c5 Bxf3; 11.gxf3 , which is a typical continuation. But Alburt had an unpleasant experience earlier in the year against the well-prepared theoretician Leonid Shamkovich at the Heraldica tournament in New York. 11...Nc8; 12.f4 b6; 13.Bd3!? and Black went wrong with 13...Bxc5?!, though 13...g6 leads only to messy complications for which Karpov might well have been prepared.

6.c4 Nb6; 7.exd6. This transposes to the Exchange Variation, which is usually reached via 4.c4 Nb6; 5.exd6. 7.e6!? is an interesting alternative.

7...exd6. This is better than capturing with the c-pawn, after which the advance to d5 is even more effective for White. **8.d5! Bxf3; 9.Bxf3 Ne5; 10.Be2 Qh4.**

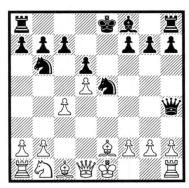

It is possible that 10...g6 is stronger than this ambitious move. **11.0–0 h5; 12.Nd2 g6.** An attempt to improve on 12...Be7, 13.f4 which is known to be better for White. **13.f4 Ng4; 14.Nf3 Qf6; 15.Re1 0-0-0; 16.a4 a5.** This just presents a target. Black should have done something about the bishop at f8 instead. **17.Qd2!**

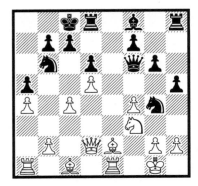

The dark squares are covered, and the White queen will sooner or later grab the weakling at a5. **17...Bg7; 18.h3 Rde8; 19.Bf1 Nh6; 20.Qxa5.** I was watching this game from time to time, since I was working at the Olympiad as one of the arbiters. Of course I was hoping the American team would do well, and was disappointed to see such a quick massacre on board one. But I knew this game would not last too much longer. **20...Nf5; 21.Rd1 Kb8; 22.Ra3 Re4; 23.Qb5 Nc8.**

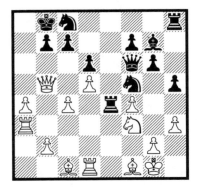

24.Rb3. Even a beginner could find the correct attacking method here! **24...b6; 25.a5! Qe7; 26.Qa6 Re8.** Now Karpov smashes through the final barrier. **27.c5! dxc5, 28.Bb5.** The light squares provide all the illumination needed for victory. **28...c6; 29.Bxc6 Bd4+; 30.Nxd4 Nxd4; 31.axb6 Nf3+; 32.Rxf3 Re1+; 33.Rxe1. White won.**

(45) NAEGELI - EUWE
Bern, 1932

1.e4 Nf6; 2.e5 Nd5; 3.d4 d6; 4.c4 Nb6; 5.f4.

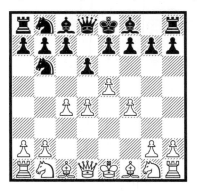

The Four Pawns Attack is what Black really wants to see in the Alekhine. Although White can manage a small positional advantage if all the complicated streams are navigated properly, it is enormously difficult to keep track of all the finesses. **5...Bf5.** These days Black usually captures at e5 first, but in this case we reach the normal lines by transposition when Black does so on the next move. **6.Nf3 dxe5; 7.fxe5 e6; 8.Nc3 Nc6; 9.Be3 Qd7.**

The current main line is 9...Bg4, which expends a tempo to pin the knight at f3, which in turn weakens the support of d4. **10.Be2.** For a while, the advance of the d-pawn was all the rage but it is now considered premature. 10.d5 exd5; 11.cxd5 Nb4; 12.Nd4 N6xd5; 13.Nxd5 Nxd5; 14.Nxf5 0-0-0; 15.Qd3 g6; 16.Nh4 Nxe3; 17.Qxe3 Bb4+ and the theoreticians give the nod to Black, despite White's extra piece. **10...0-0-0; 11.Qd2.**

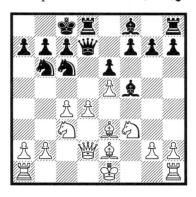

This old game is a major reason why White now prefers to castle instead. 11.0-0 Bg4; 12.c5 Nd5; 13.Nxd5 Qxd5 is the main line now. **11...f6!** The White center finally comes under attack, and the goal of the Alekhine Defense is within reach. **12.exf6 gxf6; 13.0-0 Rg8.** This open line leads directly to the White king. **14.Rfd1 Qg7; 15.Bf1 Ne5.** Black deftly exploits the pin on the d-file. **16.Nxe5 fxe5; 17.Qf2 Bg4.**

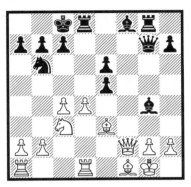

Black keeps the initiative by sniping at White's pieces. **18.Rd2 exd4; 19.Bxd4 Rxd4!** A temporary sacrifice. **20.Rxd4 Bc5.** There is only one way to break this pin, and it involves returning the exchange. **21.Rd8+ Rxd8; 22.Qxc5 Rd2.** The invasion of the seventh rank leads to a quick win. Note that White cannot play 23.b3 because the knight at c3 would fall to the Black queen. **23.Ne4 Rxb2; 24.Nd6+.** This looks good, but has no effect. The d-file is safe for the Black king because White cannot use the d1-square thanks to the bishop sitting at g4. **24...Kd7; 25.Nb5 Kc8; 26.Re1;** 26.Nd6+ would have invited a draw by repetition, so presumably Euwe would have had to retreat to the b-file instead. **26...Kb8; 27.Re5 Bf5; 28.Qd4 Rd2!**

If White grabs the rook at d2, Black takes the one at e5. **29.Qe3;** 29.Qxd2 Qxe5; 30.Qd8+ Nc8 and the queen at e5 defends the c7-square. **29...Rd1.** This pin is fatal to White. **30.Kf2 Qf6.** Threatening a strong discovered check. **31.Be2 Be4+!** White resigned, faced with the inevitable loss of material.

SCANDINAVIAN DEFENSE

The Scandinavian Defense has bubbled just below the level of respectability for most of chess history. After 1.e4 d5 White is free to capture the pawn at d5.

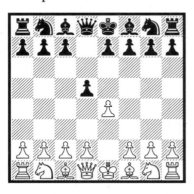

1.e4 d5

If Black recaptures immediately with 2...Qd5, then White develops a knight with tempo by playing 3.Nc3, which attacks the queen. If Black delays the capture and plays 2...Nf6, then White is free to develop while Black takes time for ...Nxd5, after which the knight at d5 can itself become a target. Yet these drawbacks are relatively minor, though they do keep the champions themselves from using the Scandinavian in their regular arsenal. In 1995, however, challenger Viswanathan Anand used it effectively against PCA World Champion Garry Kasparov. We are likely to see more such challenges at the highest level of chess play.

(46) KASPAROV - ANAND
PCA World Championship (Game 14), 1995

1.e4 d5; 2.ex d5.

2...Qxd5. 2...Nf6 is an alternative, but it is rather slow. White can meet it by simple development, for example 3.Nf3 Nxd5; 4.d4 g6; 5.c4 Nf6; 6.Nc3 Bg7; 7.h3 0-0; 8.Be3 Nbd7; 9.Qd2 c6; 10.Be2 Re8; 11.Rd1 Qa5; 12.0-0 a6; 13.a3 Qd8; 14.Qc1 b6; 15.Ne5 and White had a pleasant advantage in Tal-Bronstein, Moscow 1967. **3.Nc3 Qa5.**

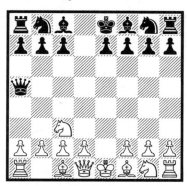

This is the main line of the Scandinavian Defense. **4.d4 Nf6.** 4...e5 is now considered to be refuted. 5.Nf3 Bb4; 6.Bd2 exd4; 7.Qe2+ Ne7; 8.Nxd4 is better for White, as Tal has demonstrated. 8...0-0; 9.a3 Bd6; 10.Ndb5 Qb6; 11.0-0-0 Be6; 12.Bg5 Ng6; 13.Nxd6 cxd6;14.h4 Nc6; 15.Be3 Qa5; 16.h5 Nge5; 17.Rh4 d5; 18.h6 g6; 19.f4 Nc4; 20.f5 Nxe3; 21.Qxe3 Bxf5; 22.Nxd5 Rad8; 23.b4 Qa4; 24.Qc3 Ne5; 25.Ne7+ Kh8; 26.Qxe5+ f6; 27.Qxf6+ and Black resigned in Tal-Skuja, Latvian Championship, 1958. **5.Nf3 c6**. The systems with the development of the bishop at f5 or g4 are too ambitious and White can obtain an advantage.

There is little doubt that 5...Nc6 is bad: 6.d5 Nb4; 7.Bb5+ c6; 8.dxc6 bxc6; 9.Ba4 Ba6; 10.a3 Rd8; 11.Bd2 Rd6; 12.axb4 Qf5; 13.Bb3 Ne4; 14.Rxa6 Rxd2; 15.Qa1 Nxc3; 16.bxc3 Rd6; 17.0-0 and Black gave up in Fischer-Seidman, New York (Rosenwald Memorial) 1959.

On the other hand, 5...Bf5 has been defended by Larsen, but not with great success. 6.Bd2 Nbd7; 7.Bc4 c6; 8.Qe2 e6; 9.d5 cxd5; 10.Nxd5 and White has a strong initiative, Spassky-Larsen, Montreal 1979; 5...Bg4; 6.h3 Bh5; 7.g4 Bg6; 8.Ne5 (8.b4 Qb6; 9.Bg2 c6; 10.Bd2 Nbd7 11.Ne5 Nxe5; 12.dxe5 Rd8; 13.Qe2 Nd5; 14.Na4 Qc7; 15.c4 and White was much better, in Kasparov's only previous game in the opening, from a 1991 simultaneous exhibition.) 8...e6; 9.h4 Bb4; 10.Rh3 c6; 11.Bd2 Qb6; 12.h5 Be4; 13.Re3 Bxc3; 14.Bxc3 Bd5; 15.g5 and White has a strong attack, Karpov-Rogers, Bath 1983.

Australian Grandmaster Ian Rogers has been a leading advocate of fringe defenses such as the Scandinavian and Budapest Defenses. **6.Ne5.** 6.Bd2 was Tal's preference, and it also looks a little better for White. **6...Be6!?** At present, this is considered Blacks best. **7.Bd3 Nbd7; 8.f4?!** A new move, but not a good one. Kasparov was probably taken by surprise, since he had so little experience with the Scandinavian. 8.Nxd7 Nxd7, 9.0-0 is surely a bit better for White.

8...g6! This is the best way of developing the bishop. **9.0–0 Bg7.**

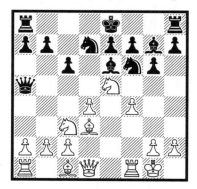

10.Kh1 Bf5!; 11.Bc4?! Kasparov tries to preserve the bishop but should have been more concerned with maintaining the balance, to which end 11.Be3 was called for. **11...e6; 12.Be2?!** Here Kasparov might have captured at d7, but it seems that Black could just capture with the king, and then bring rooks to a center and retreat the king to safety on either side of the board. **12...h5; 13.Be3 Rd8; 14.Bg1 0–0; 15.Bf3.**

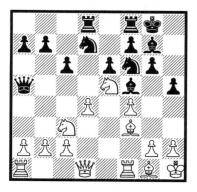

15...Nd5!; 16.Nxd5 exd5. Capturing with the c-pawn would have given White a structural advantage, and eventually the bishop at g1 would run all over the dark-squares. **17.Bf2 Qc7; 18.Rc1 f6 19.Nd3 Rfe8; 20.b3 Nb6; 21.a4! Nc8; 22.c4 Qf7; 23.a5! Bf8; 24.cxd5 cxd5; 25.Bh4 Nd6; 26.a6! b6; 27.Ne5! Qe6!; 28.g4! hxg4; 29.Nxg4 Bg7.** The bishop could also have been stationed effectively at e7, since the check at h6 would not accomplish much. **30.Rc7 Ne4?!** Capturing at g4 would have been wiser. 30...Bxg4; 31.Bxg4 f5!; 32.Bxd8 fxg4 with a complicated position in which Black's chances are no worse. **31.Ne3.**

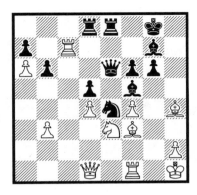

Anand cracks under the pressure. Here, and at move 32, he could have achieved a good position by heading for complications after ...Qd6. **31...Bh3?** 31...Qd6! is fine, since the sacrifice at g7 does not work: 32.Rxg7+? Kxg7; 33.Nxf5+ gxf5 is solid, for example 34.Rg1+ Kf8!; 35.Bxe4 Qxf4!; 36.Qh5 Qxe4+; 37.Rg2 Rd6 and White has exhausted all attacking possibilities. **32.Rg1 g5?!**

A serious mistake. The correct plan was to exchange the a-pawn for the f-pawn with 32...Qd6!; 33.Rxa7 Qxf4 for example 34.Rxg6 Rd7; 35.Rxd7 Bxd7; 36.Ng2 Qf5; 37.Bxe4 dxe4; 38.Rg3 e3 with counterplay. **33.Bg4! Bxg4; 34.Qxg4 Qxg4; 35.Rxg4 Nd6; 36.Bf2 Nb5 37.Rb7 Re4; 38.f5!**

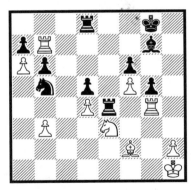

Here Anand should have played 38...Rc8, although after the rooks come off at e4 White will be able to advance the d-pawn. **38...Rxg4?!; 39.Nxg4 Rc8; 40.Rd7 Rc2?** A blunder in time pressure, but Black was in trouble anyway. **41.Rxd5.** Anand resigned, since the White rook will get to the seventh rank soon. **White won**.

9. CLOSED GAMES

INTRODUCTION

The **Closed Games** begin 1.d4 d5 (though we will include the Dutch with 1...f5 and a later ...d5 here, too). This effectively rules out the advance of either e-pawn to the center.

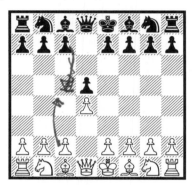

In general, these openings lead to quieter, longer struggles. For Black, they have the advantage of being very solid. White may be able to squeak out a small initiative, but the ideal pawn center remains only a dream. The vulnerable f7 square is well shielded from activity by White's bishop or queen on the a2-g8 diagonal.

Although the Closed Games all feature the same structure on the d-file, the wide variety of defensive approaches gives them less in common with each other than is the case in the Open Games. Consider that after 2.c4, Black can defend with ...e6, ...c6, ...dxc4, all of which are quite normal. The decision between a system with ...e6, locking in the bishop at c8, and ...c6, keeping the bishop mobile but slower in developing the bishop from f8, is crucial.

In the Open Games, positions from different openings often resemble each other. Here, although transpositions are possible, there are no unifying themes or typical positions.

OVERVIEW

Every World Champion has played the Black side of the Queen's Gambit which follows 2.c4, the normal response. They differ, however, with regard to their preferred defensive formation.

Some accept the challenge by capturing the pawn at c4, the **Queen's Gambit Accepted**. Declining the gambit, **Queen's Gambit Declined**, with simple development ...e6, ...Nf6, ...Be7 and kingside castling is also very popular. Kasparov and Spassky both used the **Tarrasch Defense** with ...d5, ...e6 and ...c5 in important championship events. Setting up a triangle defense with ...d5, ...e6 and ...c6, the **Semi-Slav**, was especially popular with Botvinnik. The full **Slav** where Black keeps the pawn back at e7 also had advocates in Euwe and Smyslov. Only Lasker and Spassky dared to play the radical Albin Countergambit with 2...e5!?, while none were willing to block in the c-pawn with Chigorin's 2...Nc6. Alekhine once played 2...Nf6 as an experiment, but abandoned it quickly as White gets a good game with 3.cxd5.

The last group of closed games are those which involve White adopting a formation without too much regard for move order. Black need not close the game immediately with 1...d5, but can take time to develop other pieces first. This group includes the **Torre Attack**, which we'll look at below. Some Champions, especially Capablanca, have used systems such as the Colle System (1.d4, 2.e3) and other minor openings but this was largely due to a desire to play simply against a much weaker opponent. It is easy for Black to obtain an even game against these slow openings, so they are rarely seen in critical encounters.

A related opening is the Classical Dutch, one of the two major branches of the **Dutch Defense** which begins 1.d4 f5. Although it is typically described as involving 1.d4 f5, 2.c4 e6 and only later ...d5, it is more common to see it these days after 1.d4 d5; 2.c4 e6; 3.Nf3 c6; 4.e3 f5 or 4.g3 f5. Euwe and Botvinnik used the Dutch, and many modern Grandmasters include it in their repertoire. Black essentially just sets up a stonewall formation, using an early ...f5 to discourage White from playing e4.

It is easy to see that the Queen's Gambit Declined dominates the repertoire with only Smyslov as a serious dissenter. (Morphy had so few games that his preferences are not important). This shows the staying power of the ancient and venerable lines which serve Black as well today as they did a century ago.

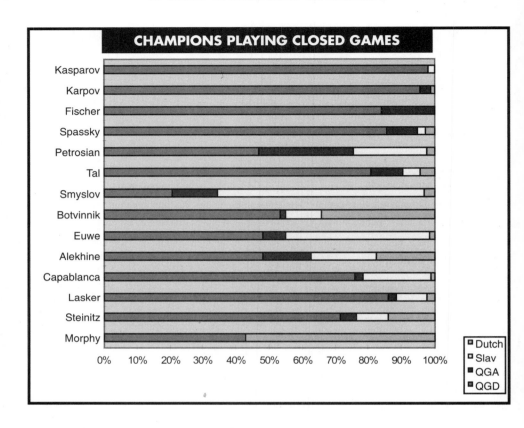

CHAMPIONS PLAYING CLOSED GAMES

Legend:
- Dutch
- Slav
- QGA
- QGD

QUEEN'S GAMBIT ACCEPTED

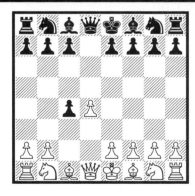

1.d4 d5
2.c4 dxc4

Not many World Champions like to defend the **Queen's Gambit Accepted**. They are willing to concede the center to White with 1.d4 d5; 2.c4 dxc4, when even 3.e4 is possible, though World Champions prefer 3.Nf3 Nf6; 4.e3. Smyslov, always seeking to combine ...d5 with ...g6, liked to defend the position after 4...g6, and I once borrowed this idea to defeat Sammy Reshevsky, one of the greatest players in American history.

I present that game here, because I think that the game both illustrates Smyslov's ideas well, and also because it contains what is most likely the refutation of that system.

(47) RESHEVSKY - SCHILLER
New York (Simultaneous Exhibition), 1972

1.d4 d5; 2.c4 dxc4; 3.Nf3 Nf6; 4.e3 g6. This is not the most common continuation. Usually Black plays an early ...e6, locking in the light-squared bishop. This can lead to great difficulties later on, and while the system is suitable for masters, it is not easy to play for beginners. On the other hand, this fianchetto is easy to play, even if not as objectively sound. **5.Bxc4 Bg7; 6.0-0 0-0; 7.Nc3 Nfd7** Smyslov's system.

The idea is to bring the knight to b6, driving back the enemy bishop, and then striking at the center with ...c5 or ...e5. **8.Qe2.** 8.e4 Nb6; 9.Be2 Bg4; 10.Be3 Nc6 was played in Evans-Smyslov, Helsinki Olympiad 1952, which was a game I had studied in preparation for this contest. Black has a lot of pressure on the center. Play continued 11.d5 Bxf3; 12.Bxf3 Ne5; 13.Be2 Nec4 with pressure on the long diagonal. After 14.Bc1 c6! Black had a strong game. **8...Nb6; 9.Bb3 Nc6!?** An attempt to improve on Golombek -Smyslov, Budapest 1952, which saw 9...a5. **10.Rd1 Bg4; 11.h3 Bxf3; 12.Qxf3 Qe8.** This move has the goal of blasting open the center. After the king moves to the h-file Black can advance both e- and f-pawns. **13.Nb5?!**

Yugoslav star Gligoric improved against me a week or two later with 13.Ne4!, with the threat of Nc5. Serves me right for getting the game published in the New York Times! **13...Rc8; 14.Bd2 a6; 15.Na3 Kh8; 16.Rac1 e5!; 17.d5 e4; 18.Qf4.**

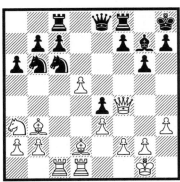

is clear that the Nc6 is headed for e5, with the possibility of jumping into f3. If only the g-file were open and a rook stood on g8... **18...g5!; 19.Qxg5 Ne5; 20.Bc3**.

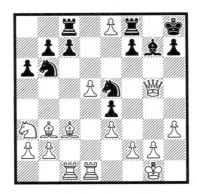

The pin looks strong — but checks have been known to break pins! **20...Nf3+!!; 21.gxf3 Bxc3 ;22.Kh1.** 22.bxc3 Rg8; **22...Rg8; 23.Qf4 Qd7; 24.Qh4 Qf5!** Black continues to make threats while improving the position of his queen, before capturing the pawn at b2. **25.f4 Bxb2; 26.Rg1 Bxc1; 27.Rxc1 Qg6.** White's position is hopeless. **28.Qg4 Qxg4; 29.hxg4 Rxg4.** White could have resigned here. **30.Rg1 Rxg1+; 31.Kxg1 Rd8; 32.d6 Rxd6; 33.Bxf7 Rd3; 34.Nc2 c5; 35.Be6 Rc3; 36.Ne1 Rc1; 37.Kf1 Nc4; 38.Ke2 b5; 39.Bd5 Ra1; 40.Bxe4 Rxa2+; 41.Kd1 Rxf2; 42.Nd3 Rd2+. 0–1**.

Yet the Queen's Gambit Accepted retains its place in the general repertoire. The ideas are simple and straightforward, and Black can't get into too much trouble if, and this is a big if, the center can be maintained.

(48) ALEKHINE - BÖÖK
Margate, 1938

1.d4 d5; 2.c4 dxc4.

By accepting the gambit, Black is willing to concede the center for rapid development. This is a dangerous strategy, however the opening was topical at the time, and had been featured in the Alekhine-Euwe World Championship match. **3.Nf3 Nf6; 4.e3 e6; 5.Bxc4 c5; 6.0–0 Nc6; 7.Qe2 a6; 8.Nc3.** 8.a4 would lead to more common lines. **8...b5; 9.Bb3.**

Alekhine correctly keeps the bishop on the queenside, as the lack of a rook at d1 means that 9.Bd3 leaves d4 without sufficient protection. **9...b4.** This came as a surprise to Alekhine, who expected Black to play 9...Be7, as in an encounter with Euwe.

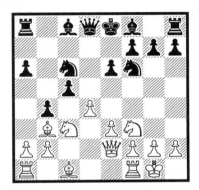

10.d5! Alekhine's judgment is probably correct, though Taimanov's preferred 10.Na4 is a worthy alternative. White's goal is to advance the e-pawn, and to do this he must somehow release the pressure at d4. **10...Na5.** 10...exd5; 11.Nxd5 Nxd5; 12.Rd1 followed by e3-e4 gives a clear advantage to White. **11.Ba4+ Bd7.** White has achieved quite a lot, but wouldn't it be great if he also had a rook on an open d-file? With this idea in mind, we can easily see how Alekhine creates one of his impressive combinations. **12.dxe6.**

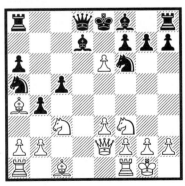

12...fxe6. 12...Bxa4; 13.exf7+ Kxf7; 14.Nxa4; **13.Rd1.** White is playing without the help of the rook at a1 and bishop at c1, but Black's pieces are even less active. **13...bxc3.**

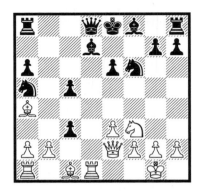

13...Be7; 14.Bxd7+ Nxd7; 15.Ne5 Ra7; 16.Qh5+ g6; 17.Nxg6 is a line given by Brinckmann. **14.Rxd7!!** Alekhine describes this as the high point of the combination. The main reason why the White attack is consequential is the position of the Na5 which cannot participate in the play. **14...Nxd7; 15.Ne5 Ra7; 16.bxc3**.

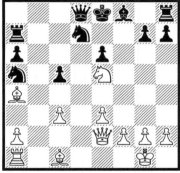

White's goal now is to get the bishop at c1 into the attack. **16...Ke7.** A strange looking move, but the alternatives are not pleasant. 16...Be7; 17.Qh5+ g6; 18.Nxg6 hxg6; 19.Qxh8+ Bf8; 20.Bc2 Qf6; 21.Qxf6 Nxf6; 22.Bxg6+ Kd8; 23.Bd2 Nc4; 24.Be1 (analysis by Brinckmann) and it is not clear that the three pawns and bishop pair will be enough to win though White is not likely to lose this position. **17.e4!** This sets up tricks with Bg5+. **17...Nf6; 18.Bg5.** And now Qh5+ is in the air. **18...Qc7; 19.Bf4 Qb6.** 19...Kd8 ; 20.Nc6+ Qxc6; 21.Bxc6 Nxc6; 22.Rd1+ Nd7; 23.e5 and the queen will pillage on the light squares; 19...Qb7; 20.Qe3! and White is threatening to win quickly, for example 20...Kd8; 21.Qd3+ Kc8; 22.Rb1 Qxe4; 23.Nf7 Rxf7; 24.Rb8 mate.

20.Rd1 g6. At this point there is nothing better. 20...Nb7; 21.Nc4; 20...Ra8; 21.Bg5 Rd8; 22.Nd7 Qc7; 23.e5 and White wins; 20...Rg8; 21.Bg5 h6; 22.Qh5 g6; 23.Nxg6+ Rxg6; 24.Qxg6 hxg5; 25.e5! Nd5; 26.Qe8 mate was pointed out by Brinckmann. **21.Bg5 Bg7.**

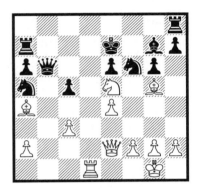

22.Nd7! The decisive, thematic thrust that brings the game to a swift conclusion. **22...Rxd7; 23.Rxd7+ Kf8; 24.Bxf6 Bxf6; 25.e5** and Black resigned, rather than walk into the obvious line: 25...Qb1+; 26.Rd1 Qf5; 27.exf6 Qxf6; 28.Qxa6 Qxc3; 29.Qxe6 to which there is simply no defense.

QUEEN'S GAMBIT DECLINED

If you want an opening that virtually every World Champion has played, look no further than the **Queen's Gambit Declined**. After **1.d4 d5; 2.c4 e6** White will have to work very hard to advance the e-pawn to e4.

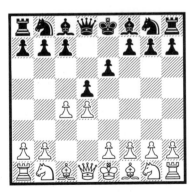

1.d4   d5
2.c4   e6

This venerable defense is based on classical principles. Black will fight vigorously for control of the central squares, and develop quickly with ...Nf6, ...Be7, and kingside castling. The lack of open lines makes it very difficult for White to mount an effective attack.

The only serious disadvantage of the opening is the blocking of the c8-bishop, which can lead to a bad bishop in the endgame. Therefore, after suitable development, Black will work toward advancing the e-pawn to e5 as a goal in the early middlegame.

The most common continuations in the Queen's Gambit Declined (often known by the initials QGD) follow **3.Nc3 Nf6; 4.Bg5 Be7** with either 5.Nf3 0-0; 6.e3 or the Exchange Variation. **5.cxd5 exd5; 6.e3**.

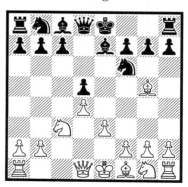

In this case Black no longer has to worry about the bishop at c8, which has a clear path to the enemy kingside. White, on the other hand, has a wide range of choices, and can adopt a strategy known as a *minority attack* where the queenside pawns will advance and undermine the enemy pawn structure.

(49) KARPOV - GEORGIEV
Tilburg, 1994

1.d4 Nf6; 2.c4 e6; 3.Nf3 d5; 4.Nc3 Be7; 5.Bg5 h6. This is played to give Black additional options, such as ...g5, and has become the normal move. **6.Bh4 0–0; 7.e3 b6**.

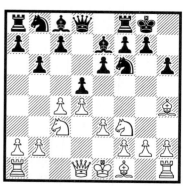

This is the Tartakower-Makagonov-Bondarevsky Variation, to name just a few of the designations in common use. The idea is to build a solid position. Karpov has battled Kasparov many times in this opening, and we'll look at some of those positions as we go along. **8.Be2 Bb7; 9.Bxf6 Bxf6; 10.cxd5 exd5; 11.b4**.

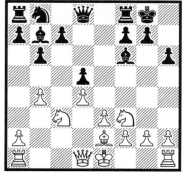

11...c6. This is often thought to be necessary, otherwise an advance of White's pawn to b5 might constrict the queenside. However, Black has a more aggressive plan, and that is the one that Kasparov, not surprisingly, prefers. 11...c5 has been seen in a number of Kasparov-Karpov games. 12.bxc5 bxc5; 13.Rb1 Bc6. Karpov tried 13...Qa5 in game 40, but it was an experiment he regretted, having to struggle for a draw. 14.0–0 Nd7; 15.Bb5 Qc7 and now let's look at the two best players in the world engaged in a multi-battle argument:

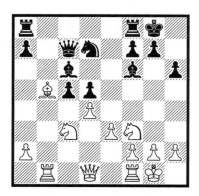

16.Qd2 Rfd8 ;17.Rfc1 Rab8; 18.Bxc6 Rxb1; 19.Nxb1 Qxc6; 20.dxc5 Nxc5; 21.Qc2 was agreed drawn in the 12th game of the 1984 match.

B) 16.Qc2 with two examples:

B1) 16...Rfd8; 17.Rfc1 Rab8; 18.a4 Qd6; 19.dxc5 Nxc5; 20.Bxc6 Qxc6; 21.Nb5 Be7; 22.Qf5 (22.Nxa7 was Karpov's choice as White in game 39 of the same match, and he squeezed out a small advantage on 22...Qa6!; 23.Nb5 Qxa4; 24.Qxa4 Nxa4; 25.Nfd4, but it was not difficult for Kasparov to hold the position.) 22...Qe8 and in the 38th game of the 1984 match Kasparov realized that capturing the pawn at a7 would allow too much counterplay after 23...Ra8, and White would get nowhere, so he tried another plan and the game ended in a draw after 23.Ne5 Rb7; 24.Nd4 Rc7; 25.Nb5 Rb7.

B2) 16...Rfc8; 17.Rfc1 Bxb5; 18.Nxb5 Qc6; 19.dxc5 Nxc5; 20.Qf5 Qe6; 21.Nfd4 Qxf5; 22.Nxf5 Ne6; 23.Rxc8+ Rxc8; 24.Nxa7 Rc2!; 25.Nb5 Rxa2; 26.h3 Ra5 was agreed drawn in game 42 of the 1984 marathon match;

16.Qd3 Rfc8; (16...Rfd8; 17.Rfd1 Rab8; 18.Bxc6 Qxc6; 19.Rxb8 Rxb8 led to an even position in game 8 of the 1985 match.) 17.Rfc1 Rab8; 18.h3 was seen in game 18 of the 1987 match. Karpov played 18...g6 here, and got a slightly worse position. **12.0–0**

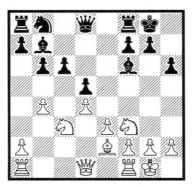

12...Qd6. There is no shortage of alternatives. 12...Re8 is considered acceptable, as are others. 12...a5; 13.a3 Qd6; 14.Qb3 axb4; 15.axb4 Nd7 was Karpov's choice as Black against Estevez at the 1973 Interzonal, en route to his first World Championship title. **13.Qb3 Nd7; 14.Rfe1.** Karpov had previously preferred 14.e4 against Ljubojevic in a rapids game at Roquebrune 1972. The text is the normal move, however. **14...Be7.** 14...Rfe8; 15.Bf1 Be7; 16.Rab1 a5; 17.bxa5 Rxa5; 18.a4 gave Karpov an advantage against Boensch, at Baden-Baden 1992. **15.Rab1 a5; 16.bxa5 Rxa5; 17.a4** White is a little better, as in the Estevez game mentioned above. **17...Re8; 18.Bf1 Bf8; 19.Qc2 g6.**

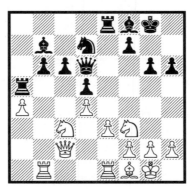

The quiet nature of the opening does not mean that play can be imprecise. Karpov demonstrates his sense of timing by blasting open the center now, and then going to work on Black's hanging pawns. **20.e4 dxe4; 21.Nxe4.** The hanging pawns at b6 and c6 are restrained by the White pawns at a4 and d4. **21...Qf4; 22.Bc4 Bg7; 23.Re2 c5.** An attempt to gain counterplay, but Karpov shuts it down. **24.d5! Raa8; 25.Rbe1.** White is setting up tactical threats. Black now tries to reorganize to go after the pawn at d5. **25...Rad8; 26.Qb3 Ba8; 27.g3 Qb8.**

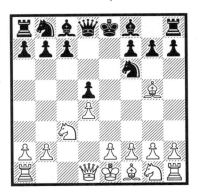

28.d6! Suddenly the age-old weakness at f7 plays a role. **28...Rf8; 29.Bxf7+ Rxf7; 30.Neg5!!** Karpov is known for positional play, but can explode some fireworks when the position calls for them. **30...hxg5; 31.Nxg5 Rdf8.** Black is trying to hang on, but Karpov finishes with a series of hammer blows. **32.Re8 Qxd6; 33.Qxf7+ Kh8; 34.Ne6. White won**.

(50) EUWE - FISCHER
New York, 1957

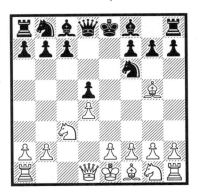

1.d4 Nf6; 2.c4 e6; 3.Nc3 d5; 4.cxd5 exd5; 5.Bg5. This is the normal continuation of the Exchange Variation. Black usually plays 5...Be7, but Fischer decided to try something different. **5...Bb4.** This move still isn't listed in the opening encyclopedias! Spassky once tried a similar plan to achieve an early...c5. But these experiments did not succeed, and both players abandoned them. **6.e3 h6; 7.Bh4 c5.** The idea is to get this pawn into the game before planting a knight at c6. **8.Bd3 Nc6; 9.Nge2 cxd4; 10.exd4 0–0; 11.0–0.**

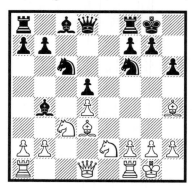

Despite the symmetrical pawn structure, Black has not achieved equality. White has a small lead in development and pressure at d5. **11...Be6.** This misplaces the other bishop, which is now a target for Nf4. He should try 11...Be7, though White keeps some edge. **12.Bc2 Be7; 13.Nf4 Qb6.** A bad move in a difficult position. **14.Bxf6! Bxf6.**

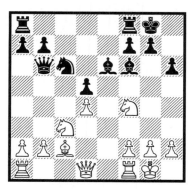

15.Qd3. Now Black can't play 15...g6 because of 16 Nxe6, so he has to let White's queen into his kingside. **15...Rfd8; 16.Rae1.** A master appreciates that the infiltration at h7 is going to happen sooner or later, so he places a rook on the e-file to keep the enemy king from fleeing to the queenside. **16...Nb4.** Accepting the inevitable. **17.Qh7+ Kf8; 18.a3! Nxc2.** Now the d5-square lacks sufficient support. **19.Ncxd5 Rxd5; 20.Nxd5.** The young Bobby Fischer resigned since Euwe was ready to play Qh8 mate, and advancing the g-pawn would only offer temporary respite after the bishop on f6 is captured by the knight. **White won.**

SEMI-SLAV

The positions which arise in the **Semi-Slav** are among the strategically richest in all of chess. While these are definitely not for beginners, World Champions are found on both sides of the board.

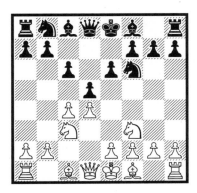

1.d4	d5
2.c4	e6
3.Nc3	Nf6
4.Nf3	c6

Black has a simple idea: capture the pawn at c4 and hold onto it by advancing the b-pawn to b5. The bishop at c8 can find a home at b7, and an eventual ...c5 will give it powerful scope on the long diagonal. White can choose to preserve the pawn with 5.e3, at the cost of shutting in the bishop at c1, or allow Black to carry out the plan, receiving in return an ideal pawn center as the pawn at e2 lunges to e4.

The positions which arise are very messy, and can feature such obscure items as four queens on the board (two for each side) and outrageous pawn structures Both tactical prowess and positional ability are required to solve the puzzles that lie in virtually every position.

(51) KARPOV - KRAMNIK
Linares, 1994

1.d4 d5; 2.c4 c6; 3.Nf3 Nf6; 4.Nc3 e6. This is the Semi-Slav Defense to the Queen's Gambit. It leads to complicated play where Black often allows a great deal of damage to be done to the queenside pawn structure, but achieves very active piece play in return. **5.e3.** The Botvinnik System with 5.Bg5 leads to wild complications. This is the calmer move, though things get interesting in the middlegame here too. **5...Nbd7; 6.Bd3 dxc4.** With this capture Black concedes central territory but gains time for a flank advance. **7.Bxc4 b5.**

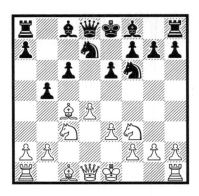

8.Bd3 a6. This provides support to b5, so that the c-pawn can safely advance. **9.e4.** White has achieved the ideal pawn center, but the pawns cannot remain at d4 and e4 after Black issues a central challenge with the next move. 9.0–0 is an older move, which Alekhine used against Bogoljubow in the 2nd game of their 1934 Championship match. Now it is considered more important to advance the pawn to e4.

9...c5; 10.d5. 10.e5 is a serious alternative which has been used by Botvinnik and Alekhine. For example 10...Nd5; 11.Ng5 cxd4; 12.Nxd5 exd5; 13.0–0 Be7; 14.e6 Ne5; 15.exf7+ Kf8; 16.Nxh7+ Kxf7; 17.Qh5+ g6; 18.Qxe5 Rxh7; 19.Qxd4 Rh4; 20.Qe3 Qh8; 21.Bxg6+ Kxg6; 22.Qxe7 Ra7; 23.Qxa7 Rxh2; 24.Qb6+ Kf5; 25.g4+ and Black resigned in Alekhine-Te Kolste, played in the famous tournament at Baden-Baden Germany 1925.

10...c4. This prevents White from playing 11.b3, which would otherwise hold up Black's queenside play. **11.dxe6** 11.Bc2 is an acceptable alternative. Here is an example: 11.Bc2 e5; 12.0–0 Qc7; 13.Ne2 Rb8; 14.Ng3 h6; 15.Bd2 g6; 16.Rc1 Bd6; 17.h3 Kf8; 18.Bb1 a5; 19.b3 Ba6 with a complicated position which was eventually drawn in Karpov-Kamsky, Las Palmas 1994. **11...fxe6.** 11...cxd3; 12.exd7+ Qxd7 is also common, but Karpov has been very effective against it.

13.0–0 Bb7; 14.Re1 Bb4 (14...Be7! is better, but even so, Karpov was able to gain an advantage after 15.e5 Nd5; 16.Ne4 0–0; 17.Qxd3 in Karpov-Lutz, Dortmund 1994.) 15.Ne5 Qe6; 16.Nxd3 Bxc3; 17.Nf4 Qd7; 18.bxc3 Nxe4; 19.Qxd7+ Kxd7; 20.Ba3 was eventually won by White in Karpov-Tal, Bugojno 1980. **12.Bc2 Bb7; 13.0–0 Qc7**.

Black has a weak e-pawn and an insecure king, but there is compensation in the form of queenside counterplay and potential use of the d-file. Indeed, Black's pieces deftly exploit that file in the course of this game. **14.Ng5.** 14.Qe2 is less ambitious and 14...Bd6 is a good reply. **14...Nc5.**

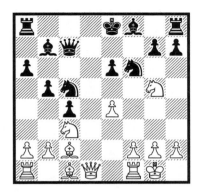

15.e5. 15.f4 is too slow after 15...h6! driving back the enemy knight. **15...Qxe5!** A fearless capture, but one which seems safe at first. **16.Re1 Qd6.** Black, having eaten the pawn, is content to offer an exchange of queens, which is usually declined by 17.Be3.

But Karpov has a surprise in store. **17.Qxd6! Bxd6; 18.Be3 0–0; 19.Rad1.** White is content to play the position a pawn down for a while, counting on the well-placed forces to provide compensation. **19...Be7; 20.Bxc5 Bxc5; 21.Nxe6.** White has the pawn back with beautifully placed pieces. **21...Rfc8; 22.h3 Bf8; 23.g4 h6; 24.f4.** White methodically advances on the kingside, seeking to establish a passed pawn there. **24...Bf3; 25.Rd2 Bc6; 26.g5 hxg5; 27.fxg5 Nd7; 28.Nxf8 Nxf8.** Now Black no longer even enjoys the advantage of the bishop pair and White owns the central files.

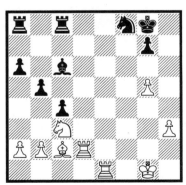

29.Rd6 b4; 30.Ne4 Be8; 31.Ng3! This knight is coming to d6 via f5. **31...Rd8; 32.Nf5 Rxd6; 33.Nxd6 Bg6.** Black offers up the extra queenside pawn to release the pressure. **34.Bxg6 Nxg6; 35.Nxc4 Rd8; 36.Re4 b3.** A temporary sacrifice. Black will regain this pawn quickly.

37.axb3 Rd3; 38.Kg2 Rxb3; 39.h4 Nf8. Not the best defense, though Black was probably lost anyway. **40.Re8.** The pin cannot be broken because 40...Kf7 is met by 41.Nd6. The endgame is lost. **White won.**

(52) DENKER - BOTVINNIK
Match (USA vs. USSR), 1945

1.d4 d5; 2.c4 e6; 3.Nc3 c6; 4.Nf3 Nf6; 5.Bg5.

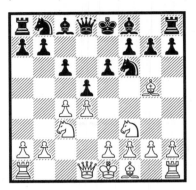

This is sometimes known as the Botvinnik Variation, but here we find him on the Black side. **5...dxc4.** Black can hold on to the extra pawn, but at the cost of conceding the center. **6.e4 b5; 7.e5.** This forces the play, but it does not win material because Black can counterattack the bishop. **7...h6; 8.Bh4 g5.**

Black must keep attacking, or part with the knight. But it is time for White to strike back — with a sacrifice! **9.Nxg5 hxg5; 10.Bxg5.** The pin on the knight at f6 insures that White will regain the piece with a material profit on the kingside. Nevertheless, Black has plenty of resources on the queenside with which to maintain the balance.

10...Nbd7; 11.exf6 Bb7; 12.Be2. In modern games, 12.g3 is preferred. The bishop belongs on the h1–a8 diagonal, and is not needed for support of the advance of the h-pawn. **12...Qb6.** After more than half a century, this game stands as the reason White's plan is no longer seen. **13.0-0.** Whether the king goes to the kingside or the queenside, it will be the target of a fierce attack. **13...0-0-0.**

14.a4. A new move at the time. Botvinnik had faced 14.h4 against Ragozin. **14...b4; 15.Ne4 c5**. This opens up the long diagonal for an eventual kingside attack. **16.Qb1**. 16.Nxc5 would be a blunder. 16...Nxc5; 17.dxc5 and now instead of taking the White queen, Black simply retreats with 17...Qc7! threatening mate at h2. **16...Qc7; 17.Ng3**. 17.h4 Bh6 would still leave the White king with insufficient defenses. **17...cxd4; 18.Bxc4 Qc6**. Threatening mate at g2. **19.f3 d3!** When one diagonal closes, another opens up! **20.Qc1 Bc5+; 21.Kh1**.

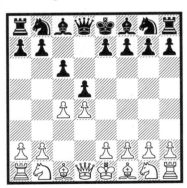

Black's pieces are trained on the White kingside, and the game cannot last long. **21...Qd6; 22.Qf4 Rxh2+; 23.Kxh2 Rh8+; 24.Qh4 Rxh4+; 25.Bxh4 Qf4. Black won**.

SLAV

The full **Slav Defense** is an uncompromising opening, beloved by Smyslov and Euwe, generally shunned by the other World Champions. After 1.d4 d5; 2.c4 c6; Black is ready to bring the bishop at c8 into the game at f5 or g4.

1. d4	**d5**
2. c4	**c6**

There is also a direct threat — the capture of the pawn at c4 and subsequent support from a pawn at b5. This theme is seen in the main line of the Slav: 3.Nc3 Nf6; 4.Nf3 dxc4 4.a4, where White eventually regains the pawn as in the Queen's Gambit Accepted. The gambit approach with 5.e4 has a good reputation, too.

The most serious drawback to the Slav is that after the boring 3.cxd5 cxd5; 4.Nf3, the game can be rather dull. On 4.Nc3, however, Black can use the Winawer Countergambit 4...e5 (another version is 1.d4 d5; 2.c4 c6; 3.Nc3 e5) to gain interesting counterplay.

The Slav is not recommended for beginners, because it concedes too much of the center. If an intermediate level player wants to try it, it is best to follow 3.Nf3 Nf6, 4.Nc3 with Smyslov's 4...g6.

(53) KASPAROV - TIMMAN
Riga (Tal Memorial), 1995

1.d4 d5; 2.c4 c6; 3.Nf3 Nf6; 4.Nc3 dxc4; 5.a4 Bf5.

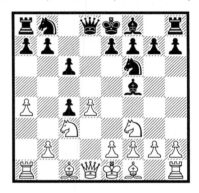

This is the main line of the Slav. **6.Ne5**. This leads to exciting play. The idea is to occupy important squares. The pawn at c4 just happens to sit on the target square.. **6...Nbd7; 7.Nxc4 Nb6**. 7...e6 is more natural. After 8.e3 Bb4, a game Keene-Birnboim, Beersheva, 1978, continued 9.Qb3!? a5; 10.e4 Bg6; 11.Be2 0–0; 12.0–0 b5; 13.axb5 cxb5; 14.Ne3 e5; 15.d5 and White had control of more space, although Black was not without counterplay. **8.Ne5 Nbd7?** A new idea, but not an improvement over more normal paths. 8...e6 would lead back to more normal lines.

9.Qb3. This idea may have been inspired by a game played by one of the world's foremost authorities on the opening, English grandmaster Raymond Keene, who retired from active play to become the most prolific author in chess history. Keene and Kasparov are the authors of Batsford Chess Openings, on which I have served as research editor since 1980. That game was mentioned in the note to Black's 8th move. Amazingly, it seems that there is no way for Black to meet this move.

9...Nxe5; 10.dxe5 Ng4. 10...Ne4; 11.Qxb7 Qc8; 12.Qxc8+ Rxc8; 13.g4 Bg6; 14.Nxe4 Bxe4; 15.f3 Bg6; 16.e4 is clearly better for White, according to Czech theoretician Ftacnik. **11.Qxb7 Nxe5; 12.f4 Ng6; 13.e4.** 13.Qxc6+ Bd7; 14.Qb7 e6 and Black will get enough play for the pawn by completing development and then placing the rooks on open files on the queenside. **13...Bd7; 14.f5 Ne5; 15.Bf4 f6; 16.Bxe5 fxe5; 17.Rd1 Rb8; 18.Qxa7 Rb4.** 18...Rxb2 is too dangerous. After 19.Bc4 Qc8; 20.Rxd7! Qxd7; 21.Qa8+ Qd8; 22.Qxc6+ Qd7; 23.Qa8+ Qd8; 24.Bf7+ Kd7; 25.Be6+ Kc7; 26.Qa5+ Rb6; 27.Nb5+ wins. This line was calculated by Ftacnik.

19.Be2 g6; 20.Rf1. 20.0-0 Qb6+, 21.Qxb6 Rxb6 gives Black additional chances. **20...Bg7**. 20...Rxb2 is still out of the question because of 21.fxg6 hxg6; 22.Bc4 e6; 23.Bxe6 Bxe6; 24.Rxd8+ Kxd8; 25.Rf7 is all but over. **21.fxg6 Rd4**. 21...hxg6 loses to 22.Rxd7 Qxd7; 23.Qa8+ Qd8; 24.Qxc6+ Qd7; 25.Qxg6+ Kd8; 26.Qxg7 Rxh2; 27.Rf8+ Kc7; 28.Qxe5+ Qd6; 29.Nd5+. **22.Bh5.** Black resigned, because of 22.Bh5. Ftacnik gave further 22...Rxd1+; 23.Nxd1 h6; 24.Rf7 Rg8; 25.Ne3+- and Black's position is indefensible.

Our next example shows the newly popular Winawer Countergambit in action:

(54) KASPAROV - NIKOLIC
Manila (Olympiad), 1992

1.d4 d5; 2.c4 c6. This is the Slav. Now on 3.Nf3 or 3.exd5 Black remains in defensive mode for some time, but against 3.Nc3, Black has an additional resource. **3.Nc3 e5!?** The Winawer Countergambit is all the rage these days. It is the subject of my book *How to Play the Winawer Countergambit*. In this example we find the reigning World Champion on the White side. **4.dxe5 d4.**

As usual, Black countergambits involve the advance of a pawn past the central dividing line. **5.Ne4 Qa5+; 6.Bd2.** Kasparov's choice led to an explosion in the theory of this line, not least because he managed to win so brilliantly. **6...Qxe5; 7.Ng3 Qd6.** The most popular move in 1995-96 was 7...c5.

8.Nf3 Nf6; 9.Qc2 Be7. There are several alternatives here, but at the time this was considered the best move.

Indeed, Black should emerge from the opening with only a very slight disadvantage which is typical of most openings at the professional level. **10.0–0-0 0-0**. Opposite wing castling usually leads to exciting play. **11.e3 dxe3; 12.fxe3!** The weak pawn at e3 is not very important, but is in any case unavoidable. 12.Bxe3 Qc7; 13.Bd3 Na6; 14.Ng5 h6 is fine for Black. **12...Qc7; 13.Bc3**.

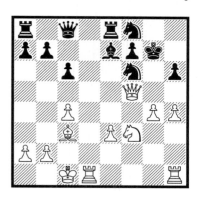

13...Bg4?! The bishop turns out to be too exposed here. 13...Na6; 14.a3 is suggested by Kasparov and White has no more than a minimal advantage. Actually, given the opposite wing castling and the pawn at e3, it seems that the concept of "slight advantage" is inoperative here. Either White will blast open the enemy king, or else the weaknesses should provide Black with a tremendous game.

14.Bd3 Nbd7; 15.Bf5! A useful way of eliminating the enemy bishop. Black must allow an exchange or there will be too much pressure on the knights. **15...Bxf5**. 15...Rfd8; 16.Bxg4 Nxg4 is the line considered best by Peters. The bishop sacrifice now fails because the king has a safe haven at f8. 17.Bxg7 Kxg7; 18.Nf5+ Kf8. **16.Nxf5** White's pieces look menacing, and they are. **16...Rfe8**. Now White closes in for the kill. **17.Nxg7!! Kxg7; 18.Qf5 Nf8; 19.h4 h6; 20.g4?!** 20.Qg4+ Kh8; 21.Ng5! Bd8; 22.Rxd8 Raxd8; 23.Bxf6+ Kg8; 24.Ne6+ Ng6; 25.Nxc7 would have been more efficient. **20...Qc8**.

21.Qxc8?. Why exchange queens when the attack is still raging? Kasparov later analyzed a superior plan. 21.Qc2 Kg8; 22.g5 Ng4; 23.gxh6 f5; 24.Rhg1 Qe6; 25.Nd4 Qxe3+; 26.Kb1 and Black's naked king cannot hold out for long. **21...Raxc8; 22.g5 N8d7; 23.e4 Rcd8?**. Black misses a chance to make White work for the win after 23...Kf8!; 24.gxf6 Nxf6; 25.Rhg1 Red8; 26.Bd2 Ng8; 27.Rdf1 Bc5; 28.Rg2 is clearly better for White. **24.Rdf1 Kf8; 25.gxf6 Bxf6; 26.e5!** Although material is level, White's control of space is decisive. **26...Bg7.** 26...Be7; 27.e6 fxe6; 28.Ng5+ Kg8; 29.Nxe6 Rc8; 30.Rhg1+ Kh7; 31.Rf7 mate. **27.Rhg1 c5; 28.Kc2 Re6; 29.Rg4 Bh8.** Black is reduced to meaningless maneuvers, and White now demonstrates superiority on the queenside too. **30.b4! b6; 31.bxc5 bxc5; 32.Rb1 Ra6; 33.Rb2 Bg7.**

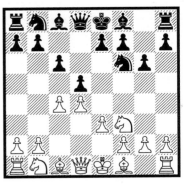

34.Rb7! The occupation of the seventh rank is decisive. **34...Rxa2+; 35.Kb3 Ra6; 36.e6 Rxe6; 37.Rxg7. White won.**

Finally, let's look at how Smyslov handles the Schlechter Variation for Black.

(55) BISGUIER - SMYSLOV
Moscow (USA vs. USSR), 1955

1.d4 d5; 2.c4 c6; 3.Nf3 Nf6; 4.e3 g6.

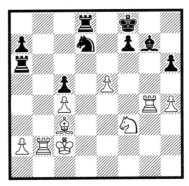

This is the Schlechter Variation of the Slav, a favorite with Smyslov. **5.Nc3 Bg7; 6.Bd3**. White has many tires here, including 6.Qb3; 6.Bd2; 6.b4 and 6.Be2, but the text remains the favorite. Since White always has the goal of advancing to e4 in the Closed Game, the position of the bishop at d3 is most logical. **6...0-0; 7.0-0**. If White stations the queen at c2, then Black has counterplay on the queenside: 7.Qc2 Na6!; 8.a3 Nc7; 9.0-0 Be6; 10.cxd5 Ncxd5; 11.h3 Nxc3; 12.bxc3 c5 and Black can be fully satisfied with the position, which was reached in Bogoljubow-Alekhine, Vilnius 1912.

7...Bg4. Smyslov's patent, introduced in this very game! **8.h3 Bxf3; 9.Qxf3 e6**. Although Black has given up the bishop pair, the position is very solid and White has no way of providing the bishop at c1 with an effective role in the game. There is another plan for Black, which Smyslov demonstrated over three decades later. 9...Qd6; 10.Rd1 Nbd7; 11.Qe2 e5; 12.dxe5 Qxe5; 13.cxd5 cxd5; 14.Bc2 Nc5, and in Hansen-Smyslov, Rome, 1988, Black had enough piece activity to compensate for the isolated pawn. **10.Rd1 Nbd7; 11.e4**.

Timing is everything when it comes to the e4 advance in the Closed Games. Here it is premature, and 11.b3 is to be preferred. 11.Bf1 Re8; 12.b3 a6; 13.Bb2 e5! was fine for Black in Panno-Smyslov, Mar del Plata 1962. 11.b4 dxc4; 12.Bxc4 Nb6; 13.Bb3 Nbd5 is also quite nice for Black, as in Korchnoi-Smyslov, USSR 1967. 11.b3 Re8; 12.Bb2 (12.Bf1 e5 is another variation on the same theme, seen in Ribli-Smyslov from their 1983 World Championship Semifinal match.) 12...Qe7; 13.Rac1 (13.Qe2 dxc4; 14.Bxc4 Nd5; 15.Rac1 Nxc3; 16.Bxc3 Nb6 and here Petrosian and Smyslov agreed to a draw in an earlier Soviet Championship.) 13...e5 is fully playable for Black, as in Bondarevsky-Smyslov, USSR 1951.

11...e5! An excellent counterthrust. One would think that players of the White pieces would not give Smyslov a chance to repeat, but he has scored a lot of points as Black. **12.dxe5**. 12.exd5 exd4; 13.dxc6 (13.Ne4 Ne5, 14.Nxf6+ Bxf6 was better for Black in Simagin-Smyslov, Chigorin Memorial 1951.) 13...Ne5; 14.Qe2 Nxd3; 15.Rxd3 bxc6 16.Bg5 Qa5; 17.Bxf6 Bxf6; 18.Ne4 Bg7 was better for Black in Polugayevsky-Smyslov, Moscow 1960. **12...Nxe5; 13.Qe2 d4; 14.Bc2 Nfd7; 15.Na4 Qa5; 16.Bd2**.

Now Smyslov exploits the clustered White formation with a bold advance. **16...d3!; 17.Bxa5?** 17.Qe3 Qa6; 18.Bb3 b5; 19.cxb5 cxb5; 20.Nc5 Nxc5; 21.Qxc5 Rac8 gives Black a lot of pressure; 17.Qxd3 Qxa4!, 18.Bxa4 Nxd3 and White remains a piece ahead; 17.Qf1 is best, but Black still enjoys a huge advantage. 17...Qa6; 18.Bb3 b5; 19.cxb5 cxb5; 20.Nc3 Nb6 and c4 beckons. **17...dxe2; 18.Re1 Nxc4; 19.Bc3 b5; 20.Bb3.** A good move, according to Smyslov, because Bisguier plays vigorously. **20...Bxc3; 21.Nxc3.** 21.bxc3 Nd2; 22.Nb2 Nxe4; 23.Rxe2 Nxc3; 24.Re7 Nc5 and Black will win without difficulty. **21...Nxb2; 22.Rxe2 Nd3.**

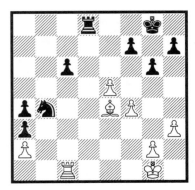

Black's extra pawn and queenside majority give Smyslov all he needs to secure victory. **23.Rd1 N7c5; 24.Red2 Nb4; 25.f4 a5!** The march of the a-pawn brings home the point. **26.e5 a4; 27.Bc2 a3; 28.Be4 Na4; 29.Rc1 Rfd8; 30.Rxd8+ Rxd8; 31.Nxa4 bxa4.**

The doubled pawns don't matter. The position is a technical win. **32.Rc3 Rd2; 33.Bxc6.** 33.Rxa3 Rxa2; 34.Rxa2 Nxa2; 35.Bxc6 a3; 36.Bd5 Nc3 and White can give up. **33...Rxa2; 34.Bxa4 Ra1+; 35.Kh2 a2; 36.e6 fxe6. Black won.**

TARRASCH DEFENSE

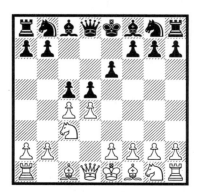

1.d4   d5
2.c4   e6
3.Nc3 c5

The **Tarrasch Defense** helped bring World Championship titles to Boris Spassky and Garry Kasparov, but has not been a favorite of most top players. You have to really value the dynamic piece play that Black obtains in return for being saddled with an isolated d-pawn which is typical in most variations.

The main line continues 4.cxd5 exd5; 5.Nf3 Nc6; 6.g3 Nf6; 7.Bg2 Be7; 8.O-O O-O; 9.dxc5 Bxc5; 10.Bg5 when it is clear that the battle must revolve around the isolated pawn at d5.

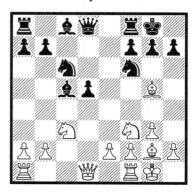

Notice that the Black forces are easily developed to useful squares. Now Black can simply protect the pawn at d5 by playing ...Be6, or can force matters by advancing the d-pawn, which is the preferred strategy among the top players. After 10...d4; 11.Bxf6 Qxf6; 12.Nd5 Qd8; 13.Nd2, we reach the starting position of the main lines. The White knights control many important squares, and the pawn at d4 is vulnerable. On the other hand, Black can place pressure on the pawn at e2, and use the active pieces to attack on the kingside.

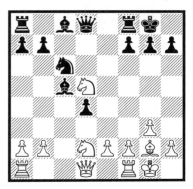

Endgame prowess is important, because sometimes Black must defend a rook endgame after losing the d-pawn. The ability to hold difficult endgames to a draw is a major asset if you choose to defend the Tarrasch.

(56) BELYAVSKY - KASPAROV
Moscow (Candidates Match, Game 2), 1983

1.d4 d5; 2.c4 e6; 3.Nc3 c5; 4.cxd5 exd5; 5.Nf3 Nc6; 6.g3 Nf6; 7.Bg2 Be7; 8.0–0 0–0; 9.Bg5 cxd4; 10.Nxd4. This is one of the most popular reactions to the Classical Tarrasch. **10...h6; 11.Be3 Re8**.

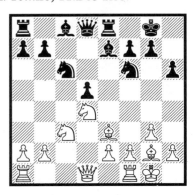

Now White has many plans. For a long time, 12.Qa4 dominated the scene, but Kasparov has demonstrated some useful ideas for Black. **12.Qa4 Bd7; 13.Rad1 Nb4; 14.Qb3 a5; 15.Rd2?!**

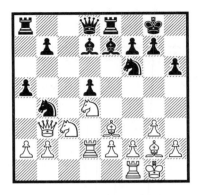

Defending the b-pawn and piling up on the d-file seems sensible, but White is really obliged here to stop the further advance of the a-pawn. **15...a4!; 16.Qd1 a3; 17.Qb1.** 17.Qb3 Qa5; 18.bxa3 Qxa3; 19.Nxd5 Nfxd5; 20.Bxd5 Nxd5; 21.Qxd5 Bh3! gives Black more than enough counterplay. **17...Bf8.** 17...Bc5 is an interesting alternative. 18.bxa3 Rxe3!; 19.fxe3 Rxa3; 20.Qb2 Qe7; 21.Kh1 Ra6; 22.a3 Qxe3; 23.axb4 Bxd4 but White has a strong resource: 24.Nd1! Bxb2; 25.Nxe3 Bc3; 26.Rd3 Bxb4; 27.Nxd5 and White is clearly better. **18.bxa3 Rxa3; 19.Qb2.** 19.Ndb5 Bxb5; 20.Nxb5 Raxe3; 21.fxe3 Qb6; 22.Nd4 Rxe3 and Black has more than enough compensation for the exchange. **19...Qa8.**

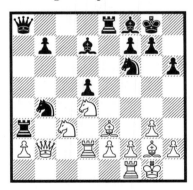

20.Nb3?! 20.Ndb5 Bxb5; 21.Nxb5 Rxa2; 22.Qb3 would have maintained equality, according to Kasparov. **20...Bc6; 21.Bd4.** 21.Nc5 d4; 22.Bxd4 Bxg2; 23.Kxg2 b6+ wins a piece. **21...Ne4; 22.Nxe4 dxe4; 23.Ra1?.** 23.Nc5! Nxa2; (23...e3; 24.Bxc6 exf2+; 25.Bxf2 Nxc63) 24.Ra1 Qa5; 25.Nxe4! Bxe4; 26.Rxa2 Bxg2; 27.Kxg2 Qd5+; 28.Kg1 Rb3 with at least a minimal advantage for Black, according to Kasparov. **23...Bd5; 24.Qb1 b6; 25.e3 Nd3; 26.Rd1.**

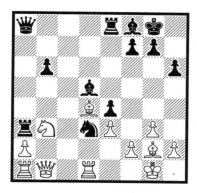

Now Kasparov improves his position by advancing the b-pawn to b4. **26...b5; 27.Bf1 b4; 28.Bxd3**. In time pressure, Belyavsky tries to get rid of the invasive knight, but now the light squares are much too weak. **28...exd3; 29.Qxd3 Rxa2; 30.Rxa2 Qxa2; 31.Nc5 Bf3! 32.Ra1 Qd5; 33.Qb3 Qh5; 34.Nd3 Bd6; 35.Ne1 Bb7; 36.Rc1 Qf5; 37.Rd1 Bf8; 38.Qb1**. White lost on time. It would have been difficult for Belyavsky to stop the advance of the b-pawn eventually.

(57) KASPAROV - HJORTH
World Junior Championship, 1980

1.d4 d5; 2.c4 e6; 3.Nf3 c5; 4.cxd5 exd5; 5.g3 Nc6; 6.Bg2 Nf6; 7.Nc3 Be7; 8.0-0 0-0; 9.Bg5 c4. This leads to quite different positions than the normal Classical Tarrasch lines. Black's game plan is simple: advance on the queenside. Of course, White has something to say in the matter, too. **10.Ne5 Be6; 11.f4 Nxe5**.

Now there is a board diagram.

12.fxe5. Kasparov introduced this move in the present game. The idea is that the f-file will be a useful asset in the attack and that a pawn at d4 may be helpful too. **12...Ne4; 13.Bxe7 Nxc3; 14.bxc3 Qxe7**. The only strategy available to White is to try to eliminate Black's pawn at d5 so that the central pawns can advance. Black will try to thrust the queenside pawns forward as quickly as possible. **15.e4! Qd7; 16.a4!** A very important move, restraining Black's queenside play. That accomplished, White can turn his attention to the kingside. **16...Rfd8; 17.Qh5 Rac8.**

The battle lines are drawn. Now White doubles rooks on the f- file. This will leave the a-pawn hanging, but if the attack is fast enough it won't matter. **18.Rf4 Rc7; 19.Raf1 Qxa4?** Black should be worrying about the defense of his kingside, so 19...Qe8 was best, although White would retain a strong initiative. **20.exd5! Rxd5.** Forced, since otherwise f7 loses its most valuable defender. The f7-square is the cornerstone of Black's position, and obviously White would like to play Rxf7 as soon as feasible. **21.Bxd5 Bxd5.**

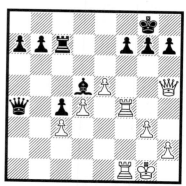

The material is not important. If White does not break through quickly Black will make a new queen on the other flank. The goal is achieved effectively. **22.e6!** What is surprising about this move is that it seems to contribute nothing to the task of deflecting the bishop from f7. In fact, however, it opens up the d5-square so that the White pawn can chase the bishop from the key square. **22...Bxe6; 23.d5 Qb5.** 23...Rc5; 24.Rxf7!; 23...g6; 24.Qh4 with the threat of Qd8+. **24.Rh4!** The simultaneous threats at e6 and h7 force victory. **24...Qc5+; 25.Rf2 Bxd5; 26.Rd4!** This breaks the pin at f2 while exploiting the pin along the 5th rank. **26...Rd7; 27.Rf5. White won.**

(58) KARPOV - HECTOR
Haninge, 1990

1.d4 d5; 2.c4 e6; 3.Nc3 c5; 4.cxd5 cxd4; 5.Qa4+ Bd7. The Schara Gambit is a sharp alternative to the main lines. **6.Qxd4 exd5; 7.Qxd5 Nc6; 8.e3 Nf6; 9.Qb3!?.**

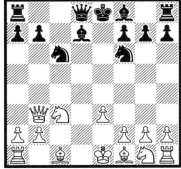

The normal move is 9.Qd1. If Hector was trying to catch Karpov by surprise, he must have forgotten that Karpov has worked for years with Igor Zaitsev, who plays the gambit as Black. **9...Bc5.** 9...Na5, 10.Qc2 just leaves the knight looking silly. **10.Nf3 0-0.** In evaluating this game it is important to keep in mind that Black chooses to castle kingside. An obvious alternative is to go the other way. 10...Qe7 intending queenside castling, is suggested by Karpov. **11.Be2 Be6; 12.Qa4.**

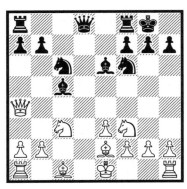

12...Qc7. Hector's new move, hoping to improve on 12...a6 which gives White a better game. **13.0-0 Rad8; 14.Bd2 Ng4.** 14...Ne5; 15.Rfd1 Nfg4; 16.Nxe5 would be much better for White, according to Karpov. **15.Rfd1 Bd6; 16.g3 Qe7; 17.Be1.**

White has a clear advantage, because Black's attack is going nowhere. An extra pawn is an extra pawn, after all. **17...f5; 18.Nd5 Qf7; 19.Ng5 Qh5; 20.h4 Bc8; 21.Nf4 Bxf4; 22.Rxd8**.

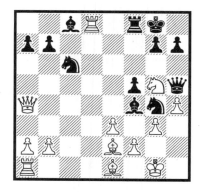

22...Nxd8. 22...Rxd8; 23.Qc4+ Kh8; 24.Nf7+ Kg8; 25.Nh6+ Kh8; 26.Nxg4 fxg4; 27.Qxf4 would have been won by White in the long run. **23.Qxf4 Nc6; 24.Qc7** Black gave up.

DUTCH DEFENSE

It almost makes no sense to talk of the **Dutch Defense** as a single opening. The style of play depends entirely on one fundamental decision: "What to do after 1.d4 f5?"

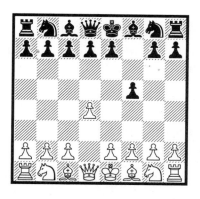

1.d4   f5

If Black chooses to fianchetto the bishop at g7, then we have the Leningrad Variation, which has not played a significant part in the opening repertoire of the World Champions. So we'll leave that approach aside here. The Classical Variation is far and away the preference of champions, especially Botvinnik, Euwe, and Alekhine. After 2.g3 (White sees opportunity along the long diagonal.) 2...Nf6; 3.Bg2 e6; 4.Nf3 d5; 5.c4 c6; 6.0-0 Black used to play 6...Be7, but now 6...Bd6 is the overwhelming favorite.

This is known as the Modern Stonewall Dutch. It is highly transpositional and Black must take great care not to entomb the bishop at c8, a fate which can befall even the most experienced Dutch fan. In the late 1980s Nigel Short, who eventually defeated Anatoly Karpov to earn a title match with Kasparov, refined this into a positional weapon for Black as well as the traditional all-out attacking method. As White, Short once gave the author a painful lesson in the consequences of not attending to the problem of the light-squared bishop, and I have played the Modern Stonewall Dutch consistently for a decade.

Yet there are great rewards for Black, especially if White does not take care to protect the king sufficiently. The pawns on the f-, g-, and h-files can come storming forward, aided by rooks, queen, knights, and even the famous bad bishop, which can emerge at h5 after visiting d7 and e8.

(58) BOTVINNIK - RAGOZIN
Leningrad (match), 1940

1.c4. The Dutch can be reached by many paths. The main feature is a White pawn at d4 and a pawn at f5 for Black. The Classical systems involve a pawn at e6 as well. Here are a few possible paths to the Classical Stonewall.
1.d4 f5; 2.Nf3 e6;3.g3 Nf6; 4.Bg2 d5; 5.0-0 Bd6; 6.c4 c6;
1.Nf3 e6; 2.g3 f5; 3.Bg2 Nf6; 4.c4 d5; 5.d4 c6; 6.0-0 Bd6;
1.g3 d5; 2.Bg2 c6; 3.d4 f5; 4.Nf3 e6; 5.0-0 Nf6; 6.c4 Bd6;
1.d4 d5; 2.c4 e6; 3.Nf3 c6; 4.g3 f5; 5.Bg2 Nf6; 6.0-0 Bd6

1...f5; 2.Nf3 Nf6; 3.g3 e6; 4.Bg2 d5; 5.0-0 c6; 6.d4 Bd6.

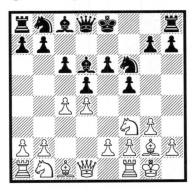

This is the starting position of the Modern Stonewall Dutch. Botvinnik played the Classical Stonewall as Black, with the bishop at e7, but now only the plan with the bishop at d6 is considered fully satisfactory. **7.Nc3.** It is perhaps a bit strange that this straightforward move is a mistake. In most cases the knight is better at d2, where it does not stand in the way of a rook at c1 or bishop at b2. Furthermore, it may wish to occupy f3 should that knight advance to e5. **7...0-0; 8.cxd5.** This exchange may be premature, but the game later transposes to known positions.

8.Bf4 Bxf4; 9.gxf4 Qe7; 10.cxd5 exd5; 11.Ne5 Ne4; 12.e3 Nd7 is similar to our game, but with the difference that there is a knight at e5 instead of d2. This was played in a game Nikolic-Psakhis, Bor 1985. **8...exd5; 9.Bf4.** This is one way of forcing the dark-squared bishops off the board, which is the goal of White's game. More common is a plan involving b3 and Ba3, but with the knight at c3, that is no longer an option. **9...Bxf4; 10.gxf4.**

White's pawn structure is not weak. A pawn at c3 will keep the twin pillars in the center from shaking. **10...Nbd7; 11.e3 Ne4; 12.Ne2.** Botvinnik decides to preserve this knight. **12...Qe7; 13.Rc1 Ndf6; 14.Qe1.** 14.Rc2 Ng4; 15.Nc1 Nexf2; 16.Rcxf2 Qxe3; 17.Qd2 was a better plan, according to Botvinnik. **14...Be6; 15.Ne5.** Botvinnik remarked that this was hasty, because this maneuver works best when the other knight can come to the support of e5. That's why, in retrospect, developing the knight at c3 in the first place is an error. **15...Nd7; 16.Kh1 a5; 17.Rc2.**

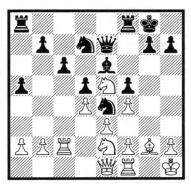

Up to now Ragozin has played well, but the next move is a serious error. **17...Qh4?.** This is not a good square for the queen, because White might have been able to reposition his knight from e2 to f3 with tempo. **18.Nc1?** Botvinnik overlooks the opportunity: 18.Nxd7! Bxd7; 19.Ng1 and the knight will get to e5 via f3. **18...Nxe5!** prevents the knight from using e5. **19.dxe5 Qe7; 20.Ne2!** Botvinnik reacts like a World Champion, though that title still lay in the future. He comes up with a deep strategic plan which Ragozin didn't pick up. **20...Bd7; 21.Rg1 b6; 22.f3 Nc5.**

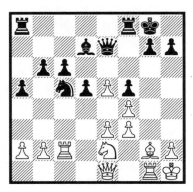

The opening of the center with e4 is not the idea here. Instead, White wants to work on the weak pawns at c6 and f5. To this end, 23.Nd4 would have been the most accurate move. **23.Rd2 Ne6; 24.Bh3 Kh8; 25.Ng3 g6; 26.Bf1.**

White spends a little time reorganizing the position. **26...Rad8; 27.Qf2 Bc8; 28.Ne2 c5; 29.Bg2 Bb7; 30.Rgd1 Bc6; 31.h3 b5; 32.Kh2 b4; 33.h4**. Finally a new contour emerges. White is attacking on the kingside while Black is concerned with the other side of the board. The center remains tense. **33...Ng7; 34.Bh3 Ba4; 35.Rc1 Bb5; 36.Rcd1**.

Black could now accept the invitation to repeat the position with ...Ba4, but Ragozin felt he had the advantage, and decided to wait until adjournment before doing anything serious, like ending the game. Indeed, he also rejected capturing at e2 on the grounds that the evaluation of the consequences would be more easily achieved on the analysis board at home. **36...Bc6; 37.Rc1 Bb7; 38.Qg3 Ne6; 39.Qf2 Ba6; 40.Rcd1 d4**.

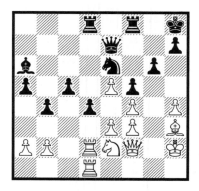

The last move of time control is a committal one. Botvinnik now had to seal his move and both sides would analyze independently at home before the resumption of the game. His move is virtually forced, usually a disadvantage since the opponent can see it coming.

In this case, however, White's reply is also forced. In the liquidation of pieces which follows, Black obtains an endgame with a strong knight against bad bishop. **41.exd4 Bxe2; 42.Rxe2 Nxf4; 43.d5**. This is the best White has. Sometimes you just have to roll the dice and hope the opponent doesn't figure out the complications properly. Botvinnik's boldness is rewarded here by Lady Fortune.

43...Nxd5? 43...Nxe2, 44.Qxe2 Qxh4 would have won for Black. For example: 45.e6 (45.d6 Rfe8; 46.d7 Qf4+; 47.Kg2 Rxe5; 48.Qb5 Qg5+; 49.Kf2 Qe7) 45...Qf4+; 46.Kg1 Rfe8; 47.Bf1 c4; 48.Qxc4 Qe3+; 49.Kg2 Rxe6 exploiting the pin on the pawn at d5, as pointed out by Botvinnik. **44.f4 Nc7; 45.Red2 Rxd2; 46.Rxd2 Ne6; 47.Bf1**.

The tables have turned, and the bishop is stronger than the knight. **47...Rd8; 48.Kg3 Kg7; 49.Bc4 Rxd2; 50.Qxd2**. Now Botvinnik infiltrates with the queen and the weak position of the Black king allows the e-pawn to advance, even though that may seem difficult from the current position where the pawn is doubly blockaded.

50...Qd8; 51.Qf2 Nd4; 52.Qg2 Qd7; 53.Qa8 a4; 54.Qg8+ Kh6; 55.Qf8+ Kh5; 56.Qf6 h6; 57.e6. The advanced pawn is danger enough, but White also threatens to capture the knight with the queen and deliver mate at e2. **White won.**

(60) KARPOV - MALANIUK
Soviet Championship, 1988

1.d4 f5; 2.g3 Nf6; 3.Bg2 g6; 4.c4 Bg7.

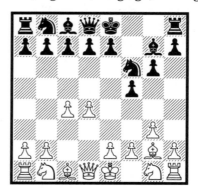

In the Leningrad Variation, Black concedes the center to White and hopes to be able to obtain counterplay later. In this game, Karpov takes on one of the leading specialists in the line. **5.Nf3 d6; 6.0–0 0–0; 7.Nc3.** White can also play 7.b3 here, though play is likely to transpose after a couple of moves. **7...Qe8; 8.b3 Na6.** Not the most respectable plan. More common is an immediate strike in the center. 8...e5!?; 9.dxe5 dxe5; 10.e4 Nc6; 11.Ba3 Rf7; 12.Nd5 looks good, but Malaniuk has been able to defend this position against his fellow Grandmasters. Unfortunately, those games came after this one. **9.Ba3.** For some reason, authoritative publications mention only 9.a4 and 9.Bb2, but this move makes a lot of sense too. **9...c6; 10.Qd3 Bd7; 11.Rfe1 Rd8; 12.Rad1.**

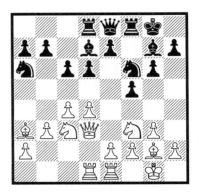

White has a magnificent position, and is ready for the central break at e4. **12...Kh8; 13.e4 fxe4; 14.Nxe4 Bf5**. The pin is defused immediately by Karpov. **15.Nxf6 Bxf6; 16.Qe3 Qf7; 17.h3 Nc7; 18.Re2**. White builds slowly, using a policy of restraining enemy pieces before trying to directly exploit the holes in Black's position. **18...Bc8; 19.Ng5 Qg8; 20.Qd2 Ne6; 21.Nxe6 Bxe6**.

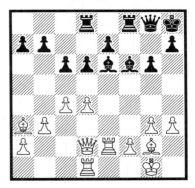

Black' bishops and pawn structure look artificial. **22.Rde1 Bd7**. Now Karpov invests an exchange to pick up the weak e-pawn, which is always a problem for Black in the Leningrad Dutch. **23.Rxe7 Bxe7; 24.Rxe7 Rf6**. Black can't afford to lose the d-pawn, too. **25.d5 Qf8; 26.Re3 Kg8; 27.Bb2 Rf5; 28.Qd4**. The dominate White battery on the a1–h8 diagonal is worth much much more than a little material. **28...Re5; 29.Rxe5 dxe5; 30.Qxe5 Kf7**. Black cannot hope to survive this position. Just look at White's bishops!

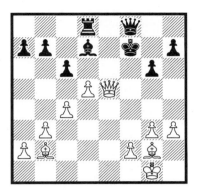

It is not surprising that White completely owns the center and can attack at will. **31.d6 Bf5; 32.c5 h5; 33.g4 hxg4; 34.hxg4 Bd3; 35.Bd5+. White won**.

Let's now look at a more unusual variation in the Dutch as a World Champion pushes the game into new territory early in the game.

(61) PETROSIAN - NIELSEN
Copenhagen, 1960

1.d4 f5; 2.Bg5. This move looks very strange, but it has a serious point. If Black wants to play a Classical Dutch, then ...e6 is needed. This move prevents that. If Black tries to prepare it with ...Nf6, then White will capture the knight and really mess up the pawn structure. A World Champion will often steer into a sideline for psychological purposes. It isn't important that the move may be less ambitious than the main lines.

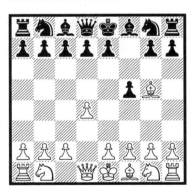

Notice, however, that unlike most unorthodox openings, these diversions by Champions involve normal, developing moves. Played in a strange order, perhaps, but never structurally weakening. **2...g6**. The most principled reply, though it is noteworthy that this is not a formation which appeals to all Dutch players. 2...h6 is playable, but does weaken the kingside, something you don't want to do against Petrosian! **3.Nd2**. The premature attack with 3.h4 is not for Petrosian! 3.Nc3 is more accurate, perhaps, because Black might be able to work the long diagonal here.

Andrew Martin, in his provocative and entertaining book on the Anti-Dutch, notes that "2.Bg5 leaves the b2 pawn weak so a quick ...c5 develops good counterplay." He has a point, but I am not sure that it applies to Petrosian's system, which is headed toward a Torre Attack.

3...Bg7; 4.c3 Nf6; 5.e3. White is going to adopt a Torre formation, but Black has a pawn at f5, so the d-pawn can be deployed at d6 instead of d5, as the e4 square is already guarded. **5...d6; 6.Ngf3 Nc6; 7.Qb3**. The weakness of the light squares will keep the Black king from escaping to the kingside. **7...h6; 8.Bxf6 Bxf6; 9.e4 e5**.

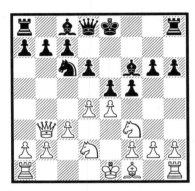

Black must have underestimated the power of the pin applied by Petrosian with his next move. **10.Bb5 Kf8**. 10...Bd7; 11.exf5 gxf5; 12.dxe5 dxe5; 13.0-0-0 Qe7; 14.Bxc6 Bxc6; 15.Nd4 Bxg2; 16.Nxf5 Qf7; 17.Nc4 sets up nasty threats at d6. **11.Bxc6 bxc6; 12.dxe5 dxe5; 13.Qa4**. Black's position is a mess. **13...Qd6; 14.Nb3 Bd7; 15.Rd1 Qe7; 16.Nc5! Be8**. 16...Qxc5; 17.Rxd7 Qb6; 18.Qc4 demonstrates the weakness of the Black king. **17.b4 Kg7**. Black has almost castled by hand.

18.0-0. White waited a long time to castle, but the position is now so overwhelming that Petrosian could take a bit of time out to get the remaining rook into the game. **18...Rf8; 19.Qa6!** The threat is primitive: Qb7! **19...fxe4; 20.Nd2 e3**. Black offers the pawn back. **21.Nde4!** This is much stronger than taking the pawn. **21...exf2+; 22.Rxf2 Bg5; 23.Rxf8 Kxf8; 24.Nxg5 hxg5**.

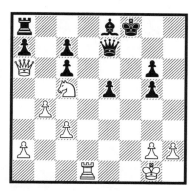

Black's extra pawn is a joke, and White now delivers the final blow. **25.Qb7**. Black resigned. The rook has no escape: 25...Rd8; 26.Rxd8 Qxd8; 27.Ne6+.

TORRE ATTACK

The **Torre Attack** is very easy to play. White's early moves are almost automatic, and there are no variations which contain maniacal complications. This makes it appealing to World Champions, because it can be played without particular preparation.

The basic elements of the Torre Attack are a pawn at d4, a knight at f3, and a bishop at g5.

White's typical formation

1.d4
2.Nf3
3.Bg5

As long as Black does not immediately engage the White forces, White will continue to develop the rest of the pieces according to plan: pawns at c3 and e3, bishop at d3, kingside castling, knight at d2, queen at e2 and rooks according to the demands of the position.

Black has many possible responses, but none lead to particularly sharp play. The Torre is a risk-free opening, but White's advantage will be minimal against a well-prepared opponent.

(62) PETROSIAN - WADE
Leipzig (Olympiad), 1991

1.d4 Nf6; 2.Nf3 b6; 3.Bg5 Bb7; 4.Nbd2 g6; 5.e3. This is a typical starting move order. Black has set up a formation which will make it difficult to construct the ideal pawn center. **5...Bg7; 6.Bd3**.

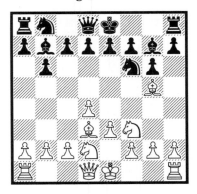

Black has chosen to fianchetto both of his bishops, a plan which has the usual drawback of making it difficult to play in the center. **6...c5; 7.c3 d6**. Taking the e5-square away from the Nf3. **8.0–0 0–0; 9.Qe2 h6; 10.Bh4 Nbd7; 11.h3 Nh5; 12.Nh2**. This move prevents Black from playing ...g5. **12...cxd4; 13.cxd4 Bf6**. An interesting decision, and probably a wise one. Even though Black parts with an important defender, he eliminates the annoying kingside pressure. **14.Bxf6 Ndxf6; 15.Rac1 Rc8; 16.Nhf3**. Now that the dark-squared bishops are gone, the knight returns to its post. **16...Rc7; 17.Nb3**. In order to overprotect c1 and allow the exchange of rooks. **17...Rxc1; 18.Rxc1 Qa8!**

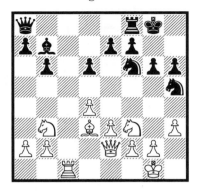

Black's position is now fully equal, but a fascinating endgame lies ahead. **19.Ba6 Rc8**. 19...Bxf3; 20.Qxf3 Qxf3; 21.gxf3 is better for White, since the powerful bishop makes up for the pawn structure and the weakness at h3 is particularly hard to exploit. Moreover, White has control of the only open file. **20.Rxc8+ Bxc8; 21.Nbd2.** 21.Qc4? would be strongly met by 21...Bxh3! **21...Qc6; 22.Bxc8 Qxc8; 23.Qc4 Qxc4; 24.Nxc4 Nd5; 25.Kf1 Nhf6.**

26.Ke2. White effectively exploits the fact that Black must take time to get his knights back into the game. The centralized king is a definite advantage, and Black will soon have to spend time to emulate it. **26...Kf8; 27.Ne1! Ke8; 28.Nd3 Kd7; 29.f3 Nc7; 30.e4**.

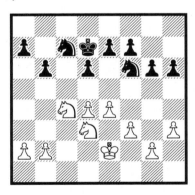

White now has firm control of the center and enjoys a significant advantage, though Black's game is by no means hopeless. **30...Nfe8; 31.h4 f6?**. Ne6 was necessary. Now White pins down the Black pieces and quashes all counterplay. **32.d5! e6.** 32...f5; 33.exf5 gxf5; 34.Ne3 Nf6; 35.Nf4 e6; 36.dxe6+ Nxe6; 37.Nxe6 Kxe6; 38.Kd3 and the superior pawn structure gives White all the chances.

33.dxe6+ Nxe6; 34.Ne3 g5; 35.Nf5?! Better was 35.h5. **35...h5!; 36.Ke3 N8g7**. 36...N8c7! was the right direction for the horse. 37.hxg5 fxg5; 38.f4 d5!; 39.Ne5+ Ke8; 40.fxg5 Nxg5; 41.Ng7+ Kf8; 42.Nxh5 Nxe4 with a probable draw, though in double knight endings nothing can be taken for granted. **37.Nxg7 Nxg7; 38.hxg5 fxg5; 39.f4**.

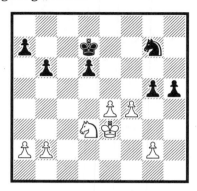

39...gxf4+?. 39...Ne6! would have saved the game. 40.fxg5 Nxg5; 41.Nf4 h4; 42.Kd4 Kc6; 43.e5 dxe5+; 44.Kxe5 Kc5; 45.Kf5 Nf7; 46.Ng6 Kd4; 47.Nxh4 Kd3; 48.g4 Nh6+; 49.Kg5 Nxg4; 50.Kxg4 Kc2 and the monarch munches the pawns. **40.Nxf4 Ke7; 41.Kd4! Kf6**. Now Petrosian gives a good endgame lesson! 41...Ne6+; 42.Nxe6 Kxe6; 43.g3! **42.Kd5 Kg5; 43.Ne2! Ne8; 44.Kc6 Nf6; 45.Kb7 Nxe4; 46.Kxa7 Kf5**. The king just can't find a way into the kingside! **47.Kxb6 Ke5; 48.a4 d5; 49.a5 d4**.

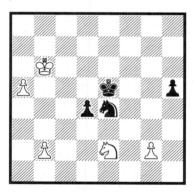

50.Nxd4! Kxd4; 51.Kc6! Nc5; 52.b4 Nd3. 52...Na6; 53.b5 Nb8+; 54.Kc7 Kc5; 55.a6!. **53.Kb5! Ke5**. 53...Nf4; 54.a6 Nd5; 55.a7 Nc7+; 56.Kc6 Na8; 57.Kb7. **54.a6 Nxb4** and Black resigned without waiting for White's reply.

(63) SPASSKY - OSNOS
USSR Championship, 1963

1.d4 Nf6; 2.Nf3 e6; 3.Bg5 c5; 4.e3. The Torre Attack and the advantage that White can usually define the contour of the middlegame. **4...Qb6**.

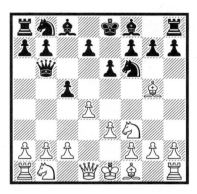

This is a provocative move, and it leads to a complex variation which is at the heart of the theory of the Torre Attack. **5.Nbd2**. The pawn sacrifice is much more promising than the cowardly 5.Qc1. **5...Qxb2.** Best. Spassky has demonstrated the inadequacy of one of the alternatives. 5...d5; 6.Bxf6 gxf6; 7.c4! cxd4; 8.exd4 dxc4; 9.Bxc4 Nc6; 10.0–0 Bd7; 11.d5! exd5; 12.Qe2+ Ne7; 13.Bxd5 0–0–0; 14.Bxf7 Ng6; 15.Nc4 Qa6; 16.Rfd1 and White had a big advantage in Spassky-A. Zaitsev, USSR 1963. **6.Bd3**.

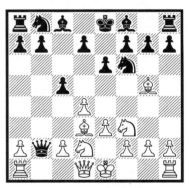

Black now chooses between retreating the queen, acting in the center, or simply developing. **6...cxd4**. This is the most aggressive move. Developing with ...Nc6 is a reasonable alternative as is 6...d5, now that White has already moved the bishop from f1. **7.exd4 Qc3**. Black doesn't fare any better with other moves. This at least keeps the knight at d2 pinned and the queen is safe here. **8.0–0 d5; 9.Re1 Be7**. 9...Nc6 is a possible alternative. **10.Re3 Qc7**.

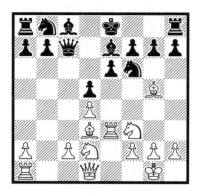

Black still has an extra pawn, but is way behind in development and the light-squared bishop has no future. **11.Ne5!** Black's pieces are in no position to stop a kingside attack, and thus the king is locked in the center. The occupation of e5 by the knight is an integral part of White's strategy in the Torre. **11...Nc6.** 11...0–0? 12.Bxf6 Bxf6 13.Bxh7+!! Kxh7 14.Qh5+ Kg8 15.Rh3 and White wins. **12.c3 Nxe5; 13.dxe5 Ng8.** An ugly retreat. Notice that after 13 moves Black only has two pieces developed.

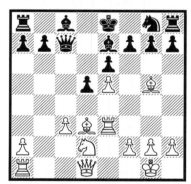

13...Ne4; 14.Nxe4 dxe4; 15.Bxe7 exd3; 16.Bd6 Qxc3; 17.Rxd3 Qa5; 18.Rc1! and the threat of Bc7 gives White the advantage, for example 18...Bd7; 19.Rc7 Qb5; 20.Be7! **14.Nf3 h6; 15.Bf4 Bd7; 16.Nd4 Bg5; 17.Bxg5 hxg5; 18.Qg4.** White's command of the center and kingside pressure is overwhelming. **18...Qxc3; 19.Nb3 Nh6; 20.Qxg5 Qb4; 21.Rg3 Qf8?.** 21...g6; 22.Qf6 Qf8 fails to prevent 23.Nc5! **22.Rc1 f6; 23.Qe3 f5; 24.Nc5!**

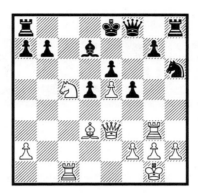

24...f4. The fork is not important, but the opening of the diagonal is!
25.Bg6+ Ke7; 26.Qa3! White won.

10. INDIAN GAMES

INTRODUCTION

The **Indian Games** (1.d4 Nf6) were given their name by the great Savielly Tartakower, to replace the derogatory term "Irregular Opening" which no longer properly applied to the newly respectable openings such as the King's Indian and Queen's Indian defenses.

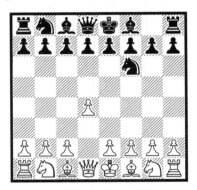

These openings tend to be highly transpositional, and can lead right back into the Closed Games if Black chooses an early ...d5. But the distinctively Indian lines are those which involve the fianchetto of one bishop, either at g7 or b7. We can call the ones with the kingside fianchetto the *West Indians*.

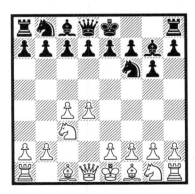

The ones where the action is on the queenside are the *East Indi-ans*.

South

North
↓

North

We are assuming that White is sitting on the North side of the board and that the battlefield and enemy Black forces are to the south. Historically, major acts of war have more often originated in the Northern Hemisphere so this is a reasonable perspective. As with the case of the first move, no racial motives should be read into the inherent advantages of the White pieces, and in fact, in the old days, White didn't always get to move first.

OVERVIEW

Most of the major Indian Games have been a serious part of the opening repertoire of our World Champions. The King's Indian, Queen's Indian, Nimzoindian and Gruenfeld are all encountered frequently at the World Championship level. Fischer and Kasparov have been devoted to the Indian Games. There is an entire book devoted to Kasparov on the King's Indian (by Kasparov and Keene, Batsford)!

The **Queen's Indian** and **Nimzoindian Defense** are among the easiest Indians to play, though the **Benko Gambit**, a positional rather than aggressive gambit, is also quite straightforward. The sharp **Benoni** has fewer fans at championship level, though the great Mikhail Tal wielded it as a powerful weapon which slew many mighty opponents.

The **Old Indian** and **Bogoindian** are a bit more boring, but they do provide interesting diversions from the major Indian Games.

When faced with the East Indians, White can choose to allow the Nimzoindian by playing 3.Nc3, avoid it with 3.Nf3, or head for the **Catalan**, a hybrid of Indian, Closed and Flank Game, with 3.g3.

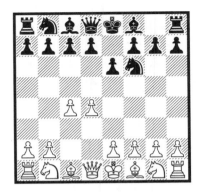

You might think that players would have a strong preference for 3.Nf3 or 3.Nc3. But look at the chart below showing how the World Champions handled the East Indians. Do keep in mind that the early champions rarely adopted 1...Nf6, which did not achieve respectability until about 1925. Also remember that Bobby Fischer was a die-hard fan of 1.e4, and the one exception is trivial.

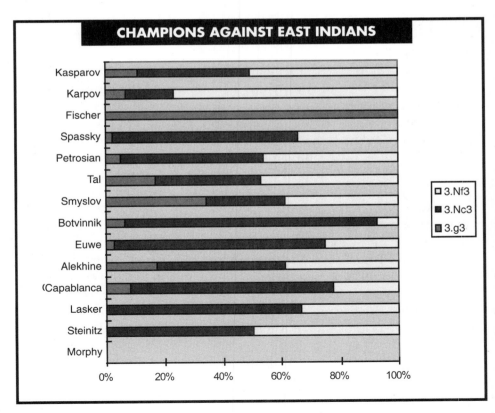

What we find, then, is that the World Champions liked to play both Nc3 and Nf3 against the East Indians. Dealing with the West Indians does not involve the same choice, and the knight is usually developed to c3 at move 3.

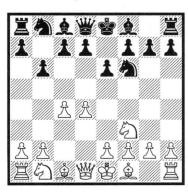

Now Black will choose between the **King's Indian** with 3...Bg7 and the **Gruenfeld** with 3...d5.

We'll start our examination of Indians in the East and follow the sun to the West. Morphy won't accompany us on this journey because he didn't play them.

QUEEN'S INDIAN

One opening which will not rattle anyone's nerves is the **Queen's Indian**, which begins 1.d4 Nf6; 2.c4 e6; 3.Nf3 b6.

1.d4	Nf6
2.c4	e6
3.Nf3	b6

It is a very respectable defense, but don't play it when you need to win. Black gets a comfortable game but unless White overextends, there are no targets for Black to aim at. For most of the last 50 years White had almost automatically fianchettoed the bishop at g2 with 4.g3, to which Black can reply with either 4...Bb7 or 4...Ba6.

At b7, the bishop battles for control of e4, as seen in the typical variation 1.d4 Nf6; 2.c4 e6; 3.Nf3 b6; 4.g3 Bb7; 5.Bg2 Be7; 6.O-O O-O; 7.Nc3 Ne4.

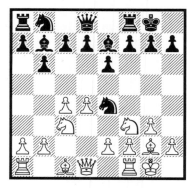

If Black chooses to put the bishop at a6, the goal is to pressure the pawn at c4, now that White's light-squared bishop is committed to g2.

Two World Champions, Petrosian and Kasparov, changed the landscape radically when they adopted a plan with a3 and Nc3 and a full assault on the center.

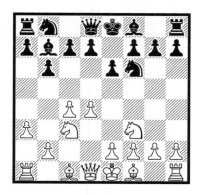

White will play Qc2 and then e4, so Black usually prevents this with 5...d5. This position dominated the Queen's Indian in the 1980s, and is still played often. Nevertheless, the Queen's Indian is a popular opening at all levels of play.

(64) KARPOV - SALOV
Linares, 1993

1.d4 Nf6; 2.c4 e6; 3.Nf3 b6; 4.g3. Karpov sticks to the traditional handling of the Queen's Indian. His arch-rival Kasparov elevated Petrosian's alternative 4.a3 or 4.Nc3 followed by 5.a3 to the main line. **4...Bb7; 5.Bg2 Be7; 6.Nc3 Ne4**.

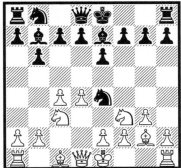

7.Bd2. 7.Qc2 is the most common move, but this alternative is frequently seen. **7...Bf6; 8.0–0 0–0; 9.Rc1 c5**. It is already established theory that this is a good move. It leads to a series of exchanges. **10.d5 exd5; 11.cxd5 Nxd2; 12.Nxd2 d6; 13.Nde4 Be7; 14.f4**. This odd-looking move is actually best, because White's plans involve a kingside pawnstorm. **14...Nd7; 15.g4 a6; 16.a4 Re8**. All this was well-known at the time, and Salov's new move is just a logical alternative to 16...Nf6. **17.g5 Bf8**.

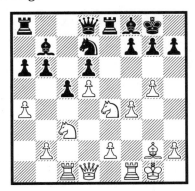

18.Kh1! Karpov's prophylactic move insures that there will be no problems when Black later stations the queen at b6. **18...b5; 19.axb5 axb5; 20.Nxb5 Qb6**. This sacrifice would have been more effective if White's king still stood at g1! **21.Nbc3 Qb4**. Black has no time for maneuvers such as 21...Ba6 because the White rook quickly penetrates the kingside with Rf1–f3 and then it can operate on the g- or h-files. **22.Qd3 Nb6; 23.Qg3 Kh8; 24.Rcd1 Nc4; 25.b3 Nb6**. Now a surprising move cracks open the Black position.

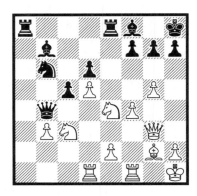

26.g6! fxg6. Taking with the other pawn also loses: 26...hxg6; 27.Qh4+ Kg8; 28.Ng5 and it is all over. **27.f5! gxf5; 28.Rxf5 Nd7.** Black cannot marshall the defensive forces in time. **29.Rdf1 Ne5; 30.R5f4 Qb6; 31.Ng5 Ng6**. Now for an elegant finish! **32.Nf7+ Kg8; 33.Qxg6!!** This brilliant sacrifice ends the game. Black resigned. There is no defense, for example 33...hxg6; 34.Rh4 Be7; 35.Rh8 mate.

Kasparov has made tremendous contributions to the theory of the Queen's Indian, so much so that he now has a major variation named after him.

(65) KASPAROV - NAJDORF
Bugojno, 1982

1.d4 Nf6; 2.c4 e6; 3.Nf3 b6; 4.a3. 4.Nc3 Bb4; 5.Bg5 Bb7; 6.e3 h6; 7.Bh4 is also popular, but after capturing at c3, Black gets counterplay. 7...Bxc3+; (7...g5; 8.Bg3 Ne4; 9.Qc2 Bxc3+; 10.bxc3 d6; 11.Bd3 f5; 12.d5 Nc5; 13.h4 g4; 14.Nd4 Qf6; 15.0–0 Nxd3; 16.Qxd3 and White was better in a game from the Kasparov-Timman match in 1985.) 8.bxc3 d6; 9.Nd2 g5; 10.Bg3 Qe7; 11.a4 a5; 12.h4 Rg8; 13.hxg5 hxg5, and Black had a fine game in game 18 of the 1986 Kasparov-Karpov World Championship match. **4...Bb7**.

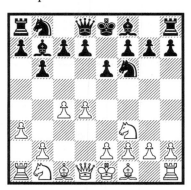

4...c5 is less effective. We have two good examples in Kasparov's crushing defeats of Van der Wiel and Fedorowicz at the 1981 World Youth Team Championship. Both games continued with 5.d5 Ba6 6.Qc2 and now:

A) 6...Qe7; 7.Bg5 exd5; 8.Nc3 Bxc4; 9.e4 h6; 10.Bxf6 Qxf6; 11.exd5 Bxf1; 12.Kxf1 d6; 13.Re1+ Be7; 14.Ne4 Qg6; 15.Qa4+ Kf8; 16.h4 and Van der Wiel eventually lost. The kingside pressure was just too much.

B) 6...exd5; 7.cxd5 g6; 8.Nc3 Bg7; 9.g3 0-0; 10.Bg2 d6; 11.0-0 Re8; 12.Re1 Qc7; 13.Bf4 Nh5; 14.Bd2 Nd7; 15.Qa4 Bb7; 16.Qh4 a6; 17.Rac1 b5; 18.b4 Qd8; 19.Bg5 f6; 20.Bd2 f5; 21.Bg5 Qb6; 22.e4 cxb4; 23.axb4 Rac8; 24.Be3 Qd8; 25.Bg5 Qb6. As team captain, I was very worried here, seeing the Black pieces drift away from the kingside. I had no idea how Kasparov would do it, but I expected a breakthrough soon. 26.exf5 Rxe1+; 27.Rxe1 Bxc3; 28.Re7 Rc4; 29.Qh3 Bc8; 30.fxg6 Ndf6; 31.Bxf6 Nxf6; 32.gxh7+ Kf8; 33.h8Q+ Kxe7; 34.Qg7+ and Fedorowicz resigned. The American team did manage to draw the match, thanks to a fine effort by Joel Benjamin.

5.Nc3. This is the Kasparov-Petrosian variation, though now it is usually just called the Kasparov Variation, since he not only rehabilitated the line, but also set a good example by racking up many points as White.

5...d5. His opponent, the great Miguel Najdorf (developer of the Najdorf Variation of the Sicilian) was not well prepared for this event. He was supposed to be the arbiter, but when one of the players couldn't make it the veteran gamely stepped in. Still, he plays well in the opening, following the main lines and improving on Petrosian's play.

5...Ne4 led to one of the most famous games in the variation, played by Kasparov against Ulf Andersson at the Tilburg Interpolis tournament of 1981. 6.Nxe4 Bxe4; 7.Nd2 Bg6; 8.g3 Nc6; 9.e3 a6; 10.b4 b5;11.cxb5 axb5; 12.Bb2 Na7; 13.h4 h6; 14.d5 exd5; 15.Bg2 c6; 16.0-0 f6; 17.Re1 Be7; 18.Qg4 Kf7; 19.h5 Bh7; 20.e4! dxe4; 21.Bxe4 Bxe4; 22.Nxe4 Nc8; 23.Rad1 Ra7; 24.Nxf6 gxf6; 25.Qg6+ Kf8; 26.Bc1 d5; 27.Rd4 Nd6; 28.Rg4 Nf7; 29.Bxh6+ Ke8; 30.Bg7. Andersson resigned.

6.cxd5 Nxd5. Black usually captures with the knight. 6...exd5; 7.g3. White gets a superior position. **7.e3.** Kasparov has also been effective with 7.Qc2, especially against Karpov. **7.Qc2 Nd7; 8.Nxd5 exd5; 9.Bg5 f6; 10.Bf4 c5; 11.g3 g6; 12.h4** with a better position in game 41 of the 1984/85 World Championship. **7...Be7; 8.Bb5+ c6; 9.Bd3 Nxc3.** 9...0–0; 10.e4 Nxc3; 11.bxc3 was better for White in Kasparov-Marjanovic, Banja Luka Yugoslavia 1979.

10.bxc3 c5; 11.0–0 Nc6. This is an attempt to improve on the simple castling, where White can get an advantage via rapid development. 11...0–0; 12.Qc2 g6; 13.e4 Nc6; 14.Bh6 and White had the advantage in Kasparov-Petrosian, Moscow 1981. Kasparov later blundered away the game in time pressure. **12.e4 0–0; 13.Be3 cxd4; 14.cxd4.**

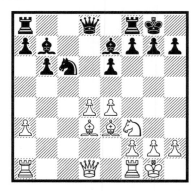

White has a good central position, but Black has no weaknesses. **14...Rc8; 15.Qe2 Na5; 16.Rfe1!** Kasparov realizes that the e-pawn will eventually need protection. **16...Qd6.** 16...Kh8; 17.h4 Bxh4; 18.Rad1 Be7; 19.d5 Bc5; 20.Bf4 led to a messy game in Kasparov-Groszpeter, also from the 1981 World Youth Team championship. **17.d5! exd5; 18.e5 Qe6; 19.Nd4! Qxe5; 20.Nf5.** White has plenty of compensation for the pawn, with active pieces and attacking changes on the kingside. Black's queenside forces are out of play. **20...Bf6; 21.Qg4 Rce8?**

I recall that as I watched this game from the audience (which was large, even in the bucolic little Yugoslav town), this move made little sense to me. I had been concentrating on a different idea. 21...Qc3 was a good move, I thought. Another spectator pointed out to me that this could invite 22.Ne7+! Bxe7; 23.Bd4 but it wasn't hard to see 23...Qxd4; 24.Qxd4 Bf6; 25.Qg4 Bxa1; 26.Rxa1, and the question is, does White have a chance to win?

It is hard to evaluate the position. White can try to attack on the h-file or get a rook to the seventh rank. If a pair of rooks are exchanged, then it is likely that the White queen will be able to infiltrate and win a pawn or two. Still, White's advantage would be pretty small, far less than in the game. **22.Bd2.** Now the queen sacrifice fails for tactical reasons. **22...Qxa1; 23.Rxa1 Bxa1; 24.Nxg7 Bxg7; 25.Bh6.**

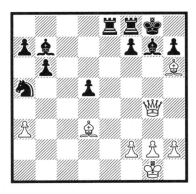

Najdorf resigned. **White won.**

NIMZOINDIAN DEFENSE

If White takes up the challenge with 3.Nc3, then Black can adopt the **Nimzoindian Defense**, a reliable weapon for Black which is undoubtedly Aron Nimzowitsch's greatest contribution to opening theory.

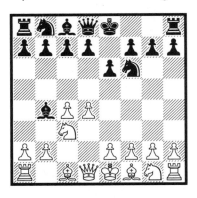

1.d4   Nf6
2.c4   e6
3.Nc3   Bb4

Once again there is a naked battle for control of e4. If White gets a pawn there without paying a penalty, then Black is in trouble. To prevent this, Black is willing to part with the dark-squared bishop to get rid of the knight at c3, and thereby undermine support of the e4-square.

There are many World Champions in the "Nimzoindian Hall of Fame." Anatoly Karpov is at the head of the class. Though almost allergic to playing the West Indians, Karpov just loves to sit on the Black side of the Nimzo. Botvinnik, Smyslov and Spassky were fans, and even Capablanca adopted this hypermodern approach. Kasparov and Fischer use it less frequently, but no less effectively.

As White, fashion is divided into two camps, those favoring 4.e3 and the stalwarts of the classical 4.Qc2. Preference here tends to pattern with the prevailing winds. 4.Qc2 was considered harmless for many years, but now takes center stage. A shift back to 4.e3 is already appearing, however.

Anyone can play the Nimzoindian, but only players with a good appreciation of the importance of the center can play it well.

We have already seen one Nimzoindian in our examination of the Caro-Kann, since the Panov Attack can, and often does, arise in the Nimzoindian. Let's examine the main alternatives here.

(66) PORTISCH - FISCHER
Santa Monica (2nd Piatigorsky Cup), 1966

1.d4 Nf6; 2.c4 e6; 3.Nc3 Bb4. Santa Monica was Nimzoindian heaven, with 13 out of the 90 games featuring the opening! **4.e3 b6**.

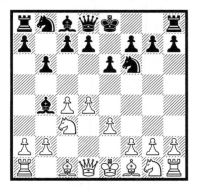

Fischer doesn't want to waste any time getting the light-squared bishop out from behind the pawns, so this variation appealed to him. **5.Nge2 Ba6; 6.Ng3**. 6.a3 is considered slightly more effective, but this move has always been popular, too. **6...Bxc3+**. 6...c5; 7.d5 0–0; 8.e4 gave White the advantage in a clash between World Championship challengers Viktor Korchnoi and Nigel Short, at Madrid 1995. **7.bxc3 d5; 8.Qf3**. Portisch noted the irony that found him on the White side of one of his favorite openings as Black. **8...0–0.**

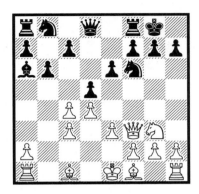

Now capturing at d5 is recommended, but thirty years ago the advance to e4 also looked promising. **9.e4.** 9.cxd5 Qxd5; 10.e4 Qa5; 11.Bxa6 Qxa6; 12.Ne2 (so that White can castle) 12...Nbd7; 13.0-0 c5 gives Black sufficient counterplay. **9...dxe4; 10.Nxe4 Nxe4; 11.Qxe4.**

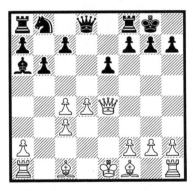

Now Fischer introduced a sacrificial plan, giving up both rooks for the White queen. Portisch admitted that it had come as a surprise — a very unpleasant one. **11...Qd7!** 11...Nd7; 12.Bd3 Nf6; 13.Qh4 gives White good attacking chances. **12.Ba3.** Portisch couldn't get the development of the other bishop to work: 12.Bd3 f5; 13.Qe2 Nc6; 14.0-0 Rae8 and the pawn at c4 is going to become a target. So Portisch decides to give up the queen for two rooks, usually about an even trade. **12...Re8; 13.Bd3 f5**.

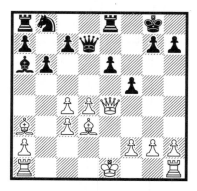

14.Qxa8 Nc6; 15.Qxe8+ Qxe8. White has the bishop pair, but the pawn at c4 is weak and the king has not yet found a safe home. **16.0–0 Na5; 17.Rfe1 Bxc4; 18.Bxc4 Nxc4; 19.Bc1.** The knight completely dominates the bishop, and the rooks are uncoordinated. Black has a huge advantage. **19...c5; 20.dxc5 bxc5; 21.Bf4 h6; 22.Re2 g5.**

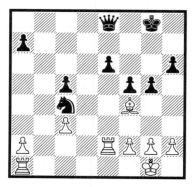

Now White must play 23.Be3 and it will still be rather difficult to win for Black. **23.Be5?; Qd8!; 24.Rae1 Kf7; 25.h3.** This gains a little space for the bishop or king, as needed. But Fischer's next play shuts down all counterplay. **25...f4!; 26.Kh2 a6; 27.Re4 Qd5; 28.h4 Ne3!**

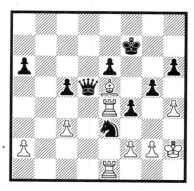

This wins more material, and leads to victory after a few more moves. **29.R1xe3 fxe3; 30.Rxe3 Qxa2; 31.Rf3+ Ke8; 32.Bg7 Qc4; 33.hxg5 hxg5; 34.Rf8+ Kd7; 35.Ra8 Kc6. Black won.**

(67) LAUTIER - KARPOV
Linares, 1995

1.d4 Nf6; 2.c4 e6; 3.Nc3 Bb4; 4.Qc2. The Classical variation has become the main line of the Nimzoindian. **4...0–0; 5.a3 Bxc3+; 6.Qxc3 b6**.

As usual, White has the bishop pair. On the other hand, Black has the lead in development. **7.Bg5 Bb7; 8.e3 d6; 9.f3 Nbd7; 10.Bd3 c5; 11.Ne2 Rc8**. This position is fairly typical of those which arise in the Qc2 lines. The most natural continuation is 12.b4, but that may lead to premature liquidation of pieces with a lot of drawing chances. Probably the best move is to retreat to d2. Lautier stations the lady at b3, but it proves to be an infelicitous post.

12.Qb3?! h6. Better than an immediate capture at d4. This gives Black an opportunity to play ...g5 later. **13.Bh4 cxd4.** Black can also play 14...d5 right away, but Karpov elects to capture. **14.exd4 d5; 15.c5?!** Lautier should simply have castled, as had been played back in 1993. This is a positionally aggressive move, but it is without foundation. 15.cxd5 Bxd5 should be fine for Black. **15...Ba8; 16.Ba6 Rc7; 17.Bg3.** If White captures at b6, Black must be careful. The best response would be to ignore the pawn and simply play 17..Rc6! since 18.b7 fails to 18...Bxb7 and now either 19.Qxb7 Qa5+ or 19.Bxb7 Rb6 picks off a piece.

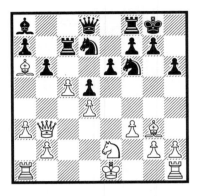

17...bxc5! Well timed! **18.Bxc7 Qxc7; 19.Qc3 e5!** Black's hypermodern opening has led to a powerful central counterattack and White is already in serious trouble. **20.Bd3.** Any capture by the d-pawn can be met by ...d4. **20...exd4; 21.Nxd4 Re8+; 22.Kf1.** White has to abandon hope of castling, and there are no further chances for survival. **22...Qb6; 23.Nf5 d4; 24.Qd2 Ne5; 25.Re1 Re6!** Black prepares to lop off the bishop at d3. This cannot be done immediately because of 26.Rxe8+ Nxe8; 27.Qxd3 Qxb2 when White can retreat the queen to e2 and it is hard to find a convincing line for Black. **26.Bb1 Bb7; 27.Kf2.** Perhaps 27.Ba2 would have held out longer. **27...d3; 28.Rhf1 c4+; 29.Kg3 Nh5+; 30.Kh3.** Black eventually gets mated if the king advances to h4. **30...Ng6!; 31.g3 Bc8; 32.Re4 Qc5; 33.g4 Ngf4+!**

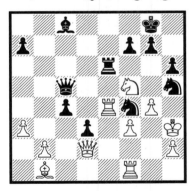

The decisive attack begins. **34.Rxf4 Re2; 35.Qc1 Nxf4+; 36.Qxf4 Bxf5; 37.gxf5 Rxb2.**

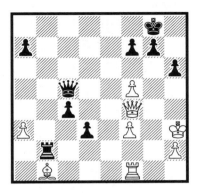

After most of the pieces have left the board, the advanced Black pawns are too difficult to stop. **38.Re1?** The only try was Qe4, but Black should still win. **38...Qf2; 39.Qg3 Qxg3+; 40.hxg3.** The queens are gone and White has a piece for two pawns. Given time, there might be some hope, but Karpov grants no extensions, and finishes the game by sacrificing the exchange and letting the pawns do the talking. **40...Rxb1! Black won.**

(68) BOTVINNIK - KERES
Hague-Moscow (World Championship Tournament), 1948

1.d4 Nf6; 2.c4 e6; 3.Nc3 Bb4; 4.e3. The Saemisch Variation can also be played immediately with 4.a3. **4...0–0; 5.a3!?** White gets an extra pawn in the center and two bishops in return for his doubled c-pawns. **5...Bxc3+; 6.bxc3.**

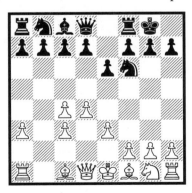

6...Re8. Black's plan is to advance the pawn to e5. This is a typical strategy. Although the pawn has already made one move, and the Black forces are not developed, the mere presence of a Black pawn at e5 puts tremendous pressure on White's center. **7.Ne2 e5; 8.Ng3.** Now if ...e4 is ever played, Botvinnik envisions putting pressure on it by f3. **8...d6; 9.Be2 Nbd7?!** If Black wants to play ...c5, the knight seems better placed on c6. **10.0–0 c5**.

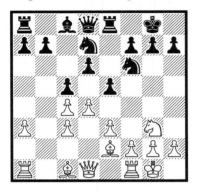

11.f3! Botvinnik pursues his plan (and the World Championship) by occupying the center with e4, possible due to the c3-pawn that protects d4 adequately. **11...cxd4; 12.cxd4 Nb6; 13.Bb2.** Now Keres was hoping to lock up the center with 13...exd4 14 exd4 (14 Qxd4 Na4!) 14...d5!. But Botvinnik understood this better than almost any player in history. **13...exd4; 14.e4!** Black has no counterplay and must worry about his isolated pawn at d6. **14...Be6; 15.Rc1 Re7.** Black plans to retreat the knight to e8. White's forces are not in a position to attack. **16.Qxd4 Qc7; 17.c5 dxc5; 18.Rxc5.** The idea is to transfer the rook to g5. **18...Qf4; 19.Bc1! Qb8; 20.Rg5 Nbd7.** Black hopes to move once more and play ...Ne8, followed by ...f6, but his kingside is ripped open immediately.

21.Rxg7+!! Kxg7; 22.Nh5+ Kg6. 22...Kf8; 23.Nxf6 Nxf6; 24.Qxf6 Ke8; 25.Bb5+ Rd7; 26.Bg5 and Black is in deep trouble. **23.Qe3!** Checkmate looms, so Black resigned.

BOGOINDIAN

Of all the candidates for most boring opening, the **Bogoindian**, named for Efim Bogoljubow (Bogoljubow-Indian being just too hard on the tongue) is the most commonly seen. The idea behind 1.d4 Nf6; 2.c4 e6; 3.Nf3 Bb4+ is to avoid the Queen's Indian or reach Queen's Indian positions after the dark-squared bishops have been removed from the board.

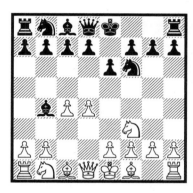

1.d4	Nf6
2.c4	e6
3.Nf3	Bb4+

Usually White interposes a bishop at d2, after which Black can exchange or defend the bishop with 3...a5 or 3...Qe7. White can get a minuscule advantage out of the position, but it is not easy to do much with it.

In the Bogoindian, Black is essentially playing for a draw. Playing it regularly can lead to a reputation as a wimp. At professional levels, of course, if the wimp gets the half-point, it is not bad. Of course if White overextends, Black can take advantage and score a good point. World Champions use it when the occasion suggests, but not with much relish.

(69) KASPAROV - YUSUPOV
Soviet Championship, 1981

1.d4. This game contains one of those moves that is pure genius, a sacrifice of great profundity. It is one of my all-time favorites. **1...Nf6; 2.c4 e6; 3.Nf3 Bb4+.** The Bogoindian Defense is considered playable, but boring, Kasparov manages to liven this one up! 3...b6; 4.g3 Bb7; 5.Bg2 Bb4+; 6.Bd2

Bxd2+; 7.Qxd2 0–0; 8.Nc3 Ne4; 9.Qc2 Nxc3; 10.Ng5 Ne4; 11.Bxe4 Bxe4; 12.Qxe4 Qxg5; 13.Qxa8 Nc6; 14.Qb7 Nxd4; 15.Rd1 used to be popular, for example. 15...Qe5; (15...c5; 16.e3 Nc2+; 17.Kd2 Qf5; 18.Qg2 Nb4; 19.e4 Qf6; 20.Kc1 Nxa2+; 21.Kb1 Nb4; 22.Rxd7 Nc6; 23.f4 e5; 24.Rhd1 Nd4; 25.Rxa7 exf4; 26.gxf4 Qxf4; 27.Re1 Nf3; 28.Re2 Nd4; 29.Re1 was agreed drawn in Euwe-Capablanca, Match Amsterdam 1931)

16.e3 Nc2+; 17.Ke2 d5; 18.Rd2 Qxb2; 19.cxd5 Qb5+; 20.Kf3 Nb4; 21.Rc1 Qa5; 22.d6 cxd6; 23.Rc8 g6; 24.Rxf8+ Kxf8; 25.Qc8+ Ke7; 26.Qc7+ Kf6; 27.Qc3+ Ke7; 28.Qc7+ was eventually drawn, Euwe-Capablanca, Match Amsterdam 1931. **4.Bd2**.

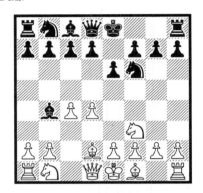

The normal reply. Now Black can exchange bishops, or defend with ...a5 or ...Qe7. **4...a5** Here are some top-level encounters featuring the alternatives.

A) 4...Bxd2+; 5.Qxd2 d5; 6.g3 0–0; 7.Bg2 Nbd7; 8.Qc2 has brought Karpov the advantage against Bogoindian specialist Ulf Andersson. 8...c6 (8...b6; 9.cxd5 Nxd5; 10.0–0 Bb7; 11.e4 N5f6; 12.Nc3 c5; 13.Rad1 cxd4; 14.Nxd4 Qe7; 15.Rfe1 Ne5; 16.f4 Nc6 and now Karpov unleashed 17.Nd5! exd5; 18.Nxc6 Bxc6; 19.exd5 Qxe1+; 20.Rxe1 Bxd5; 21.Bxd5 Nxd5; 22.Qa4 with a significant advantage for White in Karpov-Andersson, Enkoping (rapid) 1995.) 9.Nbd2 Qe7; 10.0–0 e5; 11.cxd5 Nxd5; 12.e4 N5f6; 13.Rfe1 Rd8; 14.Rad1 exd4; 15.Nxd4 Nb6; 16.N2b3 Bg4; 17.f3 Be6; 18.Qc5 and White won quickly: 18...Qe8; 19.e5 Nfd7; 20.Qc1 Nf8; 21.f4 Bxb3; 22.Nxb3 Ne6; 23.Rd6 Nc8; 24.Rxc6, Karpov-Andersson, Reykjavik (World Cup), 1991.

B) 4...Qe7; 5.g3 Nc6; 6.Bg2 Bxd2+; 7.Nbxd2 d6; 8.0–0 0–0; 9.e4 e5; 10.d5 gives White too much space, as seen in the game between Euwe and Flohr, played at the famous AVRO tournament of 1938.

C) 4...c5; 5.Bxb4 cxb4 leads to an interesting position, and again the fianchetto is correct. 6.g3 b6; 7.Bg2 Bb7; 8.0–0 0–0; 9.Qb3 a5; 10.a3 Na6; 11.Nbd2 d6; 12.Rfd1 Qe7; 13.Ne1 Bxg2; 14.Nxg2 Rfd8; 15.Ne3 Qe8; 16.Qd3 e5; 17.Ne4 Nxe4; 18.Qxe4 exd4; 19.Qxe8+ Rxe8; 20.Rxd4 and White had an endgame advantage in Karpov-Korchnoi, from the Euwe memorial in Belgium, 1987.

5.g3. The fianchetto plan is a good choice against the Bogoindian.

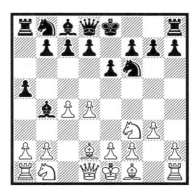

5...0–0; 6.Bg2 b6; 7.0–0 Ba6; 8.Bg5 Be7; 9.Qc2 Nc6; 10.a3. White keeps the enemy knight off of b4. **10...h6; 11.Bxf6 Bxf6.** Black's position is not bad. At present, only the h1–a8 diagonal looks dangerous. **12.Rd1 Qe7**.

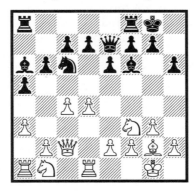

13.e3 Rae8?! In this slow opening, Black has actually outstripped White's development. But White controls the center, and d7-d5 will not be appropriate because of the position of the White queen, putting pressure on the c-file. **14.Nfd2**. A strong move which threatens to post the knight effectively at e4, while opening up lines for the Bg2 and threatening to disrupt Black's pawn structure. In addition, the c4 pawn is guarded so that the other knight can enter the game. **14...g5?!** Black overreacts to the positional strength of White's game. 14...g6 would have been more solid. **15.Nc3 Bg7**

White should probably bring Black's extended fianchetto into question by playing 16.f4, but he is concentrating on the queenside, and in particular, on the c-file. **16.Nb5 Qd8; 17.f4**.

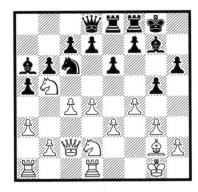

17...Ne7! Black has taken advantage of White's faulty plan by reorganizing his pieces so that the Ne7 can take part in the defense. Unfortunately, Yusupov soon forgets why he wanted the knight at e7. **18.Nf3 Nf5; 19.Qf2?!** Kasparov notes that this was not the correct square for the queen — it would have been better placed at e2, where it could protect the pawn at c4. **19...c6; 20.Nc3 gxf4; 21.gxf4 Bxc4.** Although White is a pawn down, he is at the same time almost a piece ahead, because Black's light-squared bishop is incapable of reaching the kingside to help in the defense. In addition, White now takes charge of the center.

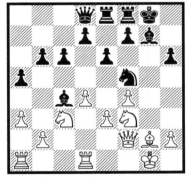

22.e4. Now Yusupov makes a major strategic error. He must return the knight to its defensive post at e7. **22...Nd6?** 22...Ne7; 23.Kh1! f5; 24.e5 brings White sufficient compensation for his pawn, because Black's kingside is very weak. The difference between this position and the game is that here the knight participates in the defense. In the game, it watches from c8. **23.Ne5 f5; 24.Nxc4 Nxc4.**

Black does not mind parting with his bishop, but the problem is that the Nc4 is far away from the kingside. Kasparov now chases it to an utterly useless position on the back rank. **25.b3! Nd6; 26.e5 Nc8.** At this point White must determine his strategy for the remainder of the game. His goal is to infiltrate the kingside, and exploit the weak light squares. 26...Ne4; 27.Bxe4 fxe4; 28.Nxe4 is clearly better for White, with a SuperKnight at e4 and threats along the g-file. **27.Bf3!** Clearly the bishop must get involved in this task.

27...Kh7. Black escapes the g-file, and hopes to use it to exchange rooks, lessening White's attacking force. **28.Bh5 Re7; 29.Kh1 Rg8?!** Although this is consistent with Black's plan, he chooses the wrong rook. The correct strategy was 29...Bh8! followed by Re7-g7. 29...Bh8; 30.Rg1 Rg7; 31.Rxg7+ Bxg7; 32.Rg1 Qe7! The point. This square is now available for the queen, which can hold the position together until the other rook reaches g8. 33.Qg3 Rg8, 34.Nb1! is given by Kasparov, with the comment that White stands better, since he will be able to swing his knight to h4, while the Nc8 is still out of play. **30.Rg1 Bh8**. If White's queen stood on f5, and were not attacked, then mate in two.

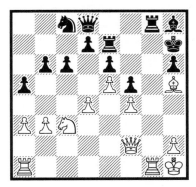

30...Bf8? 31.Qh4 sets up a very nasty pin! **31.Ne4!!** Because of the threat of Nf6+, the knight must be captured. But this gives White access to the f5-square. The sacrifice of material is not so important because Black's knight is so out of play. **31...fxe4; 32.f5 Rg5?** An error in time pressure. According to Kasparov, Black should have brought the queen over to help with the defense: 32...Qf8; 33.Rxg8 Kxg8; 34.f6! Rg7! **33.Rxg5 hxg5; 34.f6**.

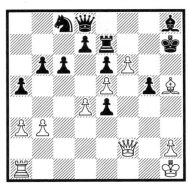

34...Kh6. 34...Qf8; 35.fxe7 Qxf2; 36.e8Q wins because Black has no checks. **35.fxe7 Qxe7**. 35...Nxe7; 36.Qf7 Bg7; 37.Rf1 Bh8; 38.Rf6+ Bxf6; 39.exf6.

36.Bf7! d6. 36...g4; 37.h4! gxh3; 38.Rg1 Bg7; 39.Qf4+ Kh7; 40.Qxe4+ Kh8; 41.Qg6. **37.Rf1 g4.** White needs to get his queen and rook into the game in order to mate. The best route is via h4, but that is covered by the Black queen. 37...dxe5 allows 38.Qe2. **38.Bxe6!! Qxe6; 39.Qh4+ Kg7** and here Black resigned before Kasparov could play 40.Rf6.

KING'S INDIAN DEFENSE

The **King's Indian Defense** is one of the most popular chess openings. It is relatively easy to play, even if you don't know all the latest fashions, because it is based on solid principles of development and counterattack that typify the Hypermodern school of chess. At the same time, the complexity of the positions which arise gives ample opportunity for spectacular creative combinations and attacks.

The current champions represent the antipodes of attitudes toward the King's Indian. Anatoly Karpov wouldn't be caught dead as Black, and Garry Kasparov plays it most of the time. Their clashes against each other have been entertaining and of high artistic merit, and Kasparov has shown that Black has nothing to complain about.

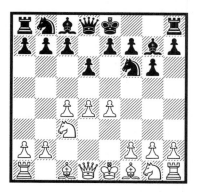

1.d4	Nf6
2.c4	g6
3.Nc3	Bg7
4.e4	d6

There are many approaches for White, but the main lines arise after 1.d4 Nf6; 2.c4 g6; 3.Nc3 Bg7; (3...d5 is the Gruenfeld which we will turn to next) 4.e4 d6. Now White can go for broke with 5.f4, but the more modest 5.Be2, 5.f3 and 5.Nf3 are all good alternatives.

(70) LARSEN - TAL
Candidates Match (5), 1969

1.Nf3 Nf6; 2.c4 g6; 3.Nc3 Bg7; 4.e4 d6; 5.d4 0-0. By a transpositional route we have landed in the territory of the King's Indian Defense. **6.Be2 e5; 7.0-0 Nc6; 8.d5 Ne7.**

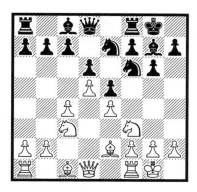

This is where the main lines of the Classical King's Indian diverge. The leading contenders are 9.Nd2 and 9.Ne1, and fashion tends to swing between them, with occasional spurts of popularity for 9.b4, too. **9.Ne1.** This is one of those openings where a horserace takes place. White will try to smash through on the queenside before Black gets to the White king on the kingside. The pace is brisk, and the closed center allows both sides to pursue their goals without much interference. **9...Nd7; 10.Nd3.** 10.f3 f5; 11.Nd3 Nf6; 12.Bd2 f4 is the more normal method of reaching the position after the twelfth move in the game. **10...f5; 11.Bd2.**

The exciting 11.g4 remains an alternative for White. **11...Nf6; 12.f3 f4; 13.c5!?** This particular move order allows White to get the attack going right away. White could also play on the kingside with 13.g4, which gives you some idea of the strategic riches of the Classical King's Indian, even this far into the opening. **13...g5; 14.Rc1.** Current Women's World Champion Zsuzsa Polgar had defended this position as Black. 14.cxd6 cxd6; 15.Rc1 (15.Nf2 Ng6; 16.Qc2 h5; 17.h3 Rf7 was successful for Kasparov as Black against Yuferov at Minsk 1978.) 15...Ng6; 16.Nb5 Rf7; 17.Qc2 Ne8; 18.a4 h5 and Black had adequate counterplay in Ftacnik-Polgar, Trencianske Teplice 1985.

14...Ng6; 15.Nb5?! This is too slow. 15.cxd6 cxd6; 16.Nb5 Rf7 is a more accurate way of getting to the desired position. **15...Rf7.** Now 15...a6! is considered more accurate, but Tal had seen previous games by Larsen and had prepared a new move which would be revealed a bit later. **16.cxd6.** If Larsen had found 16.Ba5! then Tal might have had to reveal an answer which has so far eluded the theoreticians. **16...cxd6; 17.Qc2.**

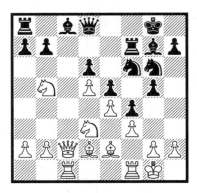

Now Tal unleashes his secret weapon. **17...g4!** This looks straightforward, but it is part of a deep and profound plan which involves sacrificing the rook at a8, and more! **18.Nc7 gxf3; 19.gxf3.** 19.Nxa8 fxe2; 20.Rf2 Bg4; 21.Nc7 Nxe4 is just too strong for Black. **19...Bh3, 20.Nxa8.** Larsen, the brave challenger to Bobby Fischer (a right earned in this match) fearlessly grabs the rook. It is not clear, however, that acceptable alternatives were at hand. 20.Ne6 Qb6+; 21.Rf2 Nf8!? (21...Bxe6; 22.dxe6 Re7; 23.Qa4 led to a draw in Podgayets-M.Gurevich, USSR 1984.) 22.Bf1 Bxe6; 23.dxe6 Nxe6 and the peripatetic knight lands eventually at d4. **20...Nxe4; 21.fxe4 Qg5+; 22.Kf2**.

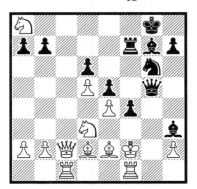

22...Qg2+. 22...Qh4+; 23.Kg1 Qg5+; 24.Kf2 would have led to a draw. In fact, that's how the game Averkin-Tal, played a bit later in the year in the Soviet Championship, ended. **23.Ke1.** This position has been assessed as simply winning for White, but massive complications lie ahead. **23...Nh4; 24.Be3?** How easy it is to go wrong in a messy position! 24.Nf2 Nf3+; 25.Kd1 Nd4; 26.Qc3 f3; 27.Bd3 Bf6; 28.Be3 Bh4; 29.Bxd4 exd4; 30.Qxd4 would have put an end to Black's chances. That's why Tal took up the drawing line in his next game in this variation. **24...Qxe4; 25.Bf2.** 25.Nxf4 loses, as pointed out by Larsen: 25...Qxe3; 26.Nxh3 Ng2+; 27.Kd1 Rxf1+; 28.Bxf1 Qe1 mate.

25...f3; 26.Bxh4 Qxh4+! Tal attacks with relentless precision. Taking the bishop at e2 would have been inferior. 26...fxe2; 27.Rxf7 Qxh4+; 28.Rf2 and Black cannot continue the attack; 26...Bxf1; 27.Nf2! Qxe2+; 28.Qxe2 Bxe2; 29.Rc8+ Bf8; 30.Nc7 and the threat of Ne6 is strong. Black does not have enough pawns to compensate for the missing piece. **27.Nf2 fxe2; 28.Qxe2.**

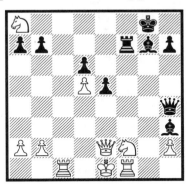

28...e4! A fine move. The pawn will march forward until it is captured, and that will open up yet another line against the White king. **29.Rg1?.** 29.Rc7! was the final resource. If Black exchanges rooks, then the knight returns to the game, but taking the rook at f1 leaves White a little better after 29...Bxf1; 30.Kxf1 Rf5; 31.Rc8+ Kf7; 32.Rc4 with a strong pin against the pawn at e4. To be fair, it is very hard to see this position when calculating back at move 29, especially the pin. **29...e3; 30.Qxe3 Re7.** Now White, in time trouble, has to return some material. **31.Rxg7+ Kxg7; 32.Rc7 Bd7; 33.Rxd7 Rxd7.**

34.Qxa7. The last straw slips from Larsen's grasp. 34.Qc3+ Qf6; 35.Qg3+ Kf8 is better for Black, but it is not easy to get at the knight at a8 without allowing perpetual checks. **34...Re7+; 35.Kd1 Qc4!** A ruthlessly efficient move. Tal was also in tremendous time pressure yet did not fail to find the best move. **36.Qb6 Qf1+; 37.Kd2 Re2+; 38.Kc3 Qc1+; 39.Kd4 Qe3+; 40.Kc4 Rc2+** and Larsen resigned, since the king would have to move to the b-file, allowing ...Rxb2+ to win the queen at b6. **Black won.**

Often White responds with a fianchetto, too, as seen in the following game.

(71) BOTVINNIK - SMYSLOV
World Championship (Game 14), 1954

1.d4 Nf6; 2.c4 g6; 3.g3.

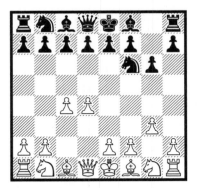

The fianchetto approach is often used against the King's Indian and Gruenfeld Defenses. The two players ignore each other for a while, but White usually winds up with more control of the center. In time, Black can stage a counterattack against the central pawns. **3...Bg7; 4.Bg2 0–0; 5.Nc3 d6; 6.Nf3 Nbd7.** The game follows well-traveled paths. **7.0–0 e5.** Black plants a stake in the center. **8.e4 c6.**

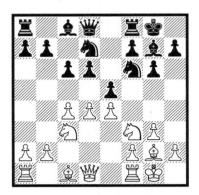

At the time, this was already a familiar position, featured in games by leading players for over a decade. **9.Be3.** It is more common to see 9.h3 here, in order to prevent Black's reply, but Smyslov had worked out an interesting plan for White. **9...Ng4; 10.Bg5 Qb6; 11.h3.** This had already been seen in Grandmaster play, and 11...Ngf6 was expected. Smyslov had a nasty surprise planned, and sprung it now. **11...exd4!; 12.Na4 Qa6.**

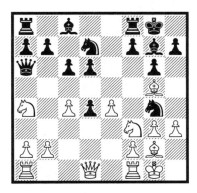

This was not anticipated by Botvinnik, and pointed to a severe flaw in his preparation. But like a true Champion, he settled down at the board and worked out a way to lead the game into messy complications. After all, just because your opponent plays an unexpected move doesn't mean it is necessarily good! **13.hxg4 b5; 14.Nxd4.** 14.Be7 Re8; 15.Bxd6 bxa4; 16.e5 (16.Nxd4 Ne5 was given by Smyslov as equal). 16...Qxc4; 17.Re1 Bb7 is a messy position, but the great Soviet theoreticians Boleslavsky and Lepeshkin combined forces to deepen the analysis: 18.b3 axb3; 19.axb3 Qc3; 20.Rc1 Qa5; 21.Qxd4 c5; 22.Qf4 h6; 23.b4 Qxb4; 24.Qxb4 cxb4; 25.Rc7 Bxf3; 26.Bxf3 Rad8 27.Bc6 Nxe5; 28.Bxe5 and here the authoritative *Encyclopedia of Chess Openings* gives 28...Rd6 and assesses the position as equal, but the rook on e8 is hanging, so they must have meant 28...Rxe5; 29.Rxe5 Bxe5; 30.Rxa7 which should be drawn. **14...bxa4; 15.Nxc6 Qxc6**.

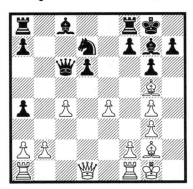

White now uses a simple tactic to win the exchange, but Smyslov had taken this into account. **16.e5 Qxc4; 17.Bxa8 Nxe5.** Black has more than enough compensation. Just look at the pawn at g4, the passed d-pawn and the general weakness of the light squares. **18.Rc1 Qb4; 19.a3 Qxb2; 20.Qxa4 Bb7**.

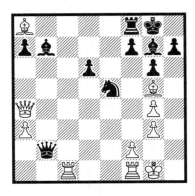

21.Rb1. 21.Bxb7 Qxb7; 22.Rc3 h6;23.Bf4 Nf3+; 24.Rxf3 Qxf3; 25.Bxd6 Rd8; 26.Bc5 is given by Smyslov as superior, leading to a game with almost level chances. **21...Nf3+.** Now the carnage begins. **22.Kh1 Bxa8!** Smyslov parts with the queen, but gets a winning position as a result. **23.Rxb2 Nxg5+; 24.Kh2 Nf3+; 25.Kh3 Bxb2; 26.Qxa7 Be4.**

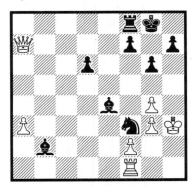

Black's three minor pieces are more than a match for the king. **27.a4 Kg7; 28.Rd1 Be5; 29.Qe7 Rc8; 30.a5 Rc2**. Everybody gets into the act! **31.Kg2 Nd4+; 32.Kf1 Bf3; 33.Rb1 Nc6**. White gave up. Even if Black can't organize an immediate checkmate, the advance of the d-pawn is inevitable. **Black won.**

The Saemisch Variation has been a favorite of most of the World Champions but not just as White. The strenuous tactical and strategic battles are usually won by the stronger player.

(72) SPASSKY - FISCHER
Sveti-Stefan (Game 8), 1992

1.d4 Nf6; 2.c4 g6; 3.Nc3 Bg7; 4.e4 d6; 5.f3 0–0; 6.Be3.

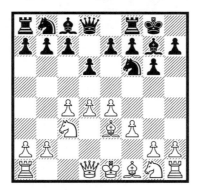

There are many ways for Black to meet the Saemisch, but the most interesting is the development of the knight at c6, where it has a great deal of influence on the center. **6...Nc6.** This is the Panno Variation. Black plans to play...Rb8, ...a6, and ...b5, with a lot of play on the queenside. That's important, because queenside castling is normal for White, who will try to march up the h-file and infiltrate with Bh6.

7.Nge2. Although it seems, at first, that this just locks in the light-squared bishop, it turns out that the bishop is fairly happy at home. This knight can go to the kingside via g3, or it can find a new home after a brief rest at c1. **7...a6; 8.Qd2 Rb8; 9.h4 h5.** Both sides are playing logically. Black can't allow White to play h5 too soon, and the last move is designed to slow the attack.

Of course, White can play an early g4 to open things up, but Black has a pawn, knight and bishop aimed at that square. Another typical reaction to the flank attack is an immediate counterblow in the center, while Black can even play on the queenside! 9...e5; 10.d5 Na5; 11.Ng3 c5; 12.h5 Bd7 is an alternative, 9...b5; 10.h5 e5; 11.d5 Na5; 12.Ng3 bxc4; 13.0–0–0 is a position that Kasparov has played as White, and as Black too! **10.Bh6**. Recently 10.Nc1 has found devotees at the top levels of chess.

10.Nc1 e5; 11.d5 Nd4; 12.Nb3 c5; 13.dxc6 bxc6; 14.Nxd4 exd4; 15.Bxd4 has been used by Karpov, for example against Kindermann at Baden-Baden 1992. **10...e5**. This move was introduced by Spassky at this game. 10...Bxh6, 11.Qxh6 e5 is considered more accurate, for example 12.0–0–0 b5; 13.g4 bxc4; 14.Ng3 and now Black can try the sacrificial 14...Bxg4!; 15.Bxc4 Bxf3; 16.Qxg6+ Kh8; 17.Qh6+ Nh7; 18.Nxh5 with a complicated game in Lerner-W.Watson, Moscow 1985. Fischer was presumably familiar with this game. **11.Bxg7 Kxg7; 12.d5**. Castling might have been wiser. **12...Ne7; 13.Ng3 c6; 14.dxc6 Nxc6**. An interesting move, but capturing with the pawn, intending to break through at d5, was also possible. Analysis by leading theoretician Leonid Shamkovich shows that life is not so simple: 14...bxc6 ;15.0–0–0 Qb6; 16.Na4 Qb4; 17.Qxb4 Rxb4; 18.b3 d5; 19.Nc5! and the knight can redeploy at d3 with a good position for White. **15.0–0–0**.

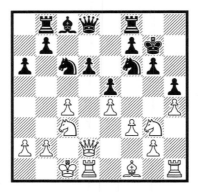

15...Be6! Spassky plays actively. The pawn at d6 cannot be taken for free. **16.Kb1.** 16.Qxd6 Qxd6; 17.Rxd6 leaves the rook in a precarious position after ...Nd4. **16...Ne8; 17.Nd5 b5!** The only source of counterplay. **18.Ne3 Rh8!** Shamkovich pointed out that Fischer is playing like the great Hypermodern hero Nimzowitsch here, restraining the enemy forces. **19.Rc1 Qb6; 20.Bd3 Nd4; 21.Nd5**. Both sides have well-placed knights. **21...Qa7; 22.Nf1 Nf6.**

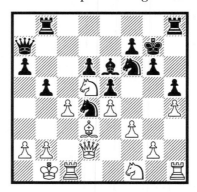

Here Spassky may have missed his chance. **23.Nfe3.** 23.Nxf6 Kxf6; 24.c5 Kg7; 25.f4 gives White a dangerous attack. **23...Bxd5; 24.cxd5 Rbc8; 25.Rcf1 Qe7.** Black is defending all the key squares now, so there is no immediate way to penetrate the Black position. **26.g4?!** 26.f4 would have been more appropriate, though Black could still defend. **26...Nd7; 27.g5 Kf8?** A serious error by Fischer. True, it does meet certain kingside threats but the communication of the rooks is interrupted. 27...Rhf8! is solid enough, and White cannot break through: 28.Nf5+ gxf5; 29.exf5 f6; 30.Rhg1 Kf7 and there is not enough to justify the investment of the piece. **28.Rf2 Ke8; 29.Bf1 Nc5; 30.Bh3 Rc7.**

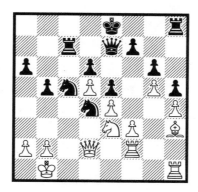

This position kept the analysts up all night after the game. After all the homework was done, it seems that Spassky made the right move here, but blew the game later on. **31.Rc1 Ncb3!** The sacrifice should not have come as a surprise. **32.axb3 Nxb3; 33.Rc6?.** This simply loses. The leading analysts published many variations, but World Champion Kasparov suggested the most promising move. 33.Qc2 Rxc2; 34.Rfxc2 Nxc1; 35.Rc8+ Qd8; 36.Kxc1! and White has the better of the endgame. But is it enough after 36...Ke7; 37.Rxd8 Rxd8; 38.Nc2 a5? That is by no means clear. **33...Nxd2+; 34.Rxd2 Kf8; 35.Rxa6.** Black is suffering all of this because of the retreat of the king to f8! **35...Ra7; 36.Rc6 Kg7; 37.Bf1 Ra1+; 38.Kxa1.**

White cannot survive. **38...Qa7+; 39.Kb1 Qxe3; 40.Kc2 b4.** Spassky resigned. Loss of further material is inevitable. **Black won.**

Finally, the Four Pawns Attack must be mentioned. Although most World Champions would not feel comfortable on the White side, as Black, they must be prepared to meet it, and usually are.

(73) KERES - SPASSKY
Riga (Candidates Match game 10), 1965

1.d4 Nf6; 2.c4 g6; 3.Nc3 Bg7; 4.e4 d6; 5.f4. This is the Four Pawns Attack, an all-out attempt to win early in the game. **5...c5.** The normal move is castling, but if Black wants to play ...c5 there is no harm in doing so now. **6.d5 0–0; 7.Nf3.**

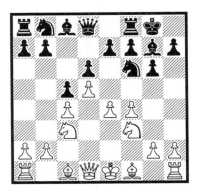

Black now has two basic approaches, which can even be combined. The first plan is to open the e-file by playing ...e6 and ...dxe5, while the other is the Benko Gambit-like ...b5 sacrifice on the queenside. In either case, it is the apparently strong pawn center which will be Black's target. **7...e6**. 7...b5; 8.cxb5 a6 has not yet been sufficiently explored. **8.Be2**. 8.dxe6 fxe6 is fine for Black, who can bring a knight to d4 via c6. **8...exd5; 9.cxd5**.

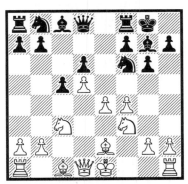

This position, which can also arise from the Benoni, is very complicated. The pawn at e4 is defended only by the knight at c3. It is important to keep that in mind. **9...b5**. At the time, this move was all the rage, but a decade later it had all but disappeared. Now Black prefers to work in the center. 9...Re8; 10.e5 dxe5; 11.fxe5 Ng4; 12.Bg5 f6; 13.exf6 Bxf6 remains controversial, but it is the approved formula at present. **10.e5 dxe5; 11.fxe5 Ng4; 12.Bf4.** 12.Bg5! is the move that put this line out of commission. 12...Qb6; 13.0-0 c4+; 14.Kh1 is better for White, since there is no smothered mate trick. 14...Nf2+; 15.Kg1 Nh3+; 16.Kh1 Qg1+; 17.Nxg1 but not 17.Rxg1??, 18.Nf2 mate. **12...Nd7.** 12...b4!; 13.Ne4 Nd7 is more accurate, for example 14.e6 fxe6; 15.dxe6 Rxf4; 16.Qd5 Kh8; 17.Qxa8 Nb6; 18.Qc6 Ne3 is still unclear, Martin-Botterill, Charlton, 1978.

Rather fitting that the game was played in Charlton, long-time home to one of Britain's great chess researchers Bob Wade, at whose home many important opening innovations were developed. **13.e6**.

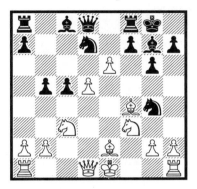

A typical motif, as we have already seen. **13...fxe6; 14.dxe6 Rxf4**. Spassky consumed over half an hour, one fifth of his entire allotment (to move 40), contemplating this move. Thirty years later, superstars usually don't settle in for a long think until around move 20 in well analyzed openings, and sometimes they can rattle off prepared moves until their 30th turn!

15.Qd5. The dual threats lead to the win of the rook. **15...Kh8; 16.Qxa8.** 16.0-0-0 Rb8, 17.Qd6 Bh6 and it is Black who threatens the discovered check! **16...Nb6; 17.Qxa7.** 17.Qc6 Ne3 would be unpleasant for the White king who would be unable to castle to safety. **17...Bxe6; 18.0-0.** 18.Rd1 is ineffective because of 18...Bd4. **18...Ne3; 19.Rf2.** 19.Rad1 is interesting. Bernard Cafferty, long-time editor of the famous British Chess Magazine gives 19...Nxd1; 20.Rxd1 Bd4+; 21.Kh1 b4; 22.Nb5 (22.Ng5 Qxg5; 23.Qxb6 bxc3; 24.Qxe6 Qe5; 25.Qc8+ Kg7; 26.bxc3 Qxe2 and Black wins.) 22...Bd5; 23.Nbxd4 cxd4; 24.Nxd4 Rxd4; 25.Rxd4 Bxg2+; 26.Kxg2 Qxd4; 27.Qe7 h5 and a draw is likely. **19...b4**.

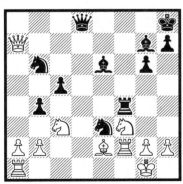

20.Nb5? 20.Nd1! would have given White a clear advantage. Instead, the position remains murky. **20...Rf7; 21.Qa5 Qb8!** This unpins the knight, freeing Black's pieces to pursue loftier goals. **22.Re1 Bd5;** 22...Ng4; 23.Bf1 Nxf2;

24.Rxe6 Nh3+; 25.gxh3 Rxf3; 26.Qxb6 Qxb6; 27.Rxb6 Bxb2; 28.Kg2 is a win for White. **23.Bf1** This was not the best way to defend, but even after 23.Bd3, 12...Nbc4 would give Black the advantage. **23...Nxf1; 24.Rfxf1 Nc4; 25.Qa6 Rf6; 26.Qa4 Nxb2.**

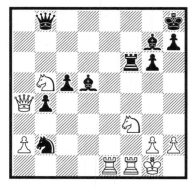

The final critical position. Keres retreats when he should have advanced. **27.Qc2?.** 27.Qa5 Nd3; 28.Re7 Qf8; 29.Qa7 Bxa2 is clearly better for Black. **27...Qxb5; 28.Re7.** 28.Qxb2 Rxf3; 29.Qd2 Bd4+; 30.Kh1 Qxf1+; 31.Rxf1 Rxf1 mate was hardly an acceptable alternative. **28...Nd3; 29.Qe2 c4; 30.Re8+ Rf8; 31.Rxf8+ Bxf8; 32.Ng5 Bc5+; 33.Kh1 Qd7; 34.Qd2 Qe7; 35.Nf3 Qe3.** Keres didn't have to resign, because he ran out of time here. **Black won.**

GRUENFELD DEFENSE

At first glance, the **Gruenfeld Defense** seems a lot like the King's Indian. But if you compare the diagram below with the previous one, you can see that there is a very important difference.

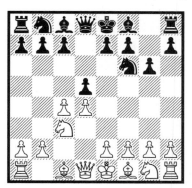

1.d4	Nf6
2.c4	g6
3.Nc3	d5

The Black pawn at d5 prevents White from establishing the ideal pawn center by playing e4. This changes the nature of the struggle, which will much more directly involve the center, which is often closed in the King's Indian. White can, and usually does, manage to get the ideal pawn center but must do so in an environment where it is hard to defend. Two main lines illustrate this.

After **1.d4 Nf6; 2.c4 g6; 3.Nc3 d5; 4.cxd5 Nxd5; 5.e4 Nxc3; 6.bxc3** we have the Exchange Variation.

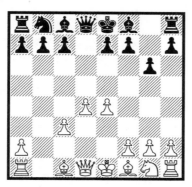

White has control of the center, but Black will strike quickly with ...c5; ...Bg7; and even ...Qa5 and ...Rd8 to place it under a lot or pressure.

In the Russian Variation, White achieves the ideal pawn center by different means. After 1.d4 Nf6; 2.c4 g6; 3.Nc3 d5; 4.Nf3 Bg7; 5.Qb3 dxc4; 6.Qxc4 O-O; 7.e4 we reach the following position:

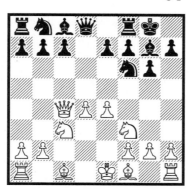

Again White has the center, but Black can chip away at the support by playing ...Bg4, moving the knight from f6, and engaging in action on the queenside. When Ernst Gruenfeld introduced his invention in the early 1920s, such a White position seemed unthinkably strong, but ways have been found to create counterplay.

The World Champion hero of the Black side is Vasily Smyslov, though many champions have contributed greatly to the legacy of the opening. Nevertheless, I strongly recommend that non-experts avoid this opening as Black. That center can become a steamroller if you don't have very good defensive technique, and the endgames that result require subtle handling, even in favorable circumstances.

(74) GLIGORIC - SMYSLOV
Yugoslavia vs. USSR, 1959

1.d4 Nf6; 2.c4 g6; 3.Nc3 d5; 4.cxd5 Nxd5; 5.e4 Nxc3; 6.bxc3 Bg7; 7.Bc4 c5.

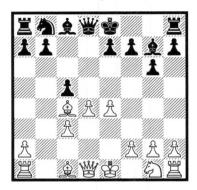

The contour of the middlegame is clear. Black will train all guns at the center, especially at d4. The c3-square is also a target. White will try to maintain the ideal pawn center. **8.Ne2**.

The plan with 8.Nf3 is another popular plan, and fashion shifts between the two. The advantage of Ne2 is that a pin with ...Bg4 can be broken by playing f3. Of course that is an asset only if the ...Bg4 plan is otherwise a good one. **8...0–0; 9.0–0 Nc6; 10.Be3 Qc7**. This was Smyslov's contribution, and the system with 10...Qc7 now bears his name. Until this time, 10...cxd4 was preferred.

Both systems are in common use today. **11.Rc1**. Capturing at c5 just weakens White's pawn structure and is not seen. **11...Rd8; 12.h3**. It is no longer considered necessary to prevent ...Bg4, so 12.Qd2 is more common. **12...b6; 13.f4**.

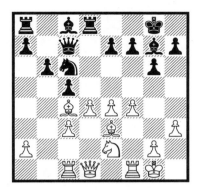

The White pawn mass looks impressive, but Black's pieces will soon start to chip away at it. **13...e6; 14.Qe1 Bb7.** 14...Na5 also holds appeal to Champions: 15.Bd3 f5; 16.g4 fxe4; 17.Bxe4 Bb7; 18.Ng3 Nc4; 19.Bxb7 Qxb7; 20.Bf2 Qc6 and Black had a good game in Spassky-Fischer, Siegen (Olympiad) 1970. **15.Qf2.** 15.f5 fails, as Smyslov demonstrated: 15...Na5; 16.Bd3 exf5; 17.exf5 Re8; 18.Qf2 because of 18...c4; 19.Bc2 Qe7 and Black wins a piece: 20.f6 Qxe3; 21.fxg7 Qxe2. **15...Na5; 16.Bd3 f5!**

Smyslov correctly calculated the effect of this move, which is a typical one in structures like this. White's center collapses. **17.e5 c4; 18.Bc2 Nc6; 19.g4**. White could not just sit passively and wait for destruction, so Gligoric tries to open up some lines. **19...Ne7; 20.Kh2 Qc6; 21.Ng3.**

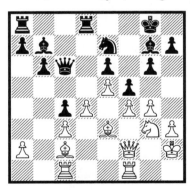

Smyslov realizes that the kingside is not the only area of operations, and starts an action on the other flank. **21...b5!; 22.a4 a6; 23.Rb1 Rab8; 24.Bd2 bxa4!** This is a move which required precise calculation. Smyslov already saw the resource at move 31, the next critical point in the game. **25.Ra1 Ba8; 26.Bxa4 Qc7; 27.Ra2 Rb6; 28.gxf5 exf5.** Black cannot afford to open the g-file, so the path for both the d-pawn and the e-pawn is cleared of pawn obstacles. Nevertheless, Black's pieces keep the situation under control. **29.Bc1 Nd5; 30.Ne2 a5!; 31.Bc2.**

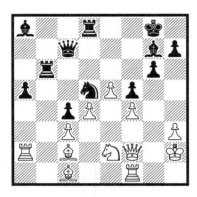

Recall that the entire opening strategy was initially built on the weakness of the White pawns at c3 and d4. Although everything looks fine now, the c-pawn is as weak as ever, as Smyslov shows with the plan launched by his next move. **31...Rb3!** The exchange is a small price to pay for two connected passed pawns on the queenside and complete domination of the light squares. **32.Bxb3 cxb3; 33.Ra4 Bf8!**

Capturing at c3 would have been a waste of time and energy. There is no hurry. 33...Nxc3? and the rook at a4 can return to the game. 34.Nxc3 Qxc3; 35.Bd2 Qb2; 36.Bxa5 Qxf2+; 37.Rxf2 Rc8; 38.Rb4 Rc2; 39.Rxc2 bxc2; 40.Rc4 Be4; 41.Rc8+ Kf7; 42.Bd2 and White will win without difficulty. **34.Bb2.** Gligoric hopes to advance the pawn to c4 and get the central pawns rolling, but Smyslov's carefully prepared reply dashes all hopes. **34...Ne3!** When you have a good position, the tactics find themselves!

35.Rfa1. 35.Qxe3 Qc6 leaves White with no defense to the threats at g2 and a4. For example: 36.d5 Rxd5!?; 37.Raa1 Rd2!; 38.Bc1 b2 and Black wins. **35...Nc4.** Again, there is no rush. Black's pieces are overwhelming their White counterparts. **36.Ng3!** 36.Rxc4 Qxc4; 37.Rxa5 Be7! and now Ng3 can be met by ...Bh4. **36...Be7!; 37.Nf1.**

Moving the queen to e2 was better, but the position was very difficult. Smyslov provided the following interesting possibility: 37.Qe2! Bd5; 38.Nf1 Ra8; 39.Ne3 Nxe3; 40.Qxe3 Bc6; 41.Rc4 Qd7; 42.Rxc6 Qxc6; 43.Qd3 a4; 44.d5 and it is difficult to evaluate the position. It seems to me that after 44...Qc5; 45.d6 Qf2+; 46.Kh1 Bh4, the Black king can find shelter at h6. The White queen must stay in the area, to prevent threats on the light squares. Black threatens ...Bg3 and ...Qh2 mate, as well as the bishop at b2. Just one sample: 47.Qd5+ Kg7; 48.Qxa8 Qxb2; 49.Rxa4 Bg3; 50.Qg2 Qc1+; 51.Qg1 Qxc3; 52.d7 b2; 53.d8Q Qf3+; 54.Qg2 b1Q+; 55.Qd1 Qbxd1 mate. **37...Qc6; 38.Rxc4 Qh1+!.** 38...Qxc4 would allow White to get some counterplay with 39.Ne3. **39.Kg3 h5!** White resigned.

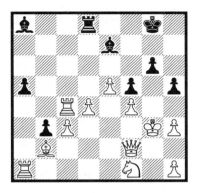

The threat of ...h4+ cannot be stopped, and if the White queen moves away then ...Qg1+ is available. 39...h5; 40.Qh2 Qf3 mate. **Black won.**

(75) BYRNE - FISCHER
New York, 1956

1.Nf3. This game has been called "The Game of the Century" and is an absolutely amazing performance by a 13-year old future World Champion! **1...Nf6; 2.c4 g6; 3.Nc3 Bg7; 4.d4 0–0; 5.Bf4 d5.** We have now reached the Gruenfeld Defense by transposition. **6.Qb3 dxc4; 7.Qxc4.**

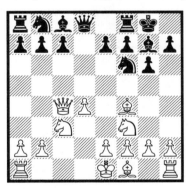

In the Russian Variations, Black has many different defensive schemes. White's move order, playing Bf4 before e4, avoids some of them. **7...c6; 8.e4.** White has the ideal pawn center, and it is up to Black to destroy it. **8...Nbd7.** 8...b5; 9.Qb3! Qa5; (9...Be6; 10.Qc2 Qa5 is Kasparov's suggestion for Black.) 10.Bd3 Be6; 11.Qd1 Rd8; 12.0–0 Bg4; 13.e5 Nd5; 14.Nxd5 cxd5; 15.Rc1 was played in Miles-Kasparov, Basel (2nd match game), 1985.

After 15...Qb6, Kasparov obtained a small advantage with 16.Rc5, but could have gotten even more with 16.e6! **9.Rd1 Nb6; 10.Qc5.** This seems to be an odd location for the queen, but in fact it is seen in many examples of the Russian Variation. **10...Bg4.** Black uses a threat on the knight at f3 to place indirect pressure on the pawn at d4. **11.Bg5 Na4; 12.Qa3.** As usual in the Gruenfeld, Black's action is at c3, d4 and e4. The fun begins now. **12...Nxc3; 13.bxc3 Nxe4; 14.Bxe7.** This is not really an exchange sacrifice, since the dark-squared bishop is far too valuable to give up for the relatively inactive rook at f8. **14...Qb6; 15.Bc4 Nxc3.**

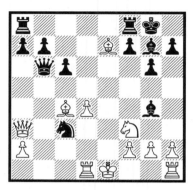

Mission accomplished! White cannot capture the knight at c3 because then Black can move a rook to e8 to pin the valuable bishop. **16.Bc5 Rfe8+.** White is forced to abandon castling and Black has threats against all three back-rank squares. The rook at e8 controls e1, the knight can come to e2 to attack g1, and the bishop can swing from g4 to the queenside, where the a6-f1 diagonal can be used. The key to White's hopes is the powerful defensive ability of the bishop at c4. **17.Kf1.**

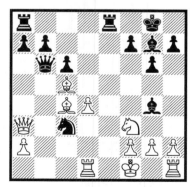

17...Be6!! A truly stunning move. In return for the queen, Black gets access to all the critical squares. **18.Bxb6.** 18.Bxe6 just draws in the powerful White queen. 18...Qb5+; 19.Kg1 Ne2+; 20.Kf1 Ng3+; 21.Kg1 and the end comes with the famous smothered mate. 21...Qf1+; 22.Rxf1 Ne2 mate. **18...Bxc4+; 19.Kg1 Ne2+.** This knight cannot give checkmate, but it can inflict mortal damage. **20.Kf1 Nxd4+; 21.Kg1 Ne2+; 22.Kf1 Nc3+; 23.Kg1 axb6**. Now Black has two pieces and two pawns for the queen, with the White queen and rook under attack and the rook at h1 locked out of the game. **24.Qb4 Ra4!**

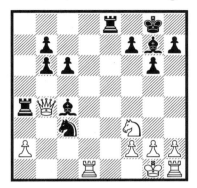

25.Qxb6 Nxd1; 26.h3. This creates a new home for the king, so that the rook can enter the game. **26...Rxa2; 27.Kh2 Nxf2; 28.Re1 Rxe1; 29.Qd8+ Bf8; 30.Nxe1 Bd5**. This position is an easy win for Black, who has a rook, two bishops and three pawns for the queen. **31.Nf3 Ne4; 32.Qb8**. The queen is out of play here, so Fischer will be able to use his massive forces to checkmate the White king. **32...b5; 33.h4 h5; 34.Ne5 Kg7; 35.Kg1 Bc5+; 36.Kf1 Ng3+; 37.Ke1 Bb4+; 38.Kd1 Bb3+; 39.Kc1 Ne2+; 40.Kb1 Nc3+; 41.Kc1 Rc2 mate.**

BENONI

The **Benoni** is a fighting defense, at least in its modern form. Black creates a central pawn structure that allows profitable use of the e5-square. After 1.d4 c5; 2.c4 c5; 3.d5 the basic contour takes shape.

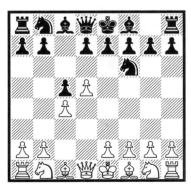

1.d4   Nf6
2.c4   c5
3.d5

Black will fianchetto the bishop at g7 and use the dark squares, especially e5, as staging posts for a kingside attack. The fighting nature of the opening gives it great appeal, but White's firm control of the light squares has discouraged most World Champions from adopting it. But Mikhail Tal, the tactical wizard, was willing to take the risks.

Although most theoreticians consider the defense slightly suspect, it can nevertheless be recommended to all amateur players who have, or wish to acquire, the tactical prowess required. The Benoni lends itself to miraculous escapes and swindling tactics.

(76) TUKMAKOV - TAL
Soviet Championship, 1969

1.d4 Nf6; 2.c4 c5; 3.d5 e6; 4.Nc3 exd5; 5.cxd5 d6. The Modern Benoni appealed to Tal as it provided excellent fighting opportunities. Nowdays it is considered slightly suspect. **6.e4 g6; 7.Nf3 Bg7; 8.Be2 0–0; 9.0–0 Re8.** This position is still highly topical, but Tal more or less abandoned the defense for other, less risky lines later in his career. **10.Nd2.** A typical theme in the Benoni. White will be able to secure the center, at least temporarily, by playing f3. **10...Nbd7** Black steers a knight toward the strong post at e5. **11.f3.** Now this is considered premature. 11.a4 a6; 12.Re1 Ne5; 13.h3 g5; 14.Nf1 h6; 15.Ne3 is perhaps a little better for White, who obtained a good game in Ivanchuk-deFirmian, Biel, 1989.

But the situation remains murky and further investigations are likely. **11...a6; 12.a4.** This is an automatic response to ...a6 in the Modern Benoni. Black cannot be allowed to advance the pawn to b5. **12...Qc7; 13.Qb3 Ne5.** Black's knights must play an active role if the Modern Benoni is to succeed. **14.a5 Rb8; 15.Nd1 Nh5.**

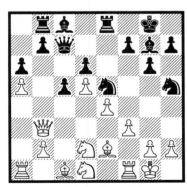

It is fair to say that the chances are equal here, which gives the advantage to the stronger player. **16.Nc4 f5; 17.exf5.**

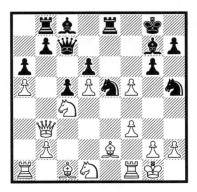

Now Tal invites a fork, but it will be some time before Tukmakov can eat! **17...Bxf5!; 18.g4**. The pawn attacks bishop and knight, but it is Black's turn to move. **18...Nxc4; 19.Bxc4 b5!** When Black can get away with this move, it is an indication that White has failed to maintain an advantage in the opening. **20.axb6 Rxb6; 21.Qa2.** 21.Qa3 Rb4; 22.b3 was evaluated as unclear by Petrosian, but Tal maintained that White has more chances there than in the game.. **21...Bd4+; 22.Kg2 Qg7.**

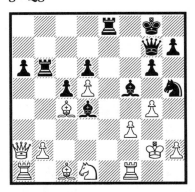

23.Nc3. The bishop is still taboo. 23.gxf5 gxf5+; 24.Kh1 Kh8! was pointed out by Petrosian. **23...Bd7; 24.Bd2.** Once again, the cleric is off-limits. 24.gxh5 gxh5+, 25.Kh1 Bh3. **24...Reb8; 25.Rab1 Nf6; 26.Rfc1 Qf7; 27.b3?** A final error, though the game was hopeless anyway. 27.Rf1 Bc8; 28.h3 Bb7 and the d-pawn will fall. **27...Nxg4!** Splendid, after luring the pawn to this square it is finally captured. Obviously White can't grab the knight because of the attack on the king. **28.Ne4.** 28.fxg4 Qf2+; 29.Kh1 Qf3 mate. **28...Ne5. Black won.**

BENKO GAMBIT

The **Benko Gambit** is very easy to play. Black sacrifices a pawn on the queenside, and uses the open files to tie down the enemy position. It has never appealed to World Champions because it is generally extraordinarily boring. For an endgame specialist like Pal Benko, the opening was perfect, since the endgame is usually the only stage of any interest in this opening.

After 1.d4 Nf6; 2.c4 c5; 3.d5 b5; 4.cxb5 a6, we have the starting position of the Benko Gambit Accepted.

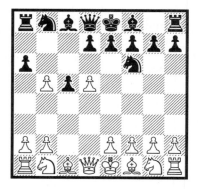

1.d4	Nf6
2.c4	c5
3.d5	b5
4.cxb5	a6

Black will fianchetto the bishop at g7, as in the Benoni, but the main focus is at b2. If White accepts the pawn, as usually the case, we reach positions like the following.

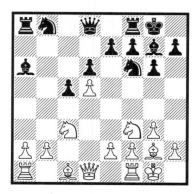

White's pawns on the queenside will find it difficult to advance. If Black can win either of them, then the endgame will bring victory due to the ideal pawn structure for Black, with no weaknesses to attack.

Perhaps it is mere prejudice, but I can't recommend the Benko Gambit for any purpose other than playing for a draw as Black. It does not lead to interesting middlegames and the World Champions have been devastatingly effective against it.

(77) PETROSIAN - ALBURT
Soviet Championship, 1977

1.d4 Nf6; 2.c4 c5; 3.d5 b5; 4.Nf3

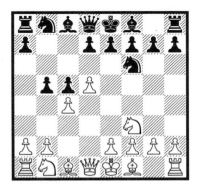

A top player will often avoid following the main lines of an opening if they tend to be too drawish. Although accepting the Benko Gambit by capturing on a6 is the normal plan, White can also get a promising game by declining, which has an additional psychological and practical advantage. The psychological advantage is that Black does not get to enter the familiar waters, with structures well known from experience.

The practical advantage is that Black is likely to have faced this move far less frequently. So even if 4.bxa6 is objectively better, and that is by no means clear, there is good motivation for using this alternative strategy. **4...g6**. This is just one of several plans, but since Black usually plays the fianchetto anyway, it might as well come now. **5.cxb5 a6; 6.e3**. Naturally capturing at a6 would lead back to the Benko Gambit Accepted. **6...Bg7; 7.Nc3 0–0; 8.a4**. This plan has become well established.

Lev Alburt, a former United States Champion and lifelong defender of the Benko, did not yet know the dangers of capturing at b5, proving that Petrosian's choice was justified. **8...axb5.** Later on, more effective plans were found for Black. Here is an example. 8...Bb7; 9.Ra3 e6; 10.dxe6 fxe6; 11.Qd6 axb5 and now 12.Bxb5 has not brought much joy to White, so the capture with the pawn should be considered. After an exchange of rooks, Black will have some targets on the queenside. 12.axb5 Rxa3; 13.bxa3 Qa5; 14.Qd2 Ng4 as suggested by Benko specialist John Fedorowicz. **9.Bxb5.**

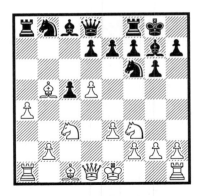

9...d6; 10.0–0 Na6; 11.Ra3 Nc7; 12.Nd2 Nd7? 12...Nfxd5; 13.Nxd5 Nxd5; 14.Bc6 Be6; 15.Bxa8 Qxa8 is given by Fedorowicz, who holds that White's advantage is minimal. Still, it is an entire exchange (rook for bishop) for White, and Black will have to keep the bishops active and the a-pawn at bay. **13.Bxd7 Bxd7; 14.Nc4 Ra6; 15.e4.** Already, it is just a matter of time until White can exploit the advantage of the extra a-pawn. This game is a good illustration of the technique required to move it up the board. **15...Qb8; 16.Qc2 Qb4; 17.Na2 Qb7; 18.Bd2 Rfa8; 19.a5.**

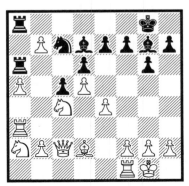

One small step for the pawn, but a big leap for the White position. Black seems to have a6 under control, but White slowly makes progress on the queenside. **19...Nb5; 20.Rb3 Qc7; 21.Bc3 Nd4.** Black cannot afford to part with the powerful bishop at g7, which is the lifeblood of the Benko Gambit. **22.Bxd4 Bxd4; 23.Nc3 Rb8.** The threat was Nb5. **24.Rb6!** White drives the enemy rook from the a6 square. **24...Raa8; 25.Qb3 Qd8; 26.Nb5 Bg7.** 26...Bxb5; 27.Qxb5 is horrible for Black. The bishop at d4 can no longer participate in the game. **27.Na7 Qe8; 28.Ra1 Bf8; 29.Nc6 Rc8; 30.a6.**

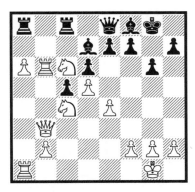

The pawn is now very difficult to stop, because Black does not have room to maneuver. **30...Rc7; 31.Rb7 Rxc6; 32.dxc6 Bxc6; 33.a7**.

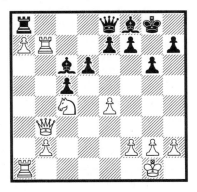

Neither the rook nor the pawn at e4 are relevant now. **33...Bxe4.** 33...Bxb7; 34.Qxb7 e6; 35.Nb6 brings the point home immediately. **34.Rb8 Qd7; 35.Rxa8 Bxa8; 36.Nb6.** Finally the hammerblow is delivered. **36...Qb7.** One last hope- the mate at g2. **37.Qf3.** End of discussion. **White won.**

CATALAN

The **Catalan** is a somewhat unusual opening which is designed to avoid the Nimzoindian and Queen's Indian Defenses. It is a hybrid of an Indian Game, Closed Game and a Flank Game.

It enjoyed a brief spate of popularity in the 1980s, when Kasparov used it in his semifinal match against Korchnoi, and the first English language monograph on the subject appeared, which was coincidentally my first solo book. Now it is considered harmless and usually leads to a draw.

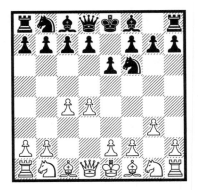

1.d4	**Nf6**
2.c4	**e6**
3.g3	

(78) EUWE - KRAMER
Match, 1941

1.d4 Nf6; 2.c4 e6; 3.g3. 3...d5. The normal reply, though 3...c5 is also good, especially for fans of the Benoni. **4.Bg2.** The "Catalan Bishop" is a powerful weapon for White, and Black must make sure it does not create havoc along the long diagonal. **4...dxc4.** Black can adopt a closed formation with 4...c6 as an alternative to opening up the game this way. **5.Qa4+.** The old main line has fallen from favor. 5.Nf3 Be7; 6.0-0 0-0; 7.Qc2 a6; 8.Qxc4 b5; 9.Qc2 Bb7 leads to a balanced game which usually ends in a draw. **5...Nbd7; 6.Nd2.** A somewhat unusual move. Euwe and Kramer, who were friends, collaborated on some fine instructional books. Perhaps they just wanted to avoid positions they may have studied together. Normal is 6.Qxc4. **6...c6; 7.Qxc4 e5**.

This is a well-established defense to the 6.Nd2 line. Black creates counterplay in the center. **8.Ngf3 Nb6.** Black can also capture at d4, but there is nothing wrong with this move. **9.Qd3 exd4; 10.Nxd4.** Capturing with the lady is actually more ambitious, even though it offers an exchange of queens. This was the plan adopted in an important game in the Women's World Championship cycle. 10.Qxd4 Qxd4; 11.Nxd4 Be7; 12.b3 0-0; 13.Bb2 and in Chiburdanidze-Akhmylovskaya, 9th match game 1986, White could have made more of her advantage.

10...Be7; 11.0–0 0–0; 12.N2b3 Bg4. Perhaps 12...Re8 is stronger, as played by Averbakh a dozen years later. **13.h3 Bd7; 14.Nf5! Be6**. The bishop has been dancing to White's tune, and the initiative is clearly with the first player. **15.Qxd8 Bxd8; 16.Nd6**.

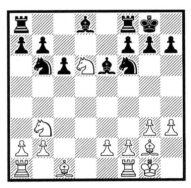

White has a clear advantage. The pawn at b7 is very weak. This is why the bishop should have stayed home. **16...Rb8; 17.Nc5**. Now the pawn falls, and White's advantage grows. It is in the nature of the Catalan that victory will take some time to achieve, usually in the endgame stage. **17...Nfd5; 18.Ndxb7 Be7; 19.Nxe6 fxe6; 20.Na5**. Black's position is riddled with weaknesses.

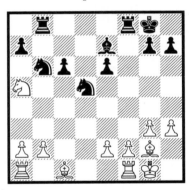

20...Rbc8; 21.Bd2 c5; 22.b3 c4; 23.bxc4 Nxc4; 24.Nxc4 Rxc4. Black has eliminated a weak pawn, but at a high cost. White has the bishop pair, and simplifying the position works well for him. **25.Rfc1 Rfc8; 26.Rxc4 Rxc4; 27.Bxd5 exd5**. Now the bishop pair is gone, but there are even fewer pieces, and the importance of White's extra pawn grows dramatically. **28.Rc1 Bf6; 29.Rxc4 dxc4**.

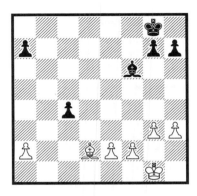

Now it is just a bishop ending which presents no real difficulties to White. It just takes a little time to score the point, since pawns walk slowly. **30.Bc1 Kf7; 31.e4 Ke6; 32.f4 Bd4+; 33.Kf1 h5; 34.Ke2 a6; 35.Be3 Bc3; 36.Kd1 g6; 37.Bf2 Kf6; 38.Kc2 Ba5; 39.Bd4+ Ke6; 40.g4 hxg4; 41.hxg4 Bb4; 42.Bc3 Bc5; 43.Kd2 Bb6; 44.Ke2 Bc5; 45.Kf3 Ba3; 46.f5+. White won.**

OLD INDIAN

The **Old Indian** is also related to the King's Indian, and can transpose easily to it if Black later plays ...g6. After 1.d4 Nf6; 2.c4 d6, we have the starting position:

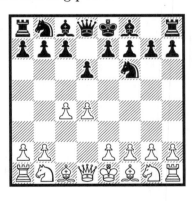

1.d4	**Nf6**
2.c4	**d6**

In the traditional approaches, Black's goal is to play an early ...e5. This is a strategy which most World Champions reject, though Mikhail Tal used it. In fact, he considered an Old Indian game, played between Rashid Nyezhmetdinov and Lev Polugayevsky, to be the best game of chess ever played. That game is far too complicated to discuss here, but it is the subject of an entire book by the author and will appear in my forthcoming *Standard Chess Openings*.

Our illustrative game is a pretty entertaining one too, if a bit one-sided!

(79) ALEKHINE - KIENINGER
Poland, 1941

1.d4 Nf6; 2.c4 d6; 3.Nc3. Now Black can try 3...Bf5, the Janowski-Indian, which often transposes to a King's Indian. The more typical Old Indians see either 3...Nbd7, or an immediate advance of the e-pawn to e5. **3...e5.**

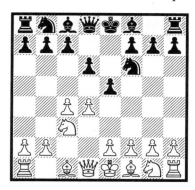

The main problem with the Old Indian is a lack of space. This game presents a rather extreme, but quite clear example of how White can use this to great advantage. **4.Nf3.** 4.dxe5 dxe5; 5.Qxd8+ Kxd8 is not particularly advantageous for White because the pawn at c4 is just in the way, and weakens the a5-e1 diagonal. **4...Nc6.** This knight belongs at d7, though that blocks the bishop at c8. Developing the knight is therefore problematic in the Old Indian. 4...e4; 5.Ng5 Qe7 is an interesting alternative for Black. **5.d5 Nb8; 6.e4.** White has a large advantage in space, which will be expanded as the game goes on. **6...Be7.** Black might have tried getting the bishop to g4 before White prevented it with his next move. **7.h3 0–0; 8.Be3 Re8.**

We can see Black struggling already. The idea behind this move is to free up f8 for use by a minor piece, for example ...Nd7-f8. We will discover that the e8 square needed to be kept available for a retreat by the knight at f6.

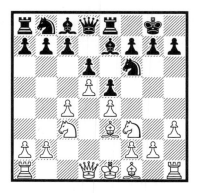

With a safe king and locked center, there is no need for White to hasten castling. The time is already ripe for a kingside pawnstorm. The king can leap to the queenside later. **9.g4! c5.** This is a bad move, because it keeps the queenside closed. But Black was worried about a retreat square for the knight, since if it went to d7 while White could advance the c-pawn to c5, the d6-square could become quite a problem. Here we see the drawback of placing the rook at e8. **10.Rg1 a6; 11.g5 Nfd7; 12.h4 Nf8; 13.h5.**

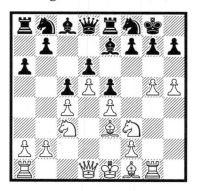

Black has just a single piece beyond the first rank, and that one is paralyzed with no available moves! **13...b6; 14.Nh4 g6; 15.Qf3 Ra7; 16.0-0-0.** White finally castles, and the end is in sight. **16...Qc7; 17.Bd3 Bd8; 18.Rg2 Kh8; 19.Rh1 Rb7.**

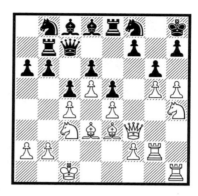

Black's pieces are almost comical. Alekhine may have had a hard time keeping a straight face here. He certainly could be forgiven a little smile when playing his next move. **20.Nf5!!** Alekhine sacrifices a knight just to get one pawn out of the way, but that pawn is the key to Black's defense. **20...gxf5.** 20...Kg8; 21.Nh6+ Kg7. **21.exf5 e4.** A desperate attempt to get some breathing room, hoping that the knight on b8 can find its way to e5. **22.Nxe4 Nbd7.**

23.Bd2. White is prepared for Black's jump to e5. The bishop will shift to c5, bearing down on the long diagonal and pinning the knight. So Black tries to close the diagonal down. **23...f6; 24.Bc3 Ne5; 25.gxf6 Qf7.** If Black had captured the queen, a nasty surprise would have been sprung by Alekhine: 25...Nxf3; 26.f7+ Ne5; 27.Rg8 mate. **26.Rhg1!!**

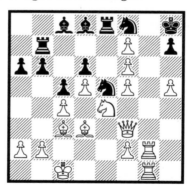

The queen is still taboo. **26...h6.** 26...Nxf3; 27.Rg8+ Qxg8; 28.f7+ Qg7; 29.Bxg7 mate. **27.Bxe5 Rxe5; 28.Rg7.** The rest is brutal. **28...Qxg7; 29.fxg7+ Rxg7; 30.Rxg7 Kxg7; 31.f6+. White won.**

11. FLANK GAMES

INTRODUCTION

Flank games are those in which White delays or avoids the occupation of the center with pawns. Usually these involve stationing a bishop at g2 and castling kingside. White's desired formation can often be achieved regardless of enemy defenses, so let's look at just the White side. Move order is not very important, because these are the most transpositional openings of all.

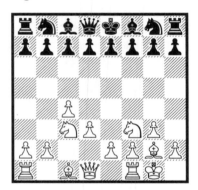

OVERVIEW

White's choice of approach is determined primarily by whether White is willing to allow Black to plant a pawn in the center. If White does not want Black to play ...d5, then 1.c4, the **English Opening**, is the best choice. If ...e5 is annoying, then 1.Nf3, leading to the **Reti Opening** (if White later plays c4) or **King's Indian Attack** (a delayed e4) is indicated.

All of the modern World Champions have played flank openings, though Botvinnik, Smyslov and Petrosian were the most enthusiastic. Playing a flank opening is often like playing a Black defense with an extra move. Because these Black defenses are not designed for attack, in most cases, the extra move is not always meaningful. Indeed, it is sometimes even awkward, as White is forced to make certain important decisions before the opponent's formation is fixed.

The following game is a good example of a Flank opening.

(80) CAPABLANCA - ALEKHINE
World Championship (3rd game), 1927

1.d4 Nf6; 2.Nf3 b6; 3.g3. This move will often lead to a Queen's Indian, if White plays c4 later. In this game Capablanca held that move back until it was particularly effective. **3...Bb7; 4.Bg2 c5; 5.0-0 cxd4; 6.Nxd4 Bxg2; 7.Kxg2 d5?!** 7...g6 is best. The players were no doubt familiar with 8.c4 Qc8, 9.b3 Bg7, 10.Bb2 Nc6 where Black had an acceptable game in Tarrasch-Grunfeld, Breslau, 1925. **8.c4! e6?** 8...dxc4 would have been strong, because 9.Qa4+ runs into 9...Qd7; 10.Nb5 Qc6+; 11.Kg1 Nfd7!! Alekhine failed to spot this resource, concentrating only on 11...Nbd7 with a level game. The retreat of the other knight is stronger, however, as the queen at c6 remains defended, as does the pawn at c4. **9.Qa4+ Qd7.** 9...Nbd7 could be met by 10.Bg5! **10.Nb5!**

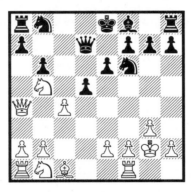

White sets up the threat of Nc7+. **10...Nc6; 11.cxd5 exd5.** Any other capture is met by the strong move 12.e4! **12.Bf4 Rc8; 13.Rc1.** A move which sets up serious threats. **13...Bc5.** 13...Nh5 allows a different threat to be executed: 14.Bc7! a6; 15.Qxa6 Rxc7; 16.Nxc7+ Qxc7; 17.Qb5 Bc5; 18.b4 and the pins are driven into Black's position; 13...Ne4!? is possible, though White should have the advantage after an immediate b4; 13...Be7; 14.Nc7+ Rxc7; 15.Bxc7 Qxc7; 16.Rxc6 Qd7; 17.Rc8+ Bd8; 18.Qxd7+ Kxd7; 19.Ra8 and White wins. **14.b4! Bxb4.** According to Lasker, Black should have taken with the knight. **15.Rxc6!** A small but fine sacrifice which obtains a sizable advantage. **15...Rxc6.** Taking with the queen would not have been any better. **16.Qxb4.**

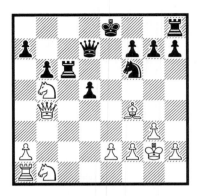

16...Ne4; 17.Nd2 Nxd2; 18.Qxd2?! A slight slip. Taking with the bishop would have been stronger, because Black would not be able to castle. **18...0–0; 19.Rd1**. The pawn at d5 is dead meat. This position is simply winning for White. **19...Rc5; 20.Nd4 Re8; 21.Nb3 Rcc8; 22.e3 Qa4**. An attempt to generate counterplay, but it fails. **23.Qxd5! Rc2**. 23...Qxa2; 24.Ra1 Qb2; 25.Rxa7 Qf6; 26.Nd4 and Black has no counterplay. **24.Rd2 Rxa2**. 24...Qxa2 was the only alternative, and now 25.Qd7 Rf8; 26.Rxc2 Qxc2; 27.Nd4 Qc5 is met by 28.Nc6! for example 28...a5; 29.Ne7+ Kh8; 30.Bd6 and here Black must play 30...Qg5 to stop Ng6+; since now Black could take with the queen and threaten to start a series of checks at e4. 31.Nf5 Rg8; 32.Qxf7 and Black, faced with the threat of Be5, can give up. 32...Qg6; 33.Qxg8+ Kxg8; 34.Ne7+ Kf7; 35.Nxg6 Kxg6; 36.Bc7 etc. **25.Rxa2 Qxa2; 26.Qc6 Rf8; 27.Nd4**.

Although Black has two connected passed pawns, the combined force of White's queen and minor pieces create too much of a threat against the enemy king, and their mobility keeps the pawns tied down. **27...Kh8; 28.Be5**. The threat of a sacrifice at g7 is in the air. **28...f6**. 28...Rd8; 29.Bxg7+ Kxg7; 30.Nf5+ Kf8; 31.Qf6 Qd5+; 32.Kh3 and White wins. **29.Ne6 Rg8; 30.Bd4 h6**. 30...Qa5 allows; 31.Nxg7! Rxg7; 32.Qa8+ Rg8; 33.Bxf6 mate. **31.h4!** A finesse. The sacrifice at g7 does not work immediately. 31.Nxg7? Rxg7; 32.Qxf6 Qd5+;

33.Kg1 Qg5!; 34.Qxg7+ Qxg7; 35.Bxg7+ Kxg7 would be much more difficult to win. 36.Kf1 a5; 37.Ke2 a4; 38.Kd2 b5; (38...a3?; 39.Kc2 a2; 40.Kb2) 39.Kc3 a3; 40.Kb3 b4 and the White pawns must handle the enemy king alone.

31...Qb1. Now the sacrifice works. **32.Nxg7! Qg6.** 32...Rxg7 loses to 33.Qxf6 Qe4+ (33...Qh7; 34.Qf8+ Qg8; 35.Bxg7+ Kh7; 36.Qxg8+) 34.Kg1 Qb7; 35.Qxh6+ Kg8; 36.Qxg7+ Qxg7; 37.Bxg7 Kxg7; 38.Kf1! and there are four pawns against the king, a simple win. 38...a5; 39.Ke2 a4; 40.Kd2 a3; 41.Kc2 b5; 42.Kb3 b4; 43.e4 Kf6; 44.h5 Kg5; 45.g4 Kf6; 46.h6 Kg6; 47.g5 Kf7; 48.e5 Kg6; 49.e6. **33.h5 Qf7.** The knight cannot be taken because of Bxf6. **34.Nf5 Kh7; 35.Qe4 Re8; 36.Qf4 Qf8; 37.Nd6 Re7.**

The f-pawn falls, and with it, the game. **38.Bxf6 Qa8+; 39.e4 Rg7; 40.Bxg7 Kxg7; 41.Nf5+ Kf7; 42.Qc7+. White won.**

ENGLISH OPENING

1.c4

The **English Opening** was developed by Howard Staunton, the Englishman who invented our standard chess pieces in the middle of the 19th century. It is only slightly inferior to 1.e4 or 1.d4, in that it does not immediately allow a bishop to get into the game.

Once considered a minor diversion, the English is now one of the main openings, and many different strategies have been developed for Black. We'll consider four of them.

KING'S ENGLISH

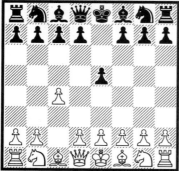

1.c4   e5

It is obvious that the **King's English** is a reversed Sicilian Defense. Given that the Sicilian is a pretty good defense to 1.e4, it doesn't seem too logical to accept the same positions with one less move. Indeed, most of the World Champions avoid it, but some players are so comfortable on the White side of the Sicilian that they don't mind the missing move. After all, Black can steer the game into lines where it is not so significant.

Their confidence seems to be justified, as the reversed Sicilian occupies a prominent place in the English. Often Black will delay advancing a pawn to d5, adopting a more closed strategy where the quiet nature of the position reduces the importance of the extra move.

(81) SIGURJONSSON - SMYSLOV
Reykjavik, 1974

1.c4 e5; 2.Nc3 Nf6; 3.Nf3 Nc6. This is the Four Knights Variation of the King's English. White has many different plans, but the kingside fianchetto, aiming for a reversed Dragon Sicilian, has always been among the most popular. **4.g3**.

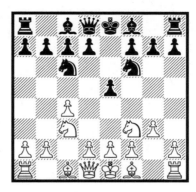

4...Bb4. Smyslov had played this against Fischer back in 1959, and got an acceptable game. **5.Bg2 0–0; 6.0–0**. Now 6...d5 would lead to the reversed Dragon, but Smyslov plays more aggressively and denies White that opportunity. **6...e4!; 7.Ng5 Bxc3; 8.bxc3 Re8**. Black has given up a bishop for a knight, but the strong pawn at e4 and uncoordinated White army is more than enough compensation. **9.f3**. Advancing the d-pawn instead would have been less risky. **9...exf3; 10.Nxf3 d5!** Only now is this an appropriate move. **11.cxd5 Qxd5** .

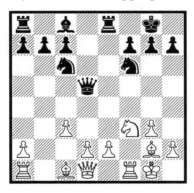

A bold but correct capture. Discovered attacks by the Nf3 are not a problem. **12.Nd4 Qh5; 13.Nxc6 bxc6; 14.e3**. 14.Bxc6 would run into 14...Qc5+. **14...Bg4; 15.Qa4 Re6; 16.Rb1 Be2**.

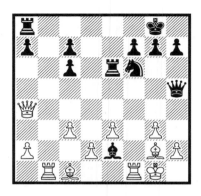

An annoying move. The rook must move, but has no happy destination. **17.Re1.** 17.Rf2 Ng4; 18.Bxc6 Nxf2; 19.Bxa8 Nh3;+ 20.Kg2 h6 and with the back rank attended to, White's king will not survive for long, according to analysis by Smyslov. **17...Ng4; 18.h3 Qf5.** The attack on the rook at b1 makes the threat at f2 unstoppable. **19.Rxe2 Qxb1; 20.Qxg4 Qxc1+; 21.Kh2 Rd8.** White has no compensation for the exchange. The d-pawn cannot advance because then the pawn at e3 would fall. **22.Qb4 h6; 23.c4 Qd1; 24.Rf2 Qe1.** The hunt is over. White resigned.

SYMMETRICAL ENGLISH

Symmetry is very dangerous for Black in the Open Games, less so in the Closed Games, and quite acceptable in the slower Flank Games. Black has often met 1.c4 with 1...c5, the **Symmetrical English**, insuring that it will be some time before White can advance the d-pawn to d4 without penalty.

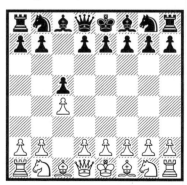

1.c4   c5

Black has not given up many options here, and is free to fianchetto bishops on either side, or neither. White usually develops in the normal flank fashion with a fianchetto at g2, and defers any direct conflict until the middlegame.

(82) PETROSIAN - PETERS
Lone Pine, 1976

1.c4 Nf6; 2.Nc3 c5; 3.g3 Nc6; 4.Bg2 e6; 5.Nf3 Be7; 6.d4 d5. Here 6...cxd4 might lead to a hedgehog, but this move leads to a Semi-Tarrasch or Tarrasch Defense. **7.cxd5 Nxd5.** Capturing with the pawn would transpose to the Classical Tarrasch. **8.0–0 0–0; 9.Nxd5 exd5**.

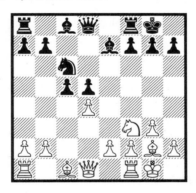

If there were still knights at c3 and f6, then we would be in the main lines of the Tarrasch, but this is a Semi-Tarrasch, which is easier to defend for Black because the knight at c3 gives rise to more possibilities than the one at f6. Their absence also gives Black more freedom to maneuver. **10.dxc5 Bxc5**. This is the main line of the formation known as the Keres-Parma Variation. **11.a3**. There are no less than eight reasonable moves for White here, and of course transpositions are possible later on. **11...a5**. This is a rather strange reaction, prompted no doubt by the fear of an advance of the White b-pawn to b4. 11...Bf5; 12.b4 Bb6 is roughly level, and Boris Spassky has defended the Black side.

For example, here is a bit of his game against Portisch at Bugojno 1978: 13.Ra2 Be4; 14.Rd2 Qe7; 15.Bb2 Rfe8; 16.Qa1 f6; 17.Rfd1 Qe6 with full equality. **12.Ne1 d4; 13.Nd3 Bb6**. Black's pieces are awkwardly placed, and White has a blockade in place. **14.Bd2 Re8; 15.Rc1 Bg4**. The pawn at e2 is a natural source of counterplay, just as in a Tarrasch Defense. **16.Re1 Rc8; 17.h3**. The pressure at e2 is diminished. **17...Bf5; 18.Qb3 Be4**. The exchange of light-squared bishops helps maintain the pawn at d4, since the knight at c6 cannot be eliminated by the bishop. At the same time, however, there are fewer resources for Black to use in any attack. **19.Bxe4 Rxe4; 20.Qb5**.

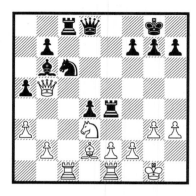

White stands better because the d-pawn is permanently blockaded and Black has no realistic attacking chances. **20...Na7; 21.Rxc8 Nxc8; 22.Bg5 Qd6; 23.Rc1**. Every one of White's pieces is on a good square, and Black's pieces are scattered and uncoordinated. **23...Na7; 24.Qf5 Re8; 25.Bf4 Qd8; 26.Rc2**. White's position gets better all the time. Still, good technique is required to convert the advantage into a win. **26...Nc6; 27.h4 h6; 28.Qb5 Na7; 29.Qf5**. Petrosian marks time, trying to figure out a way to make further progress. **29...Nc6; 30.Kf1 Re6; 31.Qb5 Na7; 32.Qb3 Nc6; 33.h5 Ne7**.

34.Ke1. Now a plan is developed. The king will head to the queenside, and then a real kingside attack can be mounted. **34...Nd5; 35.Qb5 Nf6; 36.Kd1 Nd5; 37.Be5 Ne7; 38.g4 Nc6; 39.Bg3 Na7; 40.Qb3 Nc6; 41.Kc1 Re4; 42.f3**. The slight weakening of e3 is not important. **42...Re3; 43.Kb1 Ne7; 44.Bh4 Qd6**.

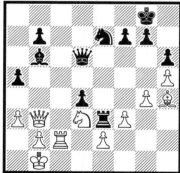

Petrosian has been slowly working out a plan, but often one needs a little help from the opponent. Perhaps Peters didn't think that White would be willing to part with the bishop, but Petrosian saw an opportunity and grabbed it. **45.Bxe7! Rxe7**. Black cannot capture with the queen because that would leave the bishop at b6 hanging. **46.Rc8+ Kh7; 47.Rf8**. The f-pawn falls and the game is quickly over. Note that this was made possible by the White pawns at g4 and h5, and those advances were made possible only after Petrosian walked the king to the queenside. **47...Qc7; 48.f4 Bc5; 49.Qd5 Re5; 50.Rxf7. White won.**

ANGLO-INDIAN AND THE HEDGEHOG

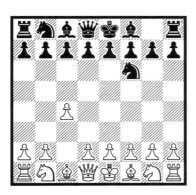

1.c4   Nf6

When Black answers 1.c4 with 1...Nf6, which is the **Anglo-Indian Defense**, there is usually an implicit message: "Look, just play 2.d4 and let's get back to the normal Indian Defenses." White can accept or decline the invitation, but if the pawn eventually goes to d3 instead of d4, it is very hard for White to obtain any advantage.

This is the most flexible approach for Black, and the World Champions generally adopt it. But there is no real significance to the choice of any first move except for 1...e5, and it is the transpositional guessing game that takes center stage.

The **Hedgehog** can be reached by a bewildering variety of move orders, and it is not easy to classify as belonging to any of them. The following position is fairly typical. Black has exchanged the c-pawn for White's d-pawn, and White has the Maroczy Bind formation (pawns at e4 and c4). Both sides castle kingside.

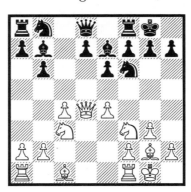

Black will try to play ...d5, just as in the Sicilian (from which the Hedgehog can be reached), but won't find it easy. Creative solutions are required in this subtle and complex opening.

(83) SMYSLOV - ANDERSSON
Biel (Interzonal), 1976

1.c4. The Hedgehog can be reached from many different openings, but the most common is the method seen in this game, which applies the Symmetrical English. **1...c5; 2.Nf3 Nf6; 3.g3 b6.** Black counters White's fianchetto plan with one of his own. **4.Bg2 Bb7; 5.0–0 e6; 6.Nc3 Be7; 7.d4 cxd4; 8.Qxd4.** Usually it is unwise to bring the queen to the center of the board so early in the game, but if White used the knight to capture, then the light-squared bishops would be exchanged at g2. Black now usually chooses between plans involving ...Nc6 and those with ...d6 and ...Nbd7. It is also possible to combine the two plans, as in this game. That strategy requires a deep knowledge of transpositional pitfalls. **8...d6**

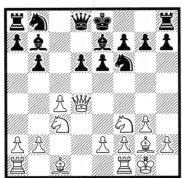

This is a hedgehog position. From here on it is difficult to determine the very best moves, and a great deal of subtlety and farsight is needed. **9.b3**. 9.e4 a6 is very common, for example 10.b3 (10.Qe3 Nbd7; 11.Nd4 Qc7; 12.b3 0–0; 13.Bb2 Rfe8 is another typical formation, which Kasparov has defended as Black.) 10...Nbd7; 11.Rd1 Qc7; 12.Ba3 Nc5; 13.e5 dxe5; 14.Qxe5 Rc8 which has been successfully defended by six-time United States Champion Walter Browne in many professional encounters. **9...0–0; 10.Bb2**. 10.Ba3! is more popular. The idea is to gang up on the pawn at d6. **10...a6; 11.Rfd1**.

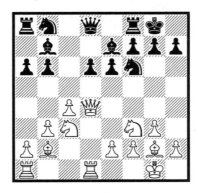

Now with 11...Nbd7 the game would transpose into well-known lines. Such are the transpositional thickets of the hedgehog. But even the finest researchers on the English, Russia's Vladimir Bagirov and America's John Watson, fail to notice that the knight can come to c6 now, transposing to a position Watson considers elsewhere in his famous monograph. That is not a criticism of either author, it is a consequence of the very highly transpositional nature of the hedgehog.

11...Nc6. 11...Nbd7 is the normal move, for example: 12.Qe3 Qc7; 13.h3 and now Black puzzles over 13...Rfc8; 13...Rac8; both played by Browne, or John Watson's preferred 13...Rfe8 after which Black can choose a position for the other rook. **12.Qf4 Qb8.** Black is adopting a normal strategy of having the queen support d6 from b8, with the possibility of bringing the rook from f8 to d8 for more support. As for the rook at a8, it can play a role at a7, defending along the seventh rank and making the a8-square available to the queen, which can team up with the bishop at b7 to slice down along the long diagonal. **13.Ng5!** A strong move. Notice how firmly White controls the e4 square. **13...Ra7; 14.Nce4 Ne5!**

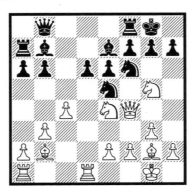

Andersson is one of the greatest exponents of the hedgehog defenses, and has an excellent sense of timing. Black is going to create counterplay by playing ...b5 and putting pressure on the pawn at c4. **15.Nxf6+ Bxf6; 16.Bxb7 Rxb7**. The exchanges have brought about a position where Black is going to need some counterplay. The pawn at d6 is now a real weakness. **17.Ne4 Be7; 18.Rd2 Ng6; 19.Qe3 Rd8; 20.Rad1 b5**.

Now the game is a real fight. Smyslov and Andersson are among the greatest positional players ever. Smyslov shows his Championship mettle by forcing the Black b-pawn to advance, relieving pressure on the center. **21.Qc3!** First, a small weakness is created on the other flank. **21...f6; 22.Qe3 Nf8**. 22...bxc4; 23.Nxd6 was given by Andersson. The point can be seen in the variation 23...Rxd6; 24.Rxd6 Bxd6; 25.Qxe6+ Rf7; 26.Rxd6 cxb3; 27.axb3 and White should win. **23.Ba3! b4; 24.Bb2**. Now Black has preserved the d-pawn, but has no source of counterplay. This does not mean the game is lost, just that no further mistakes can be made by Black. **24...Qc7; 25.Rd3 Qc6; 26.Qf3 Rc7; 27.Nd2 Qxf3; 28.Nxf3**.

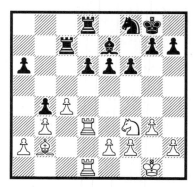

28...Kf7? Andersson probably didn't realize that he could get away with 28...Nd7, but he later published the following line. 28...Nd7!, 29.Rxd6? (I think that 29.e4!? is probably best, as after 29...Nc5; 30.Re3 White has a lock on the center. But White's advantage would be pretty small.) 29...Bxd6; 30.Rxd6 e5! the point being that 31.Rxa6 is met by 31...Nc5 and Black threatens to encircle the White bishop with ...Rd1+ and ...Rb1. **29.a3 bxa3; 30.Bxa3**. The pressure is just too much. Black's next move hastens the end. **30...Rc6?**. 30...Rb8 would have offered more resistance. **31.Nd4**. White has enough advantages to put together a winning plan. **31...Rb6; 32.Nc2 Rc6; 33.c5 e5; 34.cxd6 Bxd6; 35.Ne3**. Now it is just a matter of mopping up. **35...Bxa3; 36.Rxd8 Ne6; 37.R8d7+ Kg6; 38.Nc4 Bb4; 39.e3 Nc5. White won.**.

RETI OPENING

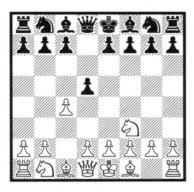

1.Nf3   d5
2.c4

The **Reti** is a cousin of the other Flank Games, and strategies are pretty much the same. The difference is that the tension between the pawn at c4 and the enemy pawn at d5 is a constant factor. If Black captures at c4, then White will be able to take over more of the center and perhaps obtain the ideal pawn center. If Black advances, we get the reversed Benoni where the additional move for White can be of great use.

Therefore Black usually shores up the defense of d5 with ...e6 or ...c6. White will then fianchetto, castle kingside, and then throw the queenside pawns forward.

Many World Champions have played the Reti, and there is no better example from them than the critical final match game of the 1987 World Championship, where Garry Kasparov desperately needed to win with White to retain the crown.

(84) KASPAROV - KARPOV
World Championship (game 24), 1987

1.c4 e6; 2.Nf3 Nf6; 3.g3 d5; 4.b3.

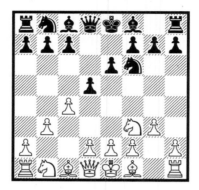

Kasparov's choice of the Reti for this critical game, which he had to win at all costs, was a big surprise. The Reti requires a lot of patience, and this contest would be a battle of nerves. **4...Be7; 5.Bg2 0–0; 6.0–0 b6; 7.Bb2 Bb7; 8.e3.** White makes it clear that he will not transpose to the Catalan. **8...Nbd7; 9.Nc3 Ne4**.

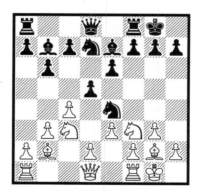

10.Ne2!? This was a new move, deviating from Geller-Kholmov, USSR Championship 1969. That game saw 10.cxd5 Nxc3; 11.Bxc3 Bxd5; 12.Qe2 Nf6; 13.Rfd1 Qc8; 14.Rac1 a5; 15.d3 c5 and White was not able to achieve anything significant. By removing his knight from c3, Kasparov is later to drive back the knight, without having to exchange. **10...a5; 11.d3 Bf6; 12.Qc2 Bxb2; 13.Qxb2**.

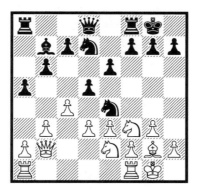

13...Nd6. Karpov has succeeded in removing a pair of pieces from the board, but now White will be able to play d2-d4 without locking in his bishop. Of the remaining bishops, White's is clearly the more powerful, and the White queen is also more active. **14.cxd5 Bxd5**. At first it seems as though White has only assisted Black by unlocking the light-squared bishop, but in fact it only becomes more exposed. **15.d4!**

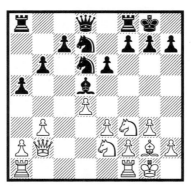

15...c5; 16.Rfd1 Rc8; 17.Nf4. It is clear now that White is trying to work the queenside, while Black is merely defending. If the bishop retreats, then White will dominate the center, e.g. **17...Bxf3**. 17...Bb7; 18.d5! exd5; 19.Nxd5; **18.Bxf3 Qe7; 19.Rac1 Rfd8; 20.dxc5 Nxc5; 21.b4! axb4; 22.Qxb4**.

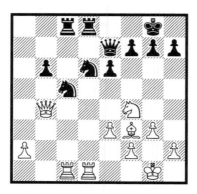

White concludes that the subsequent weakness of his a2-pawn will be less significant than the weakness of the b6-pawn. One supporting point is the strategic possibility of advancing the a-pawn and taking control of both the a-file and the b-file.

Then the advantage of bishop versus knight will be felt. **22...Qa7; 23.a3 Nf5; 24.Rb1 Rxd1+; 25.Rxd1.**

Considering that all Karpov needed was a draw to become World Champion, Kasparov is remarkably cooperative when it comes to exchanging pieces. But he has concrete strategic goals, which can, and will be met.

25...Qc7; 26.Nd3. White has a small advantage, with bishop against knight. Karpov advances the wrong pawn now. **26...h6.** 26...g6 would have been wiser, since the dark squares are safer than the light squares, because White has only a light-squared bishop. **27.Rc1 Ne7; 28.Qb5 Nf5; 29.a4!**

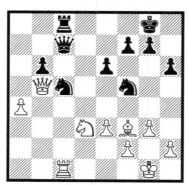

29...Nd6! White was threatening to play 30.a5, undermining the position of the c5-knight. **30.Qb1 Qa7; 31.Ne5!** White renews the threat. Now 32.a5 brings with it the threat of Ne5-c6. **31...Nxa4.** 31...Qxa4; 32.Qxb6 Qa3; 33.Rd1 gives White a big advantage: 33...Nde4; (33...Ne8; 34.Rd8 Rxd8; 35.Qxd8 Qa1+; 36.Kg2 Qxe5; 37.Qxe8+ Kh7; 38.Qxf7 and White is clearly better) 34.Bxe4 Nxe4; 35.Qb7 and White wins. **32.Rxc8+ Nxc8; 33.Qd1?** An error in time

pressure. Kasparov later pointed out that 33.Qb5! was the correct move.
33...Ne7?! Karpov returns the favor. 33...Nc5 would have held the game.

Kasparov provides the following line 34.Qd8+ Kh7; 35.Kg2 f6!; 36.Nc6
Qd7; 37.Qxd7 Nxd7; 38.Nd8 Nc5; 39.Nxe6! Nxe6; 40.Bg4 with a likely draw.
34.Qd8+ Kh7; 35.Nxf7 Ng6; 36.Qe8! ... 37.Be4 and 38.Qh8 mate! **36...Qe7.**
36...Nc5, 37.Bh5! and White is ready to unleash 38.Ng5+! **37.Qxa4 Qxf7.** The
stage is set for the remainder of the game. The weak b6-pawn will fall, and
then it will be a question of whether White can improve his position sufficiently so that Black will run out of moves. **38.Be4!**

38...Kg8; 39.Qb5 Nf8; 40.Qxb6 Qf6; 41.Qb5 Qe7; 42.Kg2

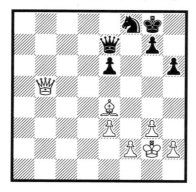

The sealed move. During the adjournment, chessboards all over the world
were subjected to energetic pounding of pieces as chessplayers debated the
probable result of the 1987 World Championship. If the Black pawns stood at
h7 and g6, then the queens could safely be exchanged with a high probability
of reaching a position which Averbakh gives as a win for White, since the
White king will be able to infiltrate. **42...g6.** This seems like an early conces-
sion, but Black obtains additional breathing room for his queen, which has an
additional square from which to protect the f8-knight. **43.Qa5 Qg7; 44.Qc5
Qf7; 45.h4! h5** Black should just have played ...Kg7. This creates permanent

weaknesses. **46.Qc6 Qe7; 47.Bd3 Qf7; 48.Qd6 Kg7**.

49.e4! An important move which launches the winning plan. The pawn will be established at e5, and the e4 square can later be used by the bishop. **49...Kg8; 50.Bc4 Kg7; 51.Qe5+ Kg8; 52.Qd6 Kg7; 53.Bb5 Kg8; 54.Bc6 Qa7; 55.Qb4! Qc7; 56.Qb7**.

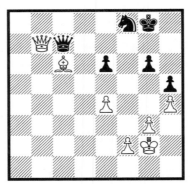

White finally offers an exchange of queens, which Karpov declines. Evidently, the advance of the e4-pawn to e5 and the excellent placement of the Bc6 would have created the requisite positional advantage for a win. Presumably, both players had analyzed the consequences of such an action at home and one must remember that Black's reply was the last move of time control. **56...Qd8; 57.e5!** Now the position is clearly winning. **57...Qa5; 58.Be8 Qc5; 59.Qf7+!** Now the White Bishop will reach the b1–h7 diagonal. There is no longer any defense. **59...Kh8; 60.Ba4 Qd5+; 61.Kh2 Qc5; 62.Bb3 Qc8; 63.Bd1 Qc5; 64.Kg2!**

Karpov resigned because there was no defense to the simple plan of bringing the bishop to e4, followed by the capture of the g6-pawn, after which the queen ending is not worth disputing. **White won.**

(85) PETROSIAN - TAL
Curacao (Candidates' Tournament), 1962

1.c4 Nf6; 2.g3 c6; 3.Nf3 d5; 4.b3 Bf5. This is another typical Reti formation.

5.Ba3. Preventing ...e6. **5...g6; 6.d3 Bg7; 7.Nbd2 Qb6.** 7...0-0 ... Re8 and e5, would have been better. Tal's tactical adventure is unsound. **8.Bg2 Ng4!?** Possibly he was attempting to unsettle his opponent, who was noted for his preference for strategic battles. **9.d4!**

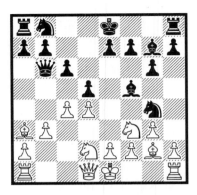

A splendid pawn sacrifice which cuts right across Black's plans. **9...Na6.** 9...Bxd4; 10.Nxd4 Qxd4; 11.0–0 leaves White with the advantage of the bishop pair, and the a1–h8 diagonal will soon belong to White. **10.0–0 Nb4.** Black aims at the vulnerable c2-square, which is usually a good plan. **11.Bb2 0–0.** 11...Nc2 cannot be played just yet because of 12.Rc1 Nxd4, 13.c5! and Black cannot avoid loss of material. **12.a3 Na6; 13.Rc1 Rad8; 14.b4 Nb8; 15.Qb3 Nf6; 16.a4** White has an advantage. The queenside pawns have plenty of support and Black does not have any significant counterplay. **16...Ne4; 17.Rfd1 Nd7; 18.cxd5 cxd5; 19.a5 Qd6.** 19...Qb5? loses to 20.e3 when Bf1 can embarrass the enemy queen. **20.b5 Nxd2; 21.Rxd2 Rc8.** Now Black seeks to reduce White's pressure through exchanges. **22.Nh4! Rxc1+; 23.Bxc1.**

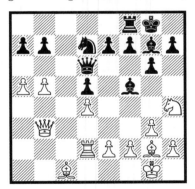

23...Qc7. 23...Rc8; 24.Ba3 Qc7; 25.Nxf5 gxf5; 26.Bxe7 and Black's pawns are wrecked. **24.Nxf5.** A neat reply to Black's double attack. **24...gxf5.** 24...Qxc1+; 25.Rd1 and Black loses material. **25.Ba3 Qxa5; 26.Qb4!** Black's pawns would fall in any endgame. **26...Qb6; 27.Bxd5 e6; 28.Bf3 Rc8; 29.Qa4 Rc7; 30.Kg2 a6.** Black hopes to have drawing chances in an ending. 30...Nf6; 31.e3 Nd5; 32.Bxd5 exd5; 33.Bc5 wins the a-pawn. **31.bxa6 Qxa6; 32.Qxa6 bxa6; 33.e3.** White has constructed a dominating position. The pawn at a6 is merely weak. **33...a5; 34.Ra2 Ra7; 35.Bb4 a4; 36.Bc6 Bf8; 37.Bxf8 Kxf8;**

38.Rxa4 Rc7. 38...Rxa4; 39.Bxa4 will lead to a win for White. **39.Bxd7 Rxd7; 40.Kf3 Kg7; 41.Kf4 Kf6; 42.h3 h5.** Preventing g4, but creating a new weakness. **43.Ra8.**

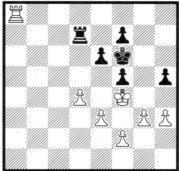

43...Rb7? The decisive mistake. 43...Kg6 was necessary when Black's position is still capable of stiff resistance. **44.Rg8! Rb2; 45.Kf3 Rd2; 46.h4 Ke7; 47.Rg5 Kf8; 48.Rxh5 Kg7; 49.Rg5+ Kh7; 50.h5.** 50.g4 f6; 51.Rh5+ Kg6; 52.gxf5+ Kxh5; 53.fxe6 Kg6; 54.h5+ etc. was Fischer's suggestion, which would have provided a more fitting finale. **50...Ra2; 51.g4 Kh6; 52.Rg8 Kh7; 53.Re8 fxg4+; 54.Kg3 Kh6; 55.Re7 Kg7; 56.Rc7 Rb2; 57.Rc5 Kf6; 58.d5 Rb4; 59.h6 exd5; 60.Rxd5 Kg6; 61.Rd6+ Kg5; 62.h7 Rb8; 63.Rd1 Rh8; 64.Rh1** and here Black, in zugzwang, lost on time.

(86) CAPABLANCA - JANOWSKI
New York, 1924

1.Nf3. Capablanca was no old fogey when it came to the openings. In the early 1920s the Hypermoderns, let by Richard Reti and Aron Nimzowitsch, were overturning a lot of conventional wisdom about the importance of the center. In this game, from the most famous tournament of 1924, Capablanca tries his hand at the new fashion. **1...d5; 2.g3 c5; 3.Bg2 Nc6.** This is a reversed King's Indian. It won't become a Reti until White advances the c-pawn to c4. **4.0–0 e5.**

5.c4 d4; 6.d3 Bd6; 7.e3. Capablanca is handling the position as if he were on the Black side of a Benoni. It is a good strategy, because the extra move as White is very important in the most dangerous lines. That's why Black chooses an unambitious and solid formation. **7...Nge7; 8.exd4 cxd4; 9.a3 a5.** Black must prevent b4 at all costs. **10.Nbd2 Ng6; 11.Re1 0–0; 12.Qc2 Re8.**

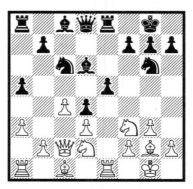

Both sides have developed logically. Capablanca now has a choice of flanks to operate on, while also maintaining the pressure on the center. **13.b3 h6?** Until this point Janowski had played well, but this creates a serious weakness which can be exploited later. Better was 13...f6 followed by ...Be6. **14.Rb1 Be6; 15.h4!?** This pawn is advanced to control squares, not to attack the enemy king. With the kingside secured, Capablanca can turn his attention to the other flank, where he enjoys a queenside pawn majority. **15...Rc8.** An obvious move, but not best. 15...Qe7 was better, to prevent White's next move and make it much harder for the queenside pawns to advance. **16.c5! Bb8; 17.Nc4.**

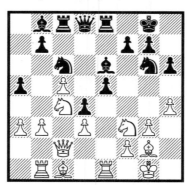

This is a magnificent post for the knight, which can survey the dark squares from a5 to e5. **17...f6; 18.Bd2 Kh8; 19.b4!** Black has failed to prevent this advance, and now Black is in deep trouble. White's pieces all have potential, while Black's are unimpressive. **19...axb4; 20.axb4 Na7.** Black will try to blockade the pawns by blockading at b5. **21.Qc1.** The weakness of the pawn at h6 becomes clear. White threatens 22.Bxh6 gxg6; 23.Qxh6+ and 24.Qxg6. **21...Nb5; 22.Nh2.** This move doesn't have much of an effect, other than to let the bishop eye the long diagonal. 22.Bxh6 Nc3; 23.Ra1 e4 would give Black a promising initiative. **22...Qe7; 23.Ra1 Rc7; 24.Ra5.** White has an effective queenside initiative. Black's pieces just aren't doing anything. **24...Bd7; 25.Nb6 Bc6; 26.Qc4 Na7; 27.Nd5! Bxd5; 28.Qxd5.**

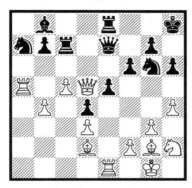

We can see that the White bishops are well-placed, and the queenside pawn majority is marching forward. **28...f5; 29.Qf3 Qf6; 30.h5 Ne7.** Black's army is in disarray. **31.g4 f4; 32.Qe4 Nec6; 33.Raa1!** The home square is now the best home for the rook. White has a decisive advantage on the queenside, and Black can only sit back and watch. **33...Rce7; 34.Qg6.**

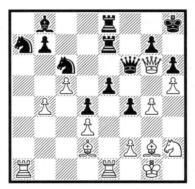

Black cannot afford to exchange queens, because the endgame would be hopeless. The White bishop will pivot at d5 and come to rest at c4, where it will support the advance of the c-pawn. But by retreating, Black invites action on the kingside, too. **34...Qf8; 35.Nf3 Re6; 36.Nh4 Rf6; 37.Be4! Qg8.** 37...Rxg6; 38.Nxg6+ Kg8; 39.Nxf8 Rxf8; 40.Bd5+ Kh8; 41.Bc4 and the pawns roll forward. **38.Bd5 Ne7.**

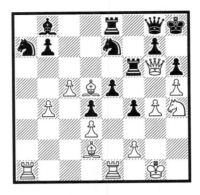

Now a small sacrifice brings the point home. **39.Qxf6! gxf6; 40.Bxg8 Rxg8; 41.f3 f5; 42.Bxf4!** The pin on the e-file adds to Black's woes. **42...Nec6; 43.Ng6+ Kh7; 44.Bxe5 Nxe5; 45.Rxe5 Bxe5; 46.Rxa7. White won.**

KING'S INDIAN ATTACK

The **King's Indian Attack** is simply a King's Indian Defense played by White. Bobby Fischer loved to attack from this formation, and it is quite simple to play, especially if you use the King's Indian as Black.

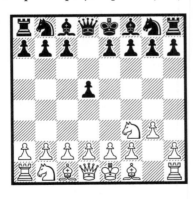

1.Nf3   d5
2.g3

Why then isn't it even more popular? The answer was hinted at in our discussion of Flank Games. Playing a defense with an extra move is not the same as playing an offense. If Black chooses the correct variations, the missing move can become almost irrelevant. In short, White gets no real advantage with this opening against a well-prepared opponent.

That said, there is no reason not to use it as White, especially since it can be used to opt out of more complicated openings. For example, if you play 1.e4 as White, but don't like facing the Sicilian or French, then you can play 2.d3; 3.g3; 4.Bg2; 5.Nf3 etc. This is one of the most common uses of the King's Indian Attack. At the same time, the King's Indian Attack is so homogenous that it deprives you of exposure to the wide variety of middlegames that arise after more standard openings.

(87) PETROSIAN - PACHMAN
Bled, 1961

1.Nf3. The King's Indian Attack can be used against many openings. Here is another fine example of play by Petrosian: 1.e4 c5; 2.Nf3 e6; 3.d3 d5; 4.Nbd2 Nc6; 5.g3 Nf6; 6.Bg2 Be7; 7.0-0 0-0; 8.Re1. This is a very common position. White will use the e-pawn as a spearhead for an attack, in which the advance of the h-pawn will play an important role. 8...dxe4; 9.dxe4 b6; 10.e5 Nd7; 11.Ne4 Ba6; 12.Bf4 b5; 13.c3 Qb6; 14.Qc2 Rfd8; 15.h4 Nf8; 16.h5 Rac8; 17.h6 Ng6; 18.hxg7 Kxg7; 19.Qc1 Rd3; 20.Bg5 Bxg5; 21.Qxg5 Rxf3; 22.Bxf3 and Black resigned in Petrosian-Kan, Soviet Championship 1955.

1...c5; 2.g3 Nc6; 3.Bg2 g6; 4.0-0 Bg7; 5.d3 e6; 6.e4. Finally White advances this pawn, which is, as we have seen, sometimes the very first move of the King's Indian Attack. **6...Nge7.** As in the Closed Sicilians, the knight is safer at e7 than f6. The f6-square is often a source of danger for Black, as we see in the present game. **7.Re1 0-0; 8.e5 d6; 9.exd6 Qxd6.**

The queen occupies d6, but it is nevertheless a weak square. **10.Nbd2 Qc7; 11.Nb3 Nd4; 12.Bf4 Qb6; 13.Ne5 Nxb3.** White could just recapture here, but there is a stronger move, played by Petrosian, which gains control of the d6-square. **14.Nc4 Qb5; 15.axb3 a5; 16.Bd6.**

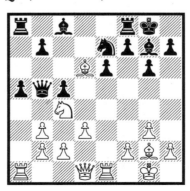

The infiltration by the White bishop draws the enemy cleric from its hiding place, and places it in a more vulnerable position. **16...Bf6; 17.Qf3.** The pressure on the dark squares d6, f6, e7 and g7 is the key to this game. **17...Kg7;**

18.Re4. Petrosian has not yet found the key to the position, but fortunately he notices it at the next move. **18...Rd8**. Black should have played ...Ng8 and settled for loss of a little material.

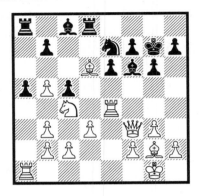

Petrosian does not let the second chance slip from his grasp. **19.Qxf6+!!** A fantastic sacrifice, one of Petrosian's best. **19...Kxf6; 20.Be5+ Kg5; 21.Bg7**.

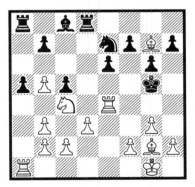

The Black king is doomed, so Pachman resigned. The conclusion might have been: 21...Nf5; 22.f4+ Kh5; 23.Bf3 mate.

12. UNORTHODOX GAMES

INTRODUCTION

There is little to say about unorthodox openings in the repertoire of World Champions. Once in a while they'll experiment with a radical idea, but never stick with them for long. Even Alekhine's once shocking 1.e4 Nf6 wasn't a major part of his repertoire, and of course now it is considered fairly mild.

It is worth pointing out to those unfamiliar with professional chess the phenomenon known as the pre-arranged or "grandmaster" draw. There are times when players have no incentive to do battle, and just go through the motions. In recent times, rules have changed to provide greater incentives to play for a win, but even the official rules note that there are circumstances where this is not appropriate. For example, if a draw clinches first place in a tournament, or secures a coveted norm toward the International Grandmaster title, then it is permissible to try to play for a draw. In addition you have to keep in mind that if a player has just played 5 straight 6-hour games, a day off is sometimes needed!

Sometimes in these circumstances, the players will fool around a bit. The best example of this was at the 1988 United States Championship in the historic town of Cambridge Springs. There, the quick draws almost all started 1.e4 d6, 2.d4 Nf6, 3.Nc3 c6, in honor of a fairly new approach for Black. Often the game would last just one move longer than the previous game, "enriching" the opening theory but without any further argument. In the funniest example, one former US Champion opened 1.c3 with White to achieve the same formation with colors reversed!

The point is that you shouldn't take an isolated experiment seriously. At the same time, observing how the World Champions handle unorthodox openings is instructive, as we saw earlier in the Karpov-Miles upset which brought jubilation to the fans of strange play.

So let's just look at a few examples of how World Champions handle unorthodox approaches. In each section I present a few different unorthodox openings in a highly subjective descending order of merit. If you'd like to examine these strange beasts in more detail, look for my upcoming book, *Unorthodox Chess Openings*.

UNORTHODOX ATTACKS

SICILIAN GRAND PRIX ATTACK

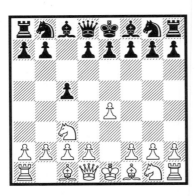

1.e4   c5
2.Nc3

or

1.e4   c5
2.f4

    The labyrinth of variations in the Sicilian often prompt White to adopt a sideline which, while not as testing to the defense, at least is easy to learn and play. In the 1980s, the **Grand Prix Attack** was developed in England by strong players who earned a living playing all over Britain in a grand prix cycle. Since one loss to a weaker player could bring disaster, the Grand Prix Attack, based on ideas by Canadian International Master Lawrence Day and elaborated on by British Grand-masters-in-waiting Julian Hodgson and Mark Hebden, among others, became all the rage. With the usual "trickle-down" effect, in the 1990s the opening is now commonly seen at amateur levels.

(88) LASKER - LEVENFISH
Moscow, 1936

1.e4 c5; 2.Nc3 Nc6; 3.f4 e6.

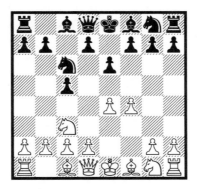

Here there is an old plan which is actually rather attractive. **4.Be2** The former World Champion was a bit past his prime when he played this game, which is not in the selected games collections. But he shows that a quiet start can still lead to a fine finish! **4...d5; 5.d3 Nge7.** 5...d4; 6.Nb1 leaves Black without a comfortable plan of development. White is, in effect, playing a reversed Dutch where he has achieved the advance of his e-pawn, cf. 1.d4 f5; 2.c4 d6; 3.Nc3 e5; 4.e3?! Be7; 5.d5. The extra tempo may not matter.

6.Nf3 Nd4?!; 7.0–0 Nec6; 8.Qd2 White can be patient. His idea is to play Nd1 and then c3, fighting for the key square d4. **8...Be7; 9.Bd1.** 9.Nd1?! doesn't work right away. 9...Nxf3+; 10.Bxf3 Nd4; 11.c3 Nxf3+; 12.Rxf3 dxe4; 13.dxe4 Qxd2; 14.Bxd2. **9...0–0; 10.Qf2 a6; 11.Re1 Bf6; 12.Ne2!** The same idea is achieved by a different route. **12...dxe4; 13.Nexd4.** 13.dxe4 is less effective. 13...Nxe2+; 14.Bxe2 Nd4; 15.Rd1 Nxf3+; 16.Bxf3 Bd4; 17.Be3 Bxe3; 18.Qxe3 Qc7 with a level game. **13...e3!?** 13...Nxd4; 14.Rxe4 Nxf3+; 15.Qxf3 Bd4+; 16.Kh1 will leave White with the better prospects. The bishop can be chased with c3, and then the pawn can advance to d4. This will clear lines for the bishop at d1, which can be stationed at c2.

14.Bxe3 cxd4; 15.Bd2. Black has a target at c2 and a potential outpost at e3, but neither is very accessible. **15...Qd5; 16.Qg3 Bd7.** Perhaps this bishop would have been more effectively stationed at b7. **17.Ne5! Rfd8; 18.c4! dxc3.** 18...Qd6; 19.Ng4 Be7; 20.b4! Nxb4 21.Rb1 Nxa2; 22.Rxb7 Nc3; 23.Bf3 and

White has a promising attack on both sides of the board. **19.bxc3 Be8; 20.Bc2!**

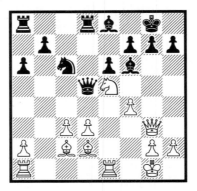

The clerics hide behind a wall of pawns, but they can easily participate in the play when the pawns move forward. **20...g6; 21.d4 Bg7; 22.h4**. Something has gone seriously wrong for Black. He is reduced to passive defense and White's game is flexible and dominant in the center. **22...Rac8; 23.Be4 Qd6; 24.Rad1! b5.** 24...Na5; 25.h5 Nc4; 26.hxg6 hxg6; 27.Bxb7 Rc7; 28.Nxc4 (28.Bxa6? allows 28...Nxd2, 29.Rxd2 Qa3 with strong counterplay.) 28...Rxc4; 29.Bxa6 Ra4; 30.Bd3 Rxa2 and White has the better game. **25.h5 b4; 26.hxg6 hxg6; 27.Re3! bxc3; 28.Bxc3 Nxe5; 29.fxe5**.

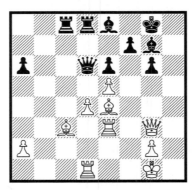

It is easy to see that White has excellent attacking prospects. Lasker demonstrates the technique required to convert the advantage into a win. **29...Bxe5; 30.Qh4! Rxc3; 31.Rxc3 Bxd4+; 32.Kh1 Ba4; 33.Rdd3 Bb5**. It seems that Black will recover the exchange and emerge with an extra pawn, but Lasker has seen deeper. **34.Bxg6! fxg6; 35.Rh3 Qd7**. 35...Bxc3 gets mated after 36.Qh7+ Kf8; 37.Rf3+ Ke8; 38.Qf7 mate. **36.Rcg3**. It is clear that one side has to get checkmated soon! **36...Bd3**. And it is clear which player it is! Consider the alternatives: 36...Be5; 37.Rxg6+ Kf7; 38.Qh7+ Kf8; 39.Rf3+ Ke8; 40.Rg8 mate; 36...Qf7 37.Qxd8+; 36...Qe8; 37.Qh7+ Kf8; 38.Rf3+; 36...Bg7; 37.Qh7+ Kf8; 38.Rf3+ Qf7; 39.Rxf7+ Kxf7; 40.Rf3+. **37.Rxd3**. Black resigned.

BIRD'S OPENING

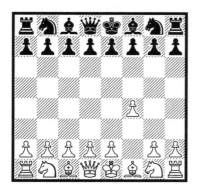

1.f4

(89) LASKER - BAUER
Amsterdam, 1889

Henry Bird's opening is rarely seen. There are two good reasons for this, and both begin 1...e5, which leads to the dangerous From Gambit on 2.fxe5 or to a King's Gambit on 2.e4! **1...d5**. This leads to a reversed Dutch Defense, which is what White is aiming for. **2.e3 Nf6; 3.b3 e6; 4.Bb2 Be7; 5.Bd3.** A somewhat artificial move, but not bad, because the c-pawn can advance to c4 and then the bishop can retreat to c2 or b1 as needed. **5...b6; 6.Nf3 Bb7; 7.Nc3 Nbd7; 8.0–0 0–0.** Black has a solid position and White has no real advantage. **9.Ne2 c5; 10.Ng3 Qc7.**

11.Ne5. White occupies this square before the Black pawn advances to e5. **11...Nxe5?.** With just one move, Black invites disaster. Moving one of the rooks to c8 would have been better. **12.Bxe5.** Just compare the relative activity of the bishops. Black is already in serious trouble. **12...Qc6; 13.Qe2 a6.** White has completed development and is ready to attack. The position of the rook at a1 cannot be improved, for the moment. Lasker starts by eliminating one of the few defenders of the Black king. But he doesn't part with the Be5. **14.Nh5 Nxh5**. White could simply recapture at h5 with a strong attack, but by sacrificing a piece, the momentum is greatly increased. **15.Bxh7+! Kxh7; 16.Qxh5+.**

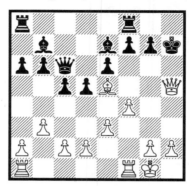

16...Kg8. Now White might like to transfer a rook to the h-file, but this is too slow, because Black is ready to play d5-d4 and threaten mate at g2. Then he could sacrifice some material in return and stay in the game. **17.Bxg7**. This threatens mate at h8. **17...Kxg7; 18.Qg4+ Kh7.** Now the queen guards g2 and White can threaten the sideways equivalent of a back rank mate. **19.Rf3 e5.** The only defense. Now the Black queen can come to h6. **20.Rh3+ Qh6; 21.Rxh6+ Kxh6**.

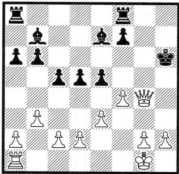

22.Qd7. This wins one of the bishops, and the game now is decisively in White's favor. **22...Bf6; 23.Qxb7 Kg7; 24.Rf1 Rab8; 25.Qd7 Rfd8; 26.Qg4+ Kf8; 27.fxe5 Bg7.** 27...Bxe5; 28.Qh5 f6; 29.Qxe5 shows another method of exploiting the pin on the f-file. **28.e6 Rb7; 29.Qg6** White exploits the pin in the maximally efficient way. **29...f6; 30.Rxf6+ Bxf6; 31.Qxf6+ Ke8; 32.Qh8+ Ke7; 33.Qg7+.** Now the rook at b7 falls, so Black gives up.

NIMZO-LARSEN ATTACK

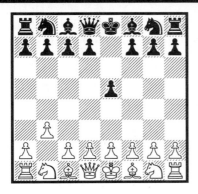

1.b3   e5

(90) LARSEN - SPASSKY
USSR vs. Rest of World, 1970

1.b3 e5! Spassky grabs the opportunity to plant a pawn at e5. That's why White usually plays 1.Nf3 before b3. **2.Bb2 Nc6; 3.c4 Nf6; 4.Nf3?!** Larsen plays his typical fighting chess in this important encounter, but this is just reckless. **4...e4.** Spassky accepts the invitation. **5.Nd4 Bc5; 6.Nxc6.** 6.e3 Bxd4; 7.exd4 d5; 8.cxd5 Qxd5 is just awful for White; 6.Nc2 d5; 7.cxd5 Qxd5 is acceptable for Black since 8.Bxf6 gxf6; 9.Nc3 Qf5; 10.Ne3 Bxe3; 11.dxe3 Be6; 12.g3 h5; 13.h4 Qe5 is not much fun for White! **6...dxc6!**

The normal instinct would lead to a capture with the other pawn, but Spassky understands that the pressure on the d-file is more valuable. **7.e3.** 7.d4 exd3; 8.Qxd3 Qxd3; 9.exd3 Bf5; 10.d4 Bxb1; 11.Rxb1 Bb4+; 12.Kd1 0–0–0 gives Black a clear advantage. **7...Bf5; 8.Qc2 Qe7; 9.Be2.** 9.d4 exd3; 10.Bxd3 Bxd3; 11.Qxd3 Rd8; 12.Qc2 0–0; 13.0–0 Ne4 and Black has considerable pressure. **9...0–0–0.**

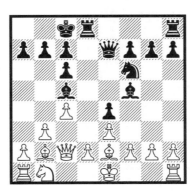

White should capture at f6, but is naturally reluctant to part with his prized bishop. Nevertheless, the plan chosen in the game leads to destruction. **10.f4?** 10.Bxf6 Qxf6; 11.Nc3 Qe5; 12.0–0 Bd6; 13.g3 h5 with a strong attack for Black. **10...Ng4; 11.g3.** 11.Bxg4 Bxg4; 12.h3 Qh4+ and Black is clearly better. **11...h5; 12.h3 h4!!; 13.hxg4.** 13.Bxg4 Bxg4; 14.hxg4 hxg3; 15.Rg1 (15.Rxh8 Rxh8 is an exchange of a defender (at h1) for a spectator (at d8), which obviously works to Black's advantage.) 15...Rh1!!; 16.Rxh1 g2; 17.Rg1 Qh4+; 18.Ke2 Qxg4+; 19.Ke1 Qg3+; 20.Ke2 Qf3+; 21.Ke1 Be7!! You have to play like a champion to get to positions that contain treasures like this! **13...hxg3; 14.Rg1.**

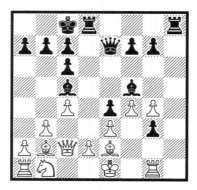

14...Rh1!! The brilliant theme works anyway! **15.Rxh1 g2; 16.Rf1.** 16.Rg1 Qh4+; 17.Kd1 Qh1!; 18.Qc3 Qxg1+; 19.Kc2 Qf2; 20.gxf5 Qxe2; 21.Na3 Bb4!! was demonstrated by Spassky after the game. His point is seen in the continuation 22.Qxb4 Qd3+; 23.Kc1 g1=R mate. **16...Qh4+; 17.Kd1 gxf1Q+** and Larsen resigned as there was no way even to get past move 20. **18.Bxf1 Bxg4+; 19.Be2.** 19.Kc1 Qe1+; 20.Qd1 Qxd1 mate. **19...Qh1 mate.**

QUEEN PAWN GAME

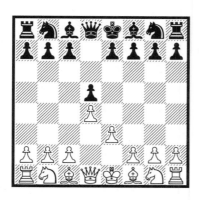

1.d4 d5
2.e3

(91) WALTER - LASKER
Mahrisch Ostrau, 1923

1.d4 d5; 2.e3. This is a dull and plodding opening, which allows Black to develop without difficulty. **2...Nf6; 3.Bd3 Bg4; 4.Nf3 e6; 5.c4.** White mixes systems. If 5.c3 instead, we have a Colle System, which is solid enough. **5...Nbd7; 6.Qb3.** White goes after a pawn but allows his kingside to get busted open. **6...Bxf3; 7.gxf3 c5; 8.cxd5 exd5.**

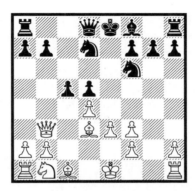

As is so often the case when the bishop leaves the monastery at c8 prematurely, the b-pawn pays the price. **9.Qxb7 cxd4; 10.exd4 Bd6; 11.Nc3 0–0.**

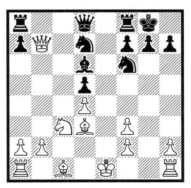

12.Nxd5. Taking this second pawn is very risky, since his king will now be permanently stuck in the center. **12...Qa5+.** By this maneuver Black prevents exchanges and gets his queen to a good attacking square. **13.Nc3 Qh5; 14.Be2** Black was threatening 14...Rab8, 15 Qc6 Rb6 when the f-pawn will fall and Black's queen will give White a major headache. **14...Rab8; 15.Qa6 Rb6; 16.Qd3 Re8**. Now White has to worry about the pin on the e-file. **17.Ne4.**

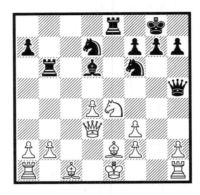

17...Nd5; 18.Nxd6 White is desperate to castle, but the knight was his only good piece, and with Black's rooks active there's no safety on the kingside. **18...Rxd6; 19.O-O Rde6; 20.Re1 Qh3; 21.Kh1**. Avoiding 21...Rg6+, but setting up a back rank mate. **21...Rxe2 Black won.**

HUNGARIAN ATTACK

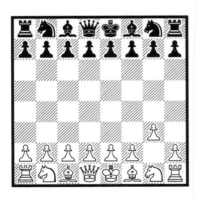

1.g3

(92) RETI - ALEKHINE
Baden Baden, 1925

1.g3. This move is more commonly preceded by 1.Nf3, which prevents Black's reply. It is sometimes known as the Benko-Barcza opening, for two Hungarian players who used it a lot, but the term Hungarian Attack is also common. **1...e5.** Never one to shirk from a challenge, Alekhine stakes out territory in the center. **2.Nf3.**

2...e4. Alekhine Defense with colors reversed, and where Alekhine himself is playing the "White" side! **3.Nd4 d5; 4.d3 exd3; 5.Qxd3.** Recapturing with a pawn would have provided a stronger central pawn formation. **5...Nf6; 6.Bg2 Bb4+; 7.Bd2 Bxd2+; 8.Nxd2 0-0.**

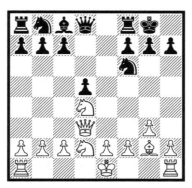

White has a lead in development but if Reti simply castled, then Black might take over the initiative, so instead he finally advances the c-pawn. **9.c4 Na6; 10.cxd5 Nb4; 11.Qc4 Nbxd5; 12.N2b3 c6.** Black's position is relatively passive, but it is solid. The power of the bishop at g2 is limited by the strong post at d5. **13.0–0 Re8; 14.Rfd1 Bg4!** A good move, because the pawn at e2, though twice defended, is a weak spot in White's armor. **15.Rd2 Qc8.** Black has the initiative, and is preparing to attack on the kingside. **16.Nc5 Bh3; 17.Bf3 Bg4.**

Now a dance begins. Under modern rules, a draw could be claimed by either side once the position has been repeated three times. **18.Bg2 Bh3; 19.Bf3 Bg4; 20.Bg2 Bh3; 21.Bf3 Bg4; 22.Bh1.** Reti finally decides to play for a win, accepting the risk of facing Black's kingside attack. **22...h5!; 23.b4 a6; 24.Rc1 h4; 25.a4.** The battle is raging on both flanks. **25...hxg3; 26.hxg3 Qc7; 27.b5?!** A poor move. 27.e4 was the correct move, according to Alekhine. **27...axb5; 28.axb5.**

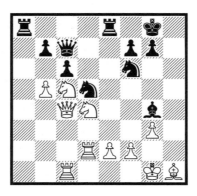

The pawn at f2 is the key to White's defense, protecting the pawn at g3. **28...Re3!!** The rook cannot be captured but White should have moved the bishop to f3 instead to eliminate its Black counterpart. **29.Nf3.** 29.fxe3 Qxg3+; 30.Kf1 (30.Bg2 Nxe3–+) 30...Nxe3 mate; 29.Bf3! Bxf3; 30.exf3 cxb5; 31.Nxb5 Qa5; 32.fxe3 Qxd2 with many dangerous threats. **29...cxb5; 30.Qxb5 Nc3; 31.Qxb7 Qxb7; 32.Nxb7 Nxe2+; 33.Kh2.** The king would not be much safer at f1.

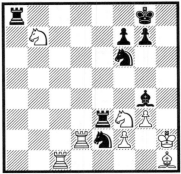

33...Ne4!! The Black knights gallop in and inflict major damage. **34.Rc4!** Best, since the alternatives lose by force. 34.fxe3 Nxd2; 35.Nxd2 Nxc1 and Black has enough left to win; 34.Rd8+ Rxd8; 35.fxe3 Rd5; 36.Re1 Rh5+; 37.Kg2 Bh3+; 38.Kh2 Bf1+; 39.Nh4 N4xg3 is terminal. **34...Nxf2!; 35.Bg2 Be6; 36.Rcc2 Ng4+; 37.Kh3 Ne5+; 38.Kh2**.

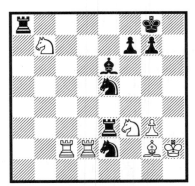

Now Alekhine brings the game home with a sacrifice. **38...Rxf3!** This sacrifice is made possible by a fork. **39.Rxe2 Ng4+; 40.Kh3 Ne3+; 41.Kh2 Nxc2; 42.Bxf3 Nd4. Black won.**

CLEMENZ OPENING

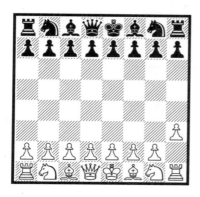

1. h3

(93) MEAD - MORPHY
New York, 1857

1.h3. There really is no point to this move. It weakens the kingside, and all Black has to do is choose an opening which does not involve placing a piece at g4. **1...e5; 2.e4 Nf6; 3.Nc3 Bc5; 4.Bc4**. So far we have a reversed Italian Game, where the move h2-h3 performs some small useful function keeping pieces out of g4. But in the Evans Gambit, that is not a key part of the strategy, so Morphy jumps right in. **4...b5!?; 5.Bxb5 c6; 6.Ba4 0–0; 7.Nge2.** 7.Nf3 would have been better. **7...d5; 8.exd5 cxd5; 9.d4.** 9.d3 Qa5; 10.a3 was suggested by Maroczy. **9...exd4; 10.Nxd4.** Knights are supposed to be used to blockade isolated pawns, but White does not have sufficient control of d4, and the king's safety has not been achieved yet. **10...Qb6; 11.Nce2 Ba6.**

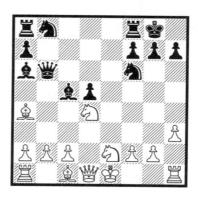

The Black bishops already exert considerable pressure. **12.c3 Bxe2; 13.Kxe2**. There is no better capture. 13.Qxe2 Bxd4; 14.cxd4 Qb4+; 15.Bd2 Qxa4; 13.Nxe2 Bxf2+; 14.Kf1 Na6 **13...Bxd4; 14.Qxd4**. Inviting an exchange of queens, which is declined. **14...Qa6+; 15.Kf3 Rc8; 16.b3 Ne4.** White cannot survive this position. **17.Bb2.** 17.Qxd5 Nxc3; 18.Qxa8 also loses: 18...Qe2+; 19.Kf4 g5+; 20.Kxg5 Rc5+; 21.Kf4 Qxf2+; 22.Qf3 Ne2+; 23.Ke4 Qd4 mate. **17...Nc6; 18.Bxc6 Rxc6.**

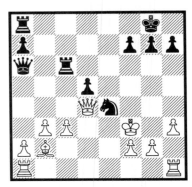

19.Ke3. Again the capture at d5 leads to rapid destruction. 19.Qxd5 Rf6+; 20.Kg4 Qe2+; 21.f3 Qxg2+; 22.Kh4 Qg3+; 23.Kh5 Rh6 mate. **19...Re8; 20.Rhe1**. The rest of the game is forced. **20...Nxc3+; 21.Kf3 Rf6+; 22.Kg3 Qd6+; 23.f4 Ne2+; 24.Rxe2 Rxe2; 25.Rf1 Rg6+; 26.Kf3 Rgxg2. Black won.**

UNORTHODOX DEFENSES

In a book on the openings of the World Champions, it makes little sense to discuss many of the more bizarre openings often seen in amateur games but not at the professional level. I have selected only a few of the many other minor openings for treatment here, and will show how the World Champions have been particularly effective against unorthodox opening strategies. Even in the most famous case of an upset, when the creative British Grandmaster Tony Miles used the odd 1...a6 to defeat Anatoly Karpov, in fact, Karpov emerged from the opening with an advantage.

Once again the openings are presented in descending order of merit, as I subjectively view them. Most strange openings have faithful fans who remain in a state of denial concerning well-known refutations, often scoring more points at the board as a result! Such colorful figures keep the chess world entertained, and once in a while score an impressive upset against an unprepared opponent.

We start with the almost fully respectable Budapest Defense and work our way down to the opening which is known mostly as the "Junk" defense, although there are even worse openings which have been spared the humiliation of being trounced by World Champions.

BUDAPEST DEFENSE

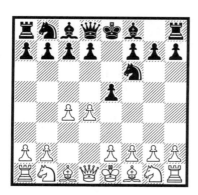

1.d4	Nf6
2.c4	e5

(94) SMYSLOV - BLACKSTOCK
London (Lloyds Bank), 1988

1.d4 Nf6; 2.c4 e5; 3.dxe5 Ng4. The Budapest borders on respectability. If White overplays the position, Black can close in quickly for the kill. With a calmer approach, however, White can maintain an advantage in the opening. **4.Nf3.** As is so often the case, development is the best reaction to an unorthodox opening strategy. **4...Nc6; 5.Bf4 Bb4+; 6.Nbd2 Qe7.** Black has developed quickly and will regain the pawn invested at the second turn. There is still some time needed to recover the pawn, and this gives White a chance to remedy the backward development. **7.e3 Ngxe5; 8.Nxe5 Nxe5; 9.Be2 0–0; 10.0–0 Bxd2; 11.Qxd2.** Now White has a permanent advantage in the form of the bishop pair, but that is not in and of itself enough to secure victory. **11...d6.**

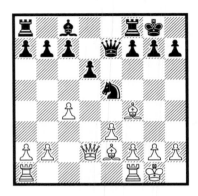

This position has been reached many times, and yet even some of the most respected authorities do not consider the move that Smyslov plays in this game! **12.b4!?** White usually plays this move in the early middlegame, so why not play it now? Smyslov really only had to take into account one additional reply, the one chosen in the game. **12...a5.** Black could try 12...b6, which would return to known paths after, say, 12.Rfd1. **13.a3 Rd8; 14.Qc3 f6; 15.Rfc1!?** This is the point of Smyslov's refined move order. Instead of going to d1, the rook operates from c1. Black must now always keep in mind the possible advance of the c-pawn. **15...Bf5; 16.f3 axb4; 17.axb4 b6; 18.e4 Bg6; 19.Rxa8 Rxa8**.

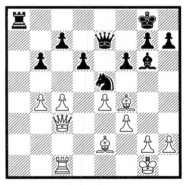

Now it is time for Smyslov to strike. **20.c5 bxc5; 21.bxc5**. The pressure on the c-file is still intense. **21...Bf7; 22.cxd6 cxd6; 23.Qd4.** Now White's advantages are clear. Smyslov holds the bishop pair and the pawn at d6 is weak. **23...h6; 24.Rd1 Rd8; 25.Qb6 Rd7; 26.Qb4 Kh7; 27.Bg3 Qe6; 28.f4 Qb3; 29.Qxb3 Bxb3**.

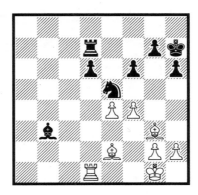

Here Smyslov wins two bishops for the rook, a substantial advantage. **30.fxe5 Bxd1; 31.e6 Re7; 32.Bxd1 Rxe6; 33.Bg4 Re8.** The e-pawn cannot be taken because of Bf5+. **34.Bxd6.** This position is a technical win, but requires good technique and will take some time. **34...g6; 35.Bf3 Kg7; 36.Kf2 Rd8; 37.e5 fxe5; 38.Bxe5+ Kh7; 39.Ke3 Re8; 40.Kd4 Rd8+; 41.Ke4 Rd2; 42.Bd4 Ra2; 43.Ke5.** White has managed to activate his king while not allowing any of the pawns to become vulnerable. The further advance of the king is now possible, with the aid of the two loyal clerics. The procession continues. **43...Ra6; 44.Bb7 Ra4; 45.Bc6 Rb4; 46.Bd5 Ra4; 47.Bc5 Ra5; 48.Bd6 Kg7; 49.Ke6 Ra6; 50.Bb7 Rb6; 51.Bc8 Kh7; 52.Ke7 Rb2.** Now it is time to get the pawns moving. **53.g4 Rf2; 54.Be6 Rf1; 55.Be5 Rf2; 56.Bf6.**

56...Rf4. 56...Rxh2 allows a mating net. 57.Kf8 Rf2; 58.Bg8 mate. **57.Kf7 Ra4; 58.Be5 Ra7+; 59.Kf6 Ra6; 60.h4 Rb6; 61.Kf7 Rb5; 62.h5.** Black resigned, for if the g-pawn moves, Bf5+ is mate. The only try is a check, but it bounces. 62...Rb7+; 63.Kf8 Rb6. 63...gxh5; 64.Bf5 mate; 63...g5; 64.Bf5 mate. **64.Bg8 mate. White won.**

ALBIN COUNTERGAMBIT

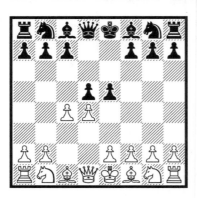

1.d4   d5
2.c4   e5

One of Black's most aggressive options is the dangerous **Albin Countergambit**. Black offers White a pawn, temporarily or permanently, in order to develop pieces quickly. After 3.dxe5 d4; 4.Nf3 Nc6, it is easy to see that Black's pawn at d4 exerts a cramping influence on White's forecourt, controlling e3 and c3, and even threatening to advance to d3 under the right circumstances.

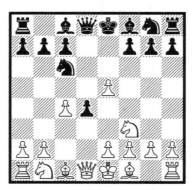

White's normal reaction is to bring the bishop at f1 into the game by placing it at g2. This does, however, create a weakness on the kingside, where White must inevitably castle. Therefore Black will castle on the queenside, and a bloody battle will ensue.

Lasker, Alekhine, Euwe and Spassky was willing to take the risks associated with this opening, but not often. It is exciting, but requires Black to exploit every available attacking opportunity. Delay often spells doom, but a premature attack will also lead to failure. Good timing is everything.

(95) NIEMALA - SPASSKY
Riga, 1959

1.d4 d5; 2.c4 e5; 3.dxe5 d4; 4.Nf3. As White, Spassky established 4.e4 as a viable alternative, and that variation now bears his name. 4.e4 Nc6; 5.f4 f6; 6.Nf3 fxe5; 7.Bd3 Bb4+; 8.Nbd2 exf4; 9.0–0 Nf6; 10.Nb3 0–0 is Spassky-Lutikov, Kharkov, 1963, but Black had no reason to complain about the position. **4...Nc6.**

Spassky is one of few recent champions who ever dabbled in dubious gambits. He did try his hand at the Albin, however. **5.a3.** This move, together with Nbd2, g3 and Bg2, form the primary plan for White. 5.g3 is probably the most popular, but the advance of the a-pawn is needed sooner or later. 5.g3 Be6; 6.Bg2 Qd7; 7.Nbd2 0–0–0; 8.a3 gives White excellent attacking prospects. **5...Bg4; 6.Nbd2 Qe7.** Black can play 6...Nge7 instead, which is another promising plan. The knight will go to g6, and then the e-pawn can be recovered. **7.g3! Nxe5; 8.Nxe5 Qxe5; 9.h3?!**

White should just continue development with 9.Bg2 0–0–0; 10.Nf3 and in my book *How to Play the Albin Countergambit,* I suggested 10...Qe8; 11.0–0 Ne7 with an unclear position. **9...Bh5; 10.Bg2 0–0–0; 11.Nf3 Qa5+; 12.Bd2 Qa6; 13.0–0 Nf6; 14.b4 Ne4; 15.c5 d3; 16.e3 f5; 17.a4 Qh6.**

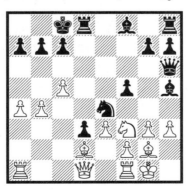

Black has plenty of compensation for the pawn. **18.Rc1 Be7; 19.a5 a6.** Now Niemala causes some damage to Black's infrastructure. **20.c6! bxc6; 21.Qa4 Be8; 22.Ne5 c5; 23.Qa2 Qf6.**

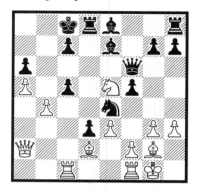

Black's position is beginning to look a little better. **24.Bxe4 fxe4; 25.Nc4 Qf5!** We can see that the weakness caused by White's 9th move has not gone away. **26.bxc5 Qxh3; 27.Nd6+.**

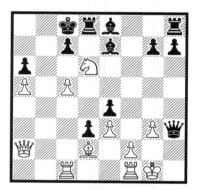

Fancy, but ineffective. **27...Bxd6; 28.cxd6 Rxd6; 29.Qc4 Bc6!; 30.Qxa6+ Kd7.** The Black king is safe. White now is threatened with the devastating advance of the h-pawn which will open up checkmating paths, so Niemala sacrifices an exchange. **31.Rxc6 Rxc6; 32.Qb5 Qe6; 33.Rc1 Ra8; 34.Rc5.**

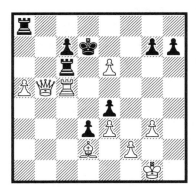

Now Spassky finds an effective way to win the game. **34...Rb8!!; 35.Rd5+ Kc8; 36.Rd8+ Kxd8; 37.Qxb8+ Kd7; 38.Qb5 Kc8; 39.Kg2 Rd6**. White is lost now. **40.Qb2 Qf7; 41.Qe5 Qf3+; 42.Kg1 Qd1+; 43.Kg2 Qxd2. Black won.**

ST. GEORGE DEFENSE

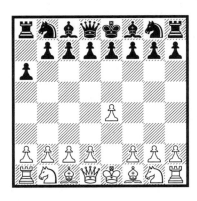

1.e4　　a6

When Miles defeated Karpov the world finally took notice of the move 1...a6, which had been championed only by the English International Master Michael Basman. The move itself is not in and of itself bad, since a great many openings involve an early ...a6.

But playing it right away allows White to establish the ideal pawn center with 2.d4. Black's idea is that after 2...b5, any White knight attempting to occupy the c3 square can be driven away by the further advance of the b-pawn. This in turn means that the pawn at e4 must be a little nervous, as Black can train the guns of a bishop at b7 and knight at f6 at it.

There are three different systems for Black in this opening. The **St.**

George proper involves Black playing ...e6. If instead Black opts for a kingside fianchetto, then play transposes into the Modern Defense, especially when Black also plays ...d6. Finally, there is the Neo-Spanish approach, where Black plays an early ...d6 and plans to play ...e5, which can reach positions similar to the Spanish Game. The latter is a personal favorite of mine.

Nevertheless, the St. George cannot be recommended as a primary weapon in your opening repertoire. It concedes White too much of the center for too long, and even the counterplay afforded by the queenside pawns is not quite enough to earn respectability for any of the 1...a6 systems.

(96) KARPOV - MILES
Skara (European Teams), 1980

1.e4 a6.

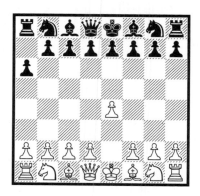

This game sent shock waves throughout the chess community. Not only did the creative English Grandmaster defeat the reigning World Champion, but he did so with one of the most impudent opening moves imaginable. Karpov called it the "Incorrect Opening," but it is now commonly known as the St. George Defense, a name given to it by its primary advocate, Michael Basman. **2.d4 b5; 3.Nf3 Bb7; 4.Bd3 Nf6; 5.Qe2 e6; 6.a4 c5; 7.dxc5 Bxc5; 8.Nbd2.** 8.axb5 axb5; 9.Rxa8 Bxa8; 10.Bxb5 Nxe4 is fine for Black. **8...b4.** Now the pawn really was in danger. **9.e5 Nd5; 10.Ne4 Be7.**

Black's pawn structure looks awkward, and one has to wonder about the long term safety of the Black king on the kingside. Sensibly, Miles keeps it in the center for a while. **11.0–0 Nc6; 12.Bd2 Qc7; 13.c4 bxc3; 14.Nxc3 Nxc3; 15.Bxc3 Nb4; 16.Bxb4 Bxb4; 17.Rac1 Qb6; 18.Be4 0–0.**

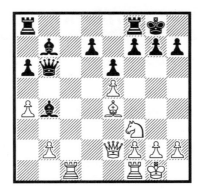

An interesting position. Many commentators suggest a classic sacrifice at h7 now, but it was dismissed by Karpov. **19.Ng5**. 19.Bxh7+ Kxh7; 20.Ng5+ Kg6; 21.Qg4 f5; 22.Qg3 Qd4 is given by Karpov, claiming that Black can defend. But in examining this position recently I found that his idea, based on the interpolation of the queen at g4, is flawed. 23.Nxe6+! Qg4; 24.Nxf8+ Rxf8; 25.Qxg4+ fxg4; 26.Rc4 a5; 27.Rxg4+ and White has a rook and three pawns for the bishop pair, definitely much better for the rooks. For example: 27...Kf7; 28.Rf4+ Ke7; 29.Rxf8 Kxf8; 30.Rd1 Bc6; 31.b3 and White's winning plan is to bring the king to a2 to defend the b-pawn, and then use the rook to support the advance of the pawns on the kingside.

19...h6; 20.Bh7+ Kh8; 21.Bb1 Be7; 22.Ne4 Rac8; 23.Qd3. Karpov claimed that this was his only serious error in the game, and that 23.Rcd1 would have maintained an advantage. **23...Rxc1; 24.Rxc1 Qxb2; 25.Re1 Qxe5; 26.Qxd7**.

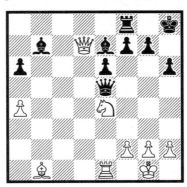

White is just a pawn down, and not even Karpov's formidable technique could save him. **26...Bb4; 27.Re3 Qd5; 28.Qxd5 Bxd5; 29.Nc3 Rc8; 30.Ne2 g5; 31.h4 Kg7; 32.hxg5 hxg5; 33.Bd3 a5; 34.Rg3 Kf6; 35.Rg4 Bd6; 36.Kf1 Be5**. The bishops dominate the board. Black would stand better even without an extra pawn. **37.Ke1 Rh8; 38.f4 gxf4; 39.Nxf4 Bc6; 40.Ne2 Rh1+; 41.Kd2 Rh2; 42.g3 Bf3**. Now the result is inevitable. **43.Rg8 Rg2; 44.Ke1 Bxe2; 45.Bxe2 Rxg3; 46.Ra8 Bc7. Black won.**

NIMZOWITSCH DEFENSE

Nimzowitsch's pet defense, answering 1.e4 with 1...Nc6, allows White to build a strong center. This is true of most of his openings, as Nimzowitsch was one of the leading exponents of the Hypermodern school. Thanks largely to the efforts of such Grandmasters as Vlastimil Hort and Tony Miles, the **Nimzowitsch Defense** has gathered a fairly large following in amateur and even professional ranks, but has yet to find an advocate among the World Champions, who score against it seemingly at will.

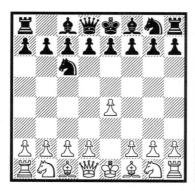

1.e4   Nc6

After 2.d4, Black can either contest the center by advancing ...d5 or ...e5, or concede it with 2...e6 or 2...d6. In any case the struggle revolves around the d5 square. White has more resources to control this square, especially since Black has at least temporarily abandoned the idea of ...c6 by stationing the knight on that square.

Here is an extremely rare example of a World Champion sitting on the Black side. Lasker defeats the relatively unknown Lennartz at Aachen, 1925. That year was a very experimental period for chess, with the Hypermoderns charging in with their radical theories. Perhaps Lasker, never a fan of that cavalier approach to the center, just wanted to try it out. Here is the game: 1.e4 Nc6; 2.Nf3 (A commonly seen alternative to 2.d4, hoping to reach an Open Game after 2...e5, reaching the position usually arrived at by 1.e4 e5 2.Nf3 Nc6) 2...Nf6; 3.Nc3 d5; 4.exd5 Nxd5; 5.Nxd5 Qxd5.

Black has a comfortable position, since White cannot harrass the Black Queen. The game continued 6.b3 Bg4; 7.Be2 Bxf3; 8.gxf3 Qc5; 9.c3 e6; 10.Bb2 Bd6; 11.d4 Qh5; 12.Qd3 Bf4; 13.Qb5 Qxb5; 14.Bxb5 O-O-O; 15.Bxc6 bxc6; 16.Bc1 Bd6; 17.Be3 h6; 18.h4 h5; 19.Ke2 Be7; 20.Rag1 g6; 21.f4 Rd5; 22.Rd1 Rhd8; 23.b4 Kb7; 24.a3 Rf5; 25.Kf3 Ka6; 26.a4 Kb7; 27.a5 Ka6; 28.Rc1 Kb5; 29.Ke4 Kc4; 30.Rc2 Re8; 31.Rcc1 Bf6; 32.Rc2 e5; 33.Kf3 exf4; 34.Bd2 Kd3; 35.Rb2 Re3+; 36.Bxe3 fxe3+; 37.Kg3 Kxc3; 38.Re2 exf2; 39.Rxf2 Rxf2; 40.Kxf2 Bxd4+; 41.Kf3 Kxb4; 42.Ke4 c5; 43.Kd5 Kxa5; 44.Kc6 Kb4; 45.Kxc7 c4; 46.Rb1+ Kc3; 47.Rc1+ Kb3; 48.Kc6 c3; 49.Kd5 c2; 50.Kxd4 Kb2; 51.Rg1 c1=Q; 52.Rxc1 Kxc1 and White resigned.

Our main game features Mikhail Tal giving a lesson on how to play the White side.

(97) TAL - CASTRO
Biel (Interzonal), 1976

1.e4 Nc6. Nimzowitsch's pet defense to 1.e4 has achieved a marginal level of respectability in professional chess, but it lacks advocates at the World Champion level. **2.Nf3.** This invites Black to return to the Open Games with 2...e5, but this is a very sensible plan, since White is usually prepared for that anyway. The alternative is 2.d4, but the ideal pawn center cannot be maintained and it is easy for White to overextend.

2...d6. Black can also try 2...d5; 2...g6; 2...e6 and the wild, but ultimately unsound, 2...f5. **3.d4 Bg4.** This position can also be reached from the Wade Defense with 1.d4 d6; 2.Nf3 Bg4; 3.e4 Nc6. It is somewhat ambitious, as Black needs the bishop to support b7 in some cases. 3...Nf6 is also seen. After 4.Nc3 Bg4 (4...a6!? deserves more investigation than it has had to date.) 5.Bb5 is sufficient for an advantage, according to many authorities.

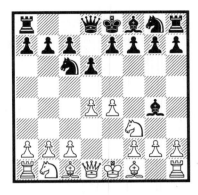

4.Bb5 a6; 5.Ba4 b5. 5...Nf6, 6.c4 is very strong for White, since 6...Nxe4? loses to 7.d5, now that the b5 square is under control. **6.Bb3 Nf6; 7.c3.** Now Black should play 7...e5, which leads to positions from the Spanish Game. Tal shows why an immediate attempt at central counterplay is premature. **7...d5?** 7...Nxe4; 8.Bd5 wins a knight. **8.e5 Ne4; 9.a4!** Tal does not castle immediately, preferring to resolve the queenside situation first. **9...e6; 10.Bc2 Na5; 11.axb5 axb5; 12.Qe2 c6; 13.0-0.**

Now development can continue normally. 13.Bxe4 dxe4; 14.Qxe4 Bf5; 15.Qe2 Nb3; 16.Rxa8 Qxa8 would give Black some play for the pawn. **13...Bf5.** Black had to address the immediate threat at e4. **14.b4!** Although this seems to lead to a symmetrical pawn structure without any advantage for White, that is not the case. **14...Nc4; 15.Rxa8 Qxa8; 16.Nh4.** The structural advantage is transferred to the other flank. **16...Qa1; 17.Nxf5 exf5; 18.Qd3.** The knight at e4 has no retreat. Black plays for complications, knowing that the coming advance of the f-pawn will weaken the a7-g1 diagonal. **18...Qa7; 19.f3.**

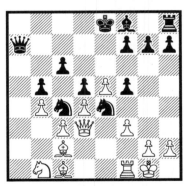

19...Nxe5; 20.Qe2 Bd6; 21.fxe4 fxe4. Black has two pawns for the piece, but it is the structure that counts. In fact, Tal quickly returns the piece to open lines toward the weak pawn at c6, finally exploiting the structure created much earlier. **22.Nd2 0-0; 23.Nxe4! dxe4; 24.Qxe4 Ng6; 25.Qxc6** The rest is simple. **25...Qb8; 26.h3 Ne7; 27.Qe4 g6; 28.Qf3.** Black resigned. The bishop will come to h6 and then the defender of f7 must flee.

CHIGORIN DEFENSE

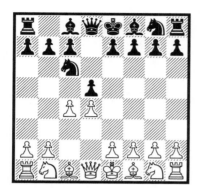

1.d4   d5
2.c4   Nc6

(98) EUWE - TARTAKOWER
Nottingham, 1936

1.d4 d5; 2.c4 Nc6. The Chigorin Defense has not had an advocate at a high level of chess since Mikhail Chigorin at the turn of the century, and no World Champion had ever shown it much respect. Euwe described it as "A rather unusual defense which can yield good results only if White makes a premature attempt to seize the advantage."

3.Nc3 e5. The main line has been 3...Bg4, but that has taken a lot of pounding in recent decades, and Tartakower's move has come to be viewed as a last salvation for Black. **4.cxd5**. This is White's most promising move. 4.dxe5 is an interesting option for White.

I managed to outplay six-time United States Champion Walter Browne as Black in the 1991 United States Blitz Championship, but the position after 4...d4; 5.Nd5 Be6; 6.e4 dxe3; 7.Bxe3 Nxe5; 8.Nf3 Nxf3+; 9.Qxf3 c6; 10.Nc3 (10.Nf4 is a losing blunder: 10...Bb4+; 11.Ke2 Bxc4+ was another game from the same event, where my opponent had to resign.) 10...Bb4; 11.Rd1 Qa5; 12.Bd4 f6; 13.a3 Be7; 14.Be2 was objectively better for White. **4...Nxd4; 5.e3 Nf5; 6.e4 Nd6; 7.Nf3**.

White is certainly better here, and the present game served as the illustration for White's best play in this variation in my 1991 book on the Chigorin. **7...Bg4; 8.Qa4+ Bd7; 9.Qb3 f6 10.Be3**. White is developing in comfort, but Black's pieces make an ugly impression. **10...Ne7; 11.Rc1 Nec8**. Necessary, if Black wants to castle. **12.Bd3 Be7; 13.0–0 0–0**. Euwe suggests 13...a6 here. **14.Nb5 Bxb5; 15.Bxb5**.

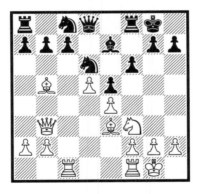

This is a crucial position for the evaluation of the line. If Black now played 15...Nf7 and 16...Ncd6, the position would not look so bad to me. Euwe, however, felt that Black should slide the king into the corner instead. **15...Nxb5?** Tartakower's choice was clearly wrong. 15...Kh8; 16.Bd3 f5; 17.Qc2 is Euwe's line, where White stands better thanks to the pressure on the c-file and on the b1–h7 diagonal. **16.d6+ Rf7**. 16...Kh8; 17.dxe7 Qxe7; 18.Qxb5 gives White an extra piece. **17.dxe7 Qd7?.**

Another error. 17...Qe8 was better, even if Black's position would still be undesirable. **18.Rfd1 Ncd6**. 18...Nbd6?; 19.Qxb7 Nxb7; 20.Rxd7 Rxe7; 21.Rxe7 Nxe7; 22.Rxc7 and one horse falls. **19.a4 Nd4; 20.Bxd4 exd4; 21.e5!** This leads to the win of material, and then Euwe displays his technical skills to bring the point home. **21...fxe5; 22.Nxe5 Qxe7; 23.Nxf7 Nxf7; 24.Qxb7 Rd8; 25.Rxc7**.

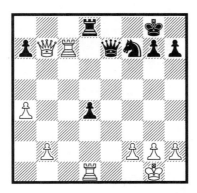

Black's resignation would be justified here. **25...Qe6; 26.Re7 Qf6; 27.Qd7 Rf8**. 27...Rxd7 gets checkmated by 28.Re8 mate. **28.Re8 Nd6; 29.Rxf8+ Kxf8; 30.Rd3 Qe5; 31.Kf1 h5; 32.Qxa7 Nf5; 33.Qd7 g6; 34.Rb3 Qf4; 35.g3 Qc1+; 36.Kg2 Ne3+; 37.Kh3 Qf1+; 38.Kh4 Nf5+; 39.Kg5 Qc1+; 40.Kf6. White won.**

ENGLISH DEFENSE

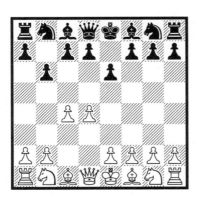

1.d4	e6
2.c4	b6

(99) PETROSIAN - KOROLKOV
Tbilisi, 1945

1.d4 Nf6. This move is usually deferred in the English Defense, which normally begins 1...e6; 2.c4 b6 and now White can establish a big center with 3.e4 Bb7; 4.Nc3 but Black can introduce some interesting complications with ...Bb4 and ...f5. Top players do not trust this defense. The highly tactical nature of the game leads to a lot of Black victories at amateur levels, but well-prepared players of the White side should be able to preserve a healthy advantage. **2.c4 e6; 3.Nf3 Be7.**

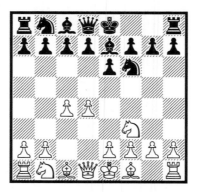

This move does not look bad, and it isn't, provided that Black does not allow White to get a pawn to e4. **4.Nc3 b6?** This leads to a variation of the English Defense which is particularly bad for Black. 4...d5 was correct, transposing to the Queen's Gambit Declined. **5.e4 d6; 6.g3 Bb7.** This bishop is about to be shut down for good. **7.d5! Nbd7; 8.Bg2 c6; 9.dxe6 fxe6.**

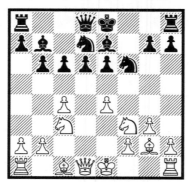

The weakness at e6 is fatal. **10.Ng5! Nf8; 11.e5!** This insures that the problem at e6 will persist for a long time. **11...dxe5; 12.Qa4 Qc8.** Now c6 needs urgent attention too. **13.Be3 Ng6; 14.0–0–0 0–0.** Both sides have castled, but now the pawn at e6 is collected by the tax man. **15.Bh3! Qe8; 16.Nxe6 b5; 17.Qb3.** Now Black simply blunders a piece, but it hardly matters, since the rook at f8 could be taken at will. **17...bxc4; 18.Qxb7. White won.**

DORY INDIAN

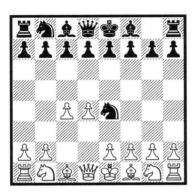

1.d4   Nf6
2.c4   Ne4

(100) ALEKHINE - MARSHALL
New York, 1927

1.d4 Nf6; 2.c4 e6; 3.Nf3 Ne4!?. The idea behind this move is to play ...Bb4+ and ...f4, after which the game can transpose to a Queen's Indian or a Dutch Defense. **4.Nfd2!** 4.Nbd2 is less good: 4...d5; 5.Nxe4 dxe4; 6.Nd2 Qxd4. **4...Bb4; 5.Qc2 d5; 6.Nc3 f5.** It looks as though Black has achieved complete domination of e4, but as long as White has an f-pawn the bind can be broken at the right time. Meanwhile, the pawn at e6 is weak. **7.Ndxe4! fxe4**.

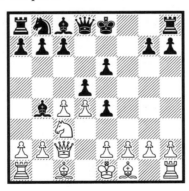

This pawn structure is not good for Black, and White will take action against it after developing and castling. **8.Bf4 0–0; 9.e3 c6; 10.Be2 Nd7; 11.a3 Be7; 12.0–0**. White's pieces are well-placed and Black has no real counterplay. Marshall should have attended to his development, but he was always one to attack as quickly as possible. **12...Bg5; 13.f3! Bxf4; 14.exf4 Rxf4; 15.fxe4 Rxf1+; 16.Rxf1.**

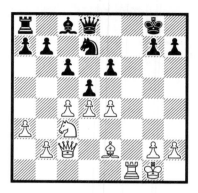

In my early days of playing the Dutch as Black I used to get in such positions and lose quickly. Marshall puts up a better fight. **16...e5!** Excellent! Now 17 dxe5 d4! gives the Black knight an outpost on e5. Alekhine comes up with a stellar reply. **17.Qd2! c5; 18.dxe5! d4.** Alekhine is prepared for this move, and has a deep sacrifice in mind. **19.Qf4!** The point is to secure the e5-square. It is actually worth a whole piece. **19...dxc3; 20.Qf7+ Kh8.**

21.bxc3! The advance of the pawn to e6 is coming, and there is not much Black can do about it. **21...Qg8; 22.Qe7 h6; 23.Bh5!** There is no point in advancing the e-pawn while the knight can escape to f6. **23...a6; 24.e6 g6.** Or 24...Nf6; 25.Bf7 Qh7; 26.Qd8+ Ng8 and now simply 27.Bxg8 Qxg8; 28.Rf8. **25.exd7 Bxd7; 26.Rf7.** There is no stopping Qf6+ so Black resigned and Alekhine got the point, and the Brilliancy Prize!

OWEN DEFENSE

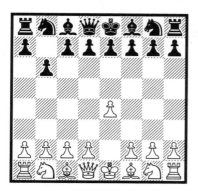

1.e4   b6

If the St. George is a rather dubious opening, then 1...b6, the **Owen Defense**, simply stinks. All of the problems of the St. George are present, but in addition the more cramped queenside formation with ...b6 (compared to ...a6 and ...b5) leaves Black with insufficient room to maneuver. This is one of the few openings for Black that were much more popular in the 19th century than they are today. No modern World Champions has even had to face it, and as Black only Alekhine, Lasker and Petrosian even dabbled with it. So for our sample game we go back to good old Steinitz, showing us how to play the White side.

(101) STEINITZ - DE VERE
Paris, 1867

1.e4 b6. The Owen Defense has virtually disappeared from play. If you recall the Steinitz-Mongredien game, you'll remember that Black had tremendous problems developing. **2.d4 Bb7; 3.Bd3 d6**. This weakens the light squares. 3...d6 would have been more logical.

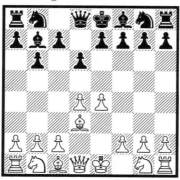

4.Ne2. There is nothing wrong with the normal 4.Nf3, but Steinitz wants to erect a strong pawn chain g2-f3-e4. **4...Nd7; 5.0–0 e5; 6.c3 Ngf6**.

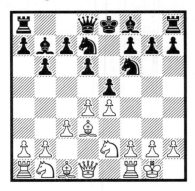

At first glance this seems to be some sort of Philidor Defense but for the abnormal position of the Black bishop at b7. **7.f3 h5?.** Sheer lunacy. There is not a single piece supporting the kingside attack. This is the sort of move only a beginner would play, but then few players beyond the early stages would ever adopt the Owen Defense anyway. **8.Be3 h4; 9.Nd2 Nh5**.

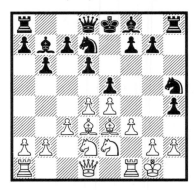

Black's forces are underdeveloped and uncoordinated. White has prepared an explosive opening of the position. **10.f4 exf4; 11.Nxf4 Nxf4; 12.Bxf4 g5?** Black continues with his feeble-minded plan. **13.Be3 Qe7; 14.Qb3!** Black wants to castle queenside, though an attack by White along the a-file after a4-a5 would be fatal in the end. But right now castling is not on, because the pawn at f7 needs the protection of the king.

You know you are in trouble when a pawn relies crucially on its monarch! **14...d5?** This will allow White to open the e-file, after one preliminary move. **15.Rae1 0–0–0; 16.exd5!** Black has no defense against the threat of d6 followed by Rxf7, as 16...Nf6 is met by 17.Bxg5. **White won.**.

JUNK DEFENSE

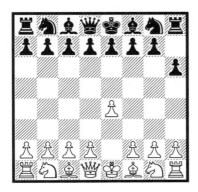

1.e4 h6

(102) MORPHY - CARR
Blindfold Game, 1858

1.e4 h6. This opening is even worse for Black than 1.h3 is for White!
2.d4 a5. A time-honored strategy when playing against a blindfolded opponent is to adopt an obscure, and often bad opening, in the hope of creating confusion. It is a bad idea and rarely works. **3.Bd3 b6; 4.Ne2 e6; 5.0–0 Ba6; 6.c4 Nf6; 7.e5 Nh7; 8.f4**. White has superior development and complete domination of the center. Morphy hardly seems to be confused by his opponent's ridiculous opening strategy. **8...Be7; 9.Ng3 d5; 10.Qg4 0–0**.

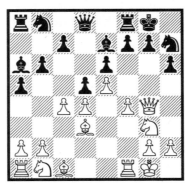

This is known as "castling into it." **11.Nh5 g5**. Black has little choice but to create this major weakness on the kingside. 11...g6; 12.Bxg6 fxg6; 13.Qxg6+ Kh8; 14.Qg7 mate. **12.fxg5 hxg5**. The Black king has only a single defender, which is easily removed. **13.Bxh7+ Kh8**. 13...Kxh7; 14.Nf6+ Bxf6; 15.Rxf6 and checkmate will follow shortly. **14.Nf6 dxc4; 15.Bc2**. We hope that you will never, ever, be in such dire straights as Black is here, even if your opponent is blindfolded. Black now uses a combination to exchange queens, but loses material. **15...Qxd4+; 16.Qxd4 Bc5**.

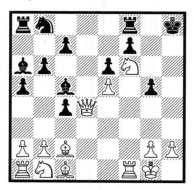

    17.Qxc5 bxc5; 18.Bxg5. Black's position cannot be said to be much improved. Fortunately, Morphy does not allow Mr. Carr to last long enough to suffer greatly. **18...Nc6; 19.Rf3 Kg7**. Now Morphy forces checkmate in 6 moves. **20.Bh6+ Kxh6; 21.Rh3+ Kg5; 22.Rh5+ Kf4; 23.Kf2 Rg8; 24.g3+ Rxg3; 25.hxg3 mate**.

13. BECOMING A BETTER CHESS PLAYER

Now that you have been introduced to the opening repertoires of the World Champions you may wish to further explore the openings. There are thousands of books available to help you. Some books are devoted to single variations or subvariations, while others promise you a complete repertoire in just one book. Two new books I've written will really get you on your way.

To start, check out *Standard Chess Openings* (SCO). In this book I present treatments of over 1,000 popular opening strategies, including 300 in greater depth. This will provide a solid foundation for your opening repertoire. Then, just for fun, take a walk on the wild side with *Unorthodox Chess Openings* (UCO), where you will learn exciting new strategies to keep your opponents off balance. With WCO, SCO and UCO in your arsenal, you'll have all the weapons you need to do battle at the chessboard!

If you supplement your knowledge of opening moves with an understanding of strategies as seen in full games, you'll be a more complete chessplayer and have more success at the chessboard. Therefore, you should study games played by the great chess masters, even if they are quite old. In these games you'll find methods of exploiting or combating small positional advantages and converting them into wins.

I hope that this book has deepened your understanding of the opening, but the task of incorporating these ideas into your own games lies ahead. Practice new openings as often as you can, whether against human opponents or one of the many fine computer chess games. If you lose a few games at first, don't worry. It takes time to adopt a new strategy early in the game.

Now it is your turn. Take your new opening knowledge and go out and win!

APPENDIX A: HOW TO READ CHESS NOTATION

INTRODUCTION

The international algebraic system of notation used for the communication of chess games and analysis is used in over 150 countries. While a full set of approximately 250 arbitrary and iconic symbols exist to provide a complete record of a chess game, in reality, far fewer symbols are needed to adequately represent a game. In this book, we have used only the most common ones. These are explained below.

THE BOARD

The chessboard is represented by a diagram containing pictures of each piece on its square. The starting position looks like this:

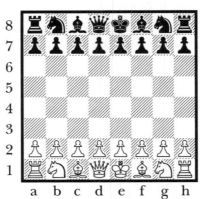

We refer to the horizontal rows as **ranks** and the vertical columns as **files**. The ranks are numbered 1-8, from White's point of view. The files are designated by letters, from a-h. After you get used to playing out chess games from the notation, you won't need any help in remembering them. For this introduction, however, we'll add the letters and numbers to help you follow the discussion.

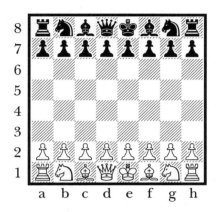

THE MOVES

Each move on the board can be described effectively with six pieces of information:

- The name of the piece being moved.
- The square the piece is moving from.
- The square the piece is moving to.
- Whether or not the move captures an enemy piece.
- Whether or not the enemy king is placed in check.
- The place in the game where the move was played.

Beginners often write 1.Pe2-e4, the *long form notation*. This is easy to understand, because the number of the move is followed by the abbreviation of the piece being moved, followed by both the square the piece is departing from and the one it is arriving at. But each move would take up a lot of space and make books more expensive. It also takes longer to write down during the game.

The most common form of notation is the *American style*. Again we start by indicating the number of the move. We use a number followed by a period. Then we add an abbreviation for the piece being moved. The abbreviations are simple to remember:

K	King
Q	Queen
R	Rook
B	Bishop
N	Knight
(nothing)	Pawn

The lowly pawn gets left out, but as long as there is no other capital letter indicated, then we understand that it must be a pawn move.

After the abbreviation for the piece, the square the piece lands on is usually indicated next. However, we can give some information about the square that the piece is moving from, but only if we have to. We will skip this for the moment, but return to it soon.

Going back to our first move, with the king pawn moving two squares forward, we now have the complete representation **1.e4.** The position after the move is shown in the diagram:

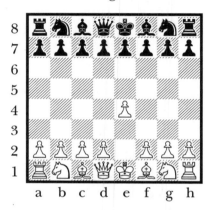

Now the pawn rests on the 4th square of the e-file. If you need to, count the letters from the left edge of the diagram (a, b, c, d, e) and count up from the bottom (1, 2, 3, 4). It will take a little time for you to master the chessboard in your mind, but you will find that it comes easily enough over time.

Now suppose we want to describe Black's reply, also moving the pawn on the kingside to a position two squares in front of the king.

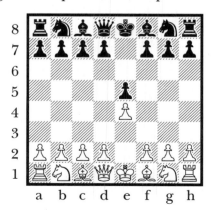

This move would be written **1...e5**. We use an ellipsis (...) to indicate that it is not White's move, but Black's. If we want to describe the entire game so far, we write simply **1.e4 e5**. In this instance, we didn't use the ellipsis, since the White and Black moves are represented together. As you can see, the White move is always shown first, then the Black move after.

Now let's say that White brings the bishop to b5.

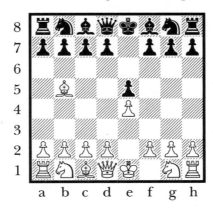

That move is written **2.Bb5**. The "2" indicates White's second move, the Bb5 shows that a bishop has moved to the b5 square. The game now reads **1.e4 e5; 2.Bb5**.

Black responds by bringing a knight to c6. We notate that as **2...Nc6**. We don't have to say which knight, because only one of the Black knights can move to c6. Let's try a few more moves. We'll let the game continue with White bringing a knight to f3, transposing, by the way, into the Spanish Game.

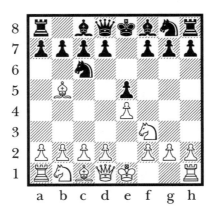

That's **3.Nf3**, giving us **1.e4 e5; 2.Bb5 Nc6; 3.Nf3**. Black responds by moving the a-pawn forward one square, attacking the White bishop. **3...a6.**

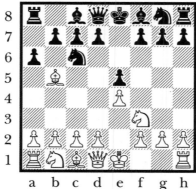

Now let us introduce a new element. We will capture the knight with our bishop. Because we are capturing an enemy piece, we add an "x" between the piece and a capture. (We place it there because that is where the verb goes in English. Germans often indicate that a piece has been captured at the end of the move, which is where the 'capture' verb would be in the past tense in German.)

We represent the move with **4.Bxc6**. Annotation of the game so far would be as follows: **1.e4 e5; 2.Bb5 Nc6; 3.Nf3 a6; 4.Bxc6.**

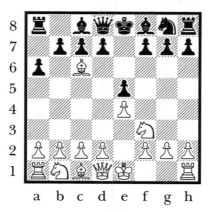

Earlier we said that we'll only mention the square the piece is leaving from if we have to. Now we have to. We can't just write 4...xc6 because that would not tell us which of the two possible pawn captures are possible.

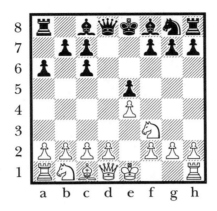

Because we need to clarify the situation, we add the file that the pawn is leaving from: **4...dxc6**. We see that it is the pawn on the *d-file* that is making the capture, not the pawn on the b-file.

Now it is White's turn, and let's suppose that the sensible move of castling takes place.

Our system has no easy way of combining the king and rook moves, so instead there is a simple convention. We use two zeros separated by a hyphen to indicate castling on the kingside (castling short): **5.0-0**. For queenside castling, we would add another hyphen and another zero "0-0-0".

Our game so far is **1.e4 e5; 2.Bb5 Nc6; 3.Nf3 a6; 4.Bxc6 dxc6; 5.0-0**. Let's try a few more moves, without commentary. **5...f6; 6.Nxe5 fxe5**. These moves should be easy to spot. We have now reached the following position:

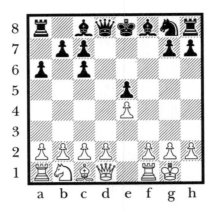

I have chosen these moves just to illustrate the last important part of the notation. If White now plays the queen to h5, the enemy king will be in check. We indicate this by appending a suffix in the form of a plus "+" sign. We are at move seven, so the notation is **7.Qh5+**. Our entire game can be described as **1.e4 e5; 2.Bb5 Nc6; 3.Nf3 a6; 4.Bxc6 dxc6; 5.0-0 f6; 6.Nxe5 fxe5;. 7.Qh5+.**

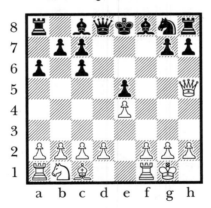

An actual checkmate will be indicated by "++" or "#".

One final point. If you are lucky enough to promote a pawn into a queen, it is written by marking the square that the pawn promotes onto, affixing an equal "=" sign, and then indicating the piece the pawn is promoted to. For example, e8=Q means that the pawn moves to the e8 square and is replaced by a queen.

THE SYMBOLS

There are hundreds of special symbols used in specialist chess literature, but in this book, words are generally used instead for easier comprehension. Still, we use a few symbols to point out moves of special, or doubtful, merit.

! A good move, probably the best available.
!! A brilliant move of artistic as well as military value.
? A mistake.
??An embarassing blunder
!? An interesting move of some merit
?! A dubious move, but one with some logic behind it.

INDEX OF GAMES • A

Listed in Order of Appearance

INDEX OF GAMES • B

Listed Alphabetically by Champion and Opponent

WORLD CHAMPION OPENINGS

WORLD CHAMPION OPENINGS

WORLD CHAMPION OPENINGS

INDEX OF CHAMPIONS

WORLD CHAMPION OPENINGS

LASKER

11, 13, 14, 18-19, 39, 40, 43, 47, 48, 62-64, 68, 96-98, 106, 110, 136, 137, 138, 139, 191, 192, 238, 291, 319-322, 325-326, 334, 340, 349

MORPHY

11, 13, 17, 23, 39, 40, 41, 43, 44, 47, 48, 68, 69, 71, 89-92, 106, 191, 192, 238, 239, 329-330, 351-352

PETROSIAN

11, 15, 21, 22-23, 39, 40, 41, 43, 44, 48, 83, 106, 140, 147, 148, 153, 161, 192, 212, 227-229, 230-232, 238, 240, 241, 243, 244, 279, 281-283, 290, 297-298, 309-311, 315-316, 345-346, 349

SMYSLOV

11, 14, 15, 21-22, 39, 40, 43, 44, 48, 83, 94-95, 106, 119, 122-123, 132-134, 156, 161, 191, 192, 193, 207, 208, 211-213, 238, 245, 262-264, 272-274, 290, 294-296, 300-302, 331-333

SPASSKY

11, 15, 22, 23-24, 39, 40, 43, 44, 48, 56, 57, 59-61, 86-87, 96, 106, 116, 117-120, 130, 132-134, 157-160, 187, 191, 192, 202, 214, 232-233, 238, 245, 265-270, 273, 297, 323-324, 334, 335-337

STEINITZ

11, 13, 14, 17, 18, 39, 40, 43, 47, 48, 49, 56, 57, 68, 69, 70-71, 96-98, 106, 143, 174-175, 192, 206, 221, 222, 238, 348, 349-350

TAL

11, 15, 21, 22, 23, 39, 40, 43, 44, 48, 49, 50-51, 55, 83, 106, 117, 118, 120, 129-130, 134, 147-149, 150, 153-155, 163-165, 172-173, 187, 192, 204, 208, 237, 238, 259-261, 278-279, 286, 309-311, 341-342

INDEX OF OPENINGS AND VARIATIONS

Page numbers in **bold** type indicate the main reference
for major discussion of this opening.

WORLD CHAMPION OPENINGS

WORLD CHAMPION OPENINGS

CARDOZA PUBLISHING
CHESS BOOKS

- OPENINGS -

WINNING CHESS OPENINGS *by Bill Robertie* - Shows concepts and best opening moves of more than 25 essential openings from Black's and White's perspectives: King's Gambit, Center Game, Scotch Game, Giucco Piano, Vienna Game, Bishop's Opening, Ruy Lopez, French, Caro-Kann, Sicilian, Alekhine, Pirc, Modern, Queen's Gambit, Nimzo-Indian, Queen's Indian, Dutch, King's Indian, Benoni, English, Bird's, Reti's, and King's Indian Attack. Examples from 25 grandmasters and champions including Fischer and Kasparov. 144 pages, $9.95

WORLD CHAMPION OPENINGS *by Eric Schiller* - This serious reference work covers the essential opening theory and moves of every major chess opening and variation as played by *all* the world champions. Reading as much like an encyclopedia of the must-know openings crucial to every chess player's knowledge as a powerful tool showing the insights, concepts and secrets as used by the greatest players of all time, *World Champion Openings (WCO)* covers an astounding 100 crucial openings in full conceptual detail (with 100 actual games from the champions themselves)! *A must-have book for serious chess players.* 384 pages, $18.95

STANDARD CHESS OPENINGS *by Eric Schiller* - The new definitive standard on opening chess play in the 20th century, this comprehensive guide covers every important chess opening and variation ever played and currently in vogue. In all, more than 3,000 opening strategies are presented! Differing from previous opening books which rely almost exclusively on bare notation, *SCO* features substantial discussion and analysis on each opening so that you learn and understand the concepts behind them. Includes more than 250 completely annotated games (including a game representative of each major opening) and more than 1,000 diagrams! For modern players at any level, this is the standard reference book necessary for competitive play. *A must have for serious chess players!!!* 768 pages, $24.95

UNORTHODOX CHESS OPENINGS *by Eric Schiller* - The exciting guide to all the major unorthodox openings used by chess players, contains more than 1,500 weird, contentious, controversial, unconventional, arrogant, and outright strange opening strategies. From their tricky tactical surprises to their bizarre names, these openings fly in the face of tradition. You'll meet such openings as the Orangutang, Raptor Variation, Halloween Gambit, Double Duck, Frankenstein-Dracula Variation, and even the Drunken King! These openings are a sexy and exotic way to spice up a game and a great weapon to spring on unsuspecting and often unprepared opponents. More than 750 diagrams show essential positions. 528 pages, $24.95

GAMBIT OPENING REPERTOIRE FOR WHITE *by Eric Schiller* - Chessplayers who enjoy attacking from the very first move are rewarded here with a powerful repertoire of brilliant gambits. Starting off with 1.e4 or 1.d4 and then using such sharp weapons such as the Göring Gambit (Accepted and Declined), Halasz Gambit, Alapin Gambit, Ulysses Gambit, Short Attack and many more, to put great pressure on opponents, Schiller presents a complete attacking repertoire to use against the most popular defenses, including the Sicilian, French, Scandinavian, Caro-Kann, Pirc, Alekhine, and other Open Game positions. 192 pages, $14.95.

GAMBIT OPENING REPERTOIRE FOR BLACK *by Eric Schiller* - For players that like exciting no-holds-barred chess, this versatile gambit repertoire shows Black how to take charge with aggressive attacking defenses against any orthodox first White opening move; 1.e4, 1.d4 and 1.c4. Learn the Scandinavian Gambit against 1.e4, the Schara Gambit and Queen's Gambit Declined variations against 1.d4, and some flank and unorthodox gambits also. Black learns the secrets of seizing the initiative from White's hands, usually by investing a pawn or two, to begin powerful attacks that can send White to early defeat. 176 pages, $14.95.

COMPLETE DEFENSE TO QUEEN PAWN OPENINGS *by Eric Schiller* - This aggressive counterattacking repertoire covers Black opening systems against virtually every chess opening except for 1.e4 (including most flank games), based on the exciting and powerful Tarrasch Defense, an opening that helped bring Championship titles to Kasparov and Spassky. Black learns to use the Classical Tarrasch, Symmetrical Tarrasch, Asymmetrical Tarrasch, Marshall and Tarrasch Gambits, and Tarrasch without Nc3, to achieve an early equality or even an outright advantage in the first few moves. 288 pgs, $16.95.

COMPLETE DEFENSE TO KING PAWN OPENINGS *by Eric Schiller* - Learn a complete defensive system against 1.e4. This powerful repertoire limits White's ability to obtain any significant opening advantage and allows Black to adopt the flexible Caro-Kann, the favorite weapon of many of great chess players. All White's options are explained in detail, and a plan is given for Black to combat them all. Analysis is up-to-date and backed by examples drawn from games of top stars. Detailed index lets you follow the opening from the point of a specific player, or through its history. 288 pages, $16.95.

SECRETS OF THE SICILIAN DRAGON by *GM Eduard Gufeld and Eric Schiller* - The mighty Dragon Variation of the Sicilian Defense is one of the most exciting openings in chess. Everything from opening piece formation to the endgame, including clear explanations of all the key strategic and tactical ideas, is covered in full conceptual detail. Instead of memorizing a jungle of variations, you learn the really important ideas behind the opening, and how to adapt them at the chessboard. Special sections on the heroes of the Dragon show how the greatest players handle the opening. The most instructive book on the Dragon written! 208 pages, $14.95.

HYPERMODERN OPENING REPERTOIRE FOR WHITE *by Eric Schiller* - Instead of placing pawns in the center of the board as traditional openings advise, this complete opening repertoire for White shows you how to stun opponents by "allowing" Black to occupy the center with its pawns, while building a crushing phalanx from the flanks, ready to smash the center apart with Black's slightest mistake. White's approach is simple to learn because White almost always develops pieces in the same manner, but can be used against all defenses no matter what Black plays! Diagrams and explanations illustrate every concept, with games from the greatest players showing the principles in action. The Réti and English openings form the basis of the Hypermodern and lead to games with brilliant sacrifices and subtle maneuvering. 288 pages, $16.95.

SECRETS OF THE KING'S INDIAN *by Eduard Gufeld and Eric Schiller* - The King's Indian is the single most popular opening and offers great opportunities for spectacular attacks and clever defenses. Readers learn the fundamental concepts, critical ideas, and hidden resources along with the opening traps and typical tactical and strategic mistakes. All major variations are covered, including the Classical, Petrosian, Saemisch, Averbakh, Four Pawns, Fianchetto and unconventional lines. Players learn how the strategies and tactics were applied in the brilliant games of the most famous players, how they can apply them to their own game. 320 pages, $14.95.

- MIDDLEGAME/TACTICS/WINNING CONCEPTS -

WINNING CHESS TACTICS *by Bill Robertie* - 14 chapters of winning ideas show the complete thinking behind every tactical concept: pins, single and double forks, double attacks, skewers, discovered and double checks, multiple threats - and other crushing tactics to gain an immediate edge over opponents. Learn the power tools of tactical play to become a better player. Includes guide to chess notation. 128 pages, $9.95.

303 TRICKY CHESS TACTICS *Fred Wilson and Bruce Alberston* - Both a fascinating challenge and great training tool, this is a fun and entertaining collection of two and three move tactical surprises for the advanced beginner, intermediate, and expert player. Tactics are arranged by difficulty so that a player may measure progress as he advances from simple to the complex positions. The examples, drawn from actual games, illustrate a wide range of chess tactics from old classics right up to the 1990's. 192 pages, $12.95.

10 MOST COMMON CHESS MISTAKES and How to Fix Them *by Larry Evans* - This fascinating collection of 218 errors, oversights, and outright blunders, not only shows the price great players pay for violating basic principles, but how to avoid these mistakes in your own game. You'll be challenged to choose between two moves, the right one, or the one actually played. From neglecting development, king safety, misjudging threats, and premature attacks, to impulsiveness, snatching pawns, and basic inattention, you receive a complete course in where you can go wrong and how to fix it. 256 pages, $14.95.

ENCYCLOPEDIA OF CHESS WISDOM, The Essential Concepts and Strategies of Smart Chess Play *by Eric Schiller* - The most important concepts, strategies, tactics, wisdom, and thinking that every chessplayer must know, plus the gold nuggets of knowledge behind every attack and defense is collected together in one volume. Step-by-step, from opening, middle and endgame strategy, to psychological warfare and tournament tactics, Schiller shows the thinking behind each essential concept, and through examples, diagrams, and discussions, shows its impact on the game. 432 pages, $19.95.

WORLD CHAMPION COMBINATIONS *by Raymond Keene and Eric Schiller* - Learn the insights, concepts, and moves of the greatest combinations ever by the best players of all time. From Morphy to Alekhine, to Fischer to Kasparov, the incredible combinations and brilliant sacrifices of the 13 World Champions are collected here in the most insightful combinations book yet. Packed with fascinating strategems, 50 annotated games, and great practical advice for your own games, this is a great companion guide to *World Champion Openings* and the other titles in the *World Champion* series. 264 pages, $16.95.

WORLD CHAMPION TACTICS *by Leonid Shamkovich and Eric Schiller* - The authors show how the greatest players who ever lived used their entire arsenal of tactical weapons to bring opponents to their knees. Packed with fascinating strategems, 50 fully annotated games, and more than 200 diagrams, players learn not only the thinking and game plan behind the moves of the champions, but the insights that will allow them to use these brilliancies in their own games. Each tactical concept is fully explained with examples and game situations from the champions themselves. 304 pages, $18.95.

100 AWESOME CHESS MOVES *By Eric Schiller* - This collection of brilliant ideas from real games are not just regular combinations or tactical swindles, but moves of stunning originality. Schiller has selected 100 *awesome* moves, and through positions, examples, and clearly explained concepts, shows you how to improve your grasp of deep positional understandings and swashbuckling tactics. You'll learn how to reinforce your gut instincts to not just reach for the best move, but the *inspired* move. 224 pgs, $18.95.

- BEGINNING AND GENERAL CHESS BOOKS -

THE BASICS OF WINNING CHESS by Jacob Cantrell - A great first book of chess, in one easy reading, beginner's learn the moves, pieces, basic rules and principles of play, standard openings, and both Algebraic and English chess notation. The basic ideas of the winning concepts and strategies of middle and end game play are also shown. Includes example games of champions. 64 pages, $4.95.

BEGINNING CHESS PLAY by Bill Robertie - Step-by-step approach uses 113 diagrams to teach the basics of chess: opening, middle and endgame strategies, principles of development, pawn structure, checkmates, openings and defenses, how to write and read chess notation, join a club, play in tournaments, use a clock, and get rated. Two annotated games reveal strategic thinking for easy learning. 144 pgs, $9.95

WHIZ KIDS TEACH CHESS Eric Schiller & the Whiz Kids - Today's greatest young stars, some perhaps to be future world champions, present a fascinating look at the world of chess. Each tells of their successes, failures, world travels, and love of chess, show off their best moves, and admit to their most embarrassing blunders. This is more than just a fascinating look at prodigies like Vinay Bhat and Irina Krush, it's also a primer featuring diagrams, explanations, and winning ideas for young players. 144 oversized pages, $14.95.

KEENE ON CHESS by Raymond Keene - Complete step-by-step course shows how to play and deepen one's understanding of chess while keeping the game fun and exciting. Fascinating chapters on chess heroes and lessons one can learn from these greats, basic chess openings, strategy, tactics, the best games of chess ever played, and the history of chess round out a player's education. Readers also learn how to use chess notation and all the basic concepts of game play – castling, pawn promotion, putting an opponent into check, the five ways of drawing or stalemating games, en passant, actual checkmate, and much more. 320 pages, $18.95.

- MATES & ENDGAMES -

303 TRICKY CHECKMATES by Fred Wilson and Bruce Alberston - Both a fascinating challenge and great training tool, this collection of two, three and bonus four move checkmates is great for advanced beginning, intermediate and expert players. Mates are in order of difficulty, from the simple to very complex positions. Learn the standard patterns and stratagems for cornering the king: corridor and support mates, attraction and deflection sacrifices, pins and annihilation, the quiet move, and the dreaded *zugzwang*. Examples, drawn from actual games, illustrate a wide range of chess tactics from classics right up to the 1990's. 192 pages, $12.95.

MASTER CHECKMATE STRATEGY by Bill Robertie - Learn the basic combinations, plus advanced, surprising and unconventional mates, the most effective pieces needed to win, and how to mate opponents with just a pawn advantage. also, how to work two rooks into an unstoppable attack; how to wield a queen advantage with deadly intent; how to coordinate pieces of differing strengths into indefensible positions of their opponents; when it's best to have a knight, and when a bishop to win. 144 pages, $9.95

BASIC ENDGAME STRATEGY: Kings, Pawns and Minor Pieces by Bill Robertie - Learn the mating principles and combinations needed to finish off opponents. From the four basic checkmates using the King with the queen, rook, two bishops, and bishop/knight combinations, to the King/pawn, King/Knight and King/Bishop endgames, you'll learn the essentials of translating small edges into decisive checkmates. Learn the 50-move rule, and the combinations of pieces that can't force a mate against a lone King. 144 pages, $12.95.

BASIC ENDGAME STRATEGY: Rooks and Queens by *Bill Robertie* - The companion guide to *Basic Endgame : Kings, Pawns and Minor Pieces*, you'll learn the basic mating principles and combinations of the Queen and Rook with King, how to turn middlegame advantages into victories, by creating passed pawns, using the King as a weapon, clearing the way for rook mates, and other endgame combinations. 144 pages, $12.95.

639 ESSENTIAL ENDGAME POSITIONS by *Eric Schiller* - From basic checkmates to sophisticated double-rook endgames, every important endgame concept is explained. Topics include every key combination of king and pawn endgames, bishops, knights, rooks, and queens, plus tricky endgames with no pawns. The thinking behind every position is explained in words (unlike diagram-only books) so that players learn which positions are winning, which are drawn, and which cannot be saved. Frequent diagrams show starting and target positions, so readers can visualize end goals and steer the middlegame to a successful conclusion. 400 pages, $18.95.

ORDER BY PHONE NOW! - (800)577-WINS
or use coupon below

KASPAROV EXPRESS™

SAITEK - The World Leader in Intelligent Electronic Games

VERSATILE AND FUN - An amazing 384 level/setting combinations includes fun levels for novices and challenging levels for experienced players. Economic powerful, and pocket size (approximately 5" x 61/2" x 1') this game is an unbeatable handheld traveling companion.

GREAT INEXPENSIVE TRAVEL COMPANION! - Features different playing styles and strengths, 5 special coach modes, and teaching levels! Sensory-style chess board, peg type pieces, folding lid, LCD screen, take back and hint features, built-in chess clock that keeps track of time for both sides, and self-rating system. Memory holds an unfinished game for up to two years, gives you the complete package in an economical, handy travel-ready unit.

To order, send just $39.95 for the Express.

COSMOS TRAVEL COMPUTER

SAITEK - The World Leader in Intelligent Electronic Games

THE WORLD'S MOST POWERFUL HAND-HELD CHESS COMPUTER! - New model features powerful RISC processor and 500 level/setting combinations. It has an **integrated training system** has an **official USCF rating of 2334**! This **awesome program** can beat over 99% of all chess players, yet it's still great for the novice. LCD shows principal variation, evaluation, search depth, and search mode counts.

64 SKILL LEVELS - 64 levels of skill and handicapping give you tons of **options** and **versatility**: Play against beginning, intermediate or advanced opponents (includes tournament time controls), play Blitz or Tournament, choose Active, Passive, or Complete style, or Tournament Opening Book, select **Brute Force** algorithm or the advanced Selective Search. Match your skill to the correct level for most **challenging** chess. You want it - it's all here!

To order, send just $119.95 for the Cosmos Travel Computer.

380

KASPAROV CHESS GK2100

SAITEK - The World Leader in Intelligent Electronic Games

THE BEST VALUE MONEY CAN BUY! - The **fabulous** Kasparov GK2100 is the **most popular** chess computer we sell. Using a super high speed **RISC** computer chip and rated at a **2334** USCF rating, you'll have consistent challenges and excitement. Coaching features and fun levels makes it suitable for novices; masters and experts will want to choose higher levels.

GREAT DESIGN - Packaged in a sleek, handsome cabinet suitable for your living room. No need to find a partner to play - **take on the Champion**!

POWERFUL PROGRAM FEATURES - **64 levels of play** include sudden death, tournament, problem solving and beginner's. Shows intended move and position evaluation, take back up to 50 moves, and user selectable **book openings library**. Also choose from **Active, Passive, Tournament, complete book, no book.** Select the high speed **Selective Search** or play against the powerful **Brute Force.** program. Thinks in opponents time for best realism. Shutoff, shut on memory - remembers game for 1 year!

GREAT FOR BEGINNERS AND MASTERS ALIKE! - This **awesome program** can beat over 99% of all regular chess players, yet it is still suitable for beginners and intermediate players: Simply set the skill level to the appropriate strength for the best challenges. Matching your skill to the correct level of play ensures a **challenging** and **exciting** game.

EVEN MORE FEATURES - Opening library of 35,000 moves, **large LCD** shows full information and keeps track of playing time. Modern ergonomic design goes well in living room.

To order, send $189.95 for the Kasparov Chess GK2100

TOURNAMENT-SYLE CHESS EQUIPMENT
Our Recommended Chess Shop

CHESS CLOCKS

A. Standard Clock - Sturdy, accurate, and dependable, the budget "king" of chess clocks. Has been used by players for decades. Hard plastic housing. Measures 5 7/8" x 3 1/4" x 1 1/2". **$44.95.**

B. Tilt-Back Rolland Blond - Stylish, functional, well-priced, and popular. Real wood, brass trim, large clock face, and accurate timers with tilt-back design for easy viewing of exact time. 5 3/4" x 3 x 1 1/8". **$59.95.**

C Tilt-Back Rolland Mahogeny - Same as "B" in beautiful mahogeny. 5 3/4" x 3 x 1 1/8". **$59.95.**

D. USCF Master Quartz - Stylish, functional, well-priced, and authorized by the United States Chess Federation, what could be better than that? In stylish Black or beautiful Midnight Blue (not shown). **$79.95.**

E. Saitek Digital Clock - The ultimate in *digital* time control for chess and board games. 21 timing combinations (FIDE, Amateur, Club, Rapid, US Active, more!) and wide choice of settings (Tournament, Blitz, Hour Glass, Bronstein, more)! Highly visible 17mm clocks. Ultramodern and stylish - shows time to the second! **$79.95.**

TOURNAMENT-STYLE CHESS PIECES

European craftsmanship

The Staunton look is the classic and standard design for chess pieces. All pieces guaranteed against defects.

Tournament Staunton - Hand-crafted wood from maple with natural and walnut finish for the tournament feel. Heavily weighted and felted - the king is 3 1/2 inches high. Popular sellers. $69.95. (Add $6 ship)

TOURNAMENT CHESS BOARD

European Crafted

The tournament board is the classic and standard board design and is a great board for playing chess.

Tournament Board - Beautiful high-polished wooden board inlaid with maple and walnut. Finished on four sides. Four felt points on back protects tables. Two inch squares. $79.95. (Add $13 ship)

TOURNAMENT-SYLE CHESS EQUIPMENT
Our Recommended Chess Shop

A. Standard Clock

B. Tilt Back Roland Blond

C. Tilt Back Roland Mahogeny

E. Saitek Digital Clock

D. USCF Master Quartz

TOURNAMENT CHESS BOARD
European Crafted